The Authentic Dissertation

The Authentic Dissertation is a road map for students who want to make their dissertation more than a series of hoop-jumping machinations that cause them to lose the vitality and meaningfulness of their research.

Students and tutors are presented with practical guidance for the kind of alternative dissertations that many educators believe are needed to move Doctoral and Master's level work beyond the limitations that currently stifle authentic contributions for a better world.

Drawing on his Cherokee/Creek heritage and his experiences with Indigenous cultures from around the world, the author explores how research can regain its authentic core and find its true place in the natural order once more. Four Arrows provides a degree of "credibility" that will help graduate students legitimize their ideas in the eyes of more conservative university committees. This inspiring book will also help academics who sincerely want to see these alternative forms but are concerned about the rigor of "alternative" dissertation research and presentation.

The featured dissertation stories tap into more diverse perspectives, more authentic experience and reflection, and more creative abilities. They are, in essence, spiritual undertakings that:

- honor the centrality of the researcher's voice, experience, creativity, and authority
- focus more on important questions than on research methodologies per se
- reveal virtues (generosity, patience, courage, respect, humility, fortitude, etc.)
- regard the *people's* version of reality.

The goal of this book is not to replace the historical values of academic research in the Western tradition, but to challenge some of these values and offer alternative ideas that stem from different, sometimes opposing, values.

Four Arrows (Don Trent Jacobs), past Dean of Education at Oglala Lakota College, is author of sixteen books. He is currently a Professor at Fielding Graduate University, USA.

The Authentic Dissertation

Alternative ways of knowing, research, and representation

Four Arrows
(aka Don Trent Jacobs)

Routledge
Taylor & Francis Group

LONDON AND NEW YORK

First published 2008
by Routledge
2 Park Square, Milton Park, Abingdon, Oxon, OX14 4RN

Simultaneously published in the USA and Canada
by Taylor & Francis Inc.
270 Madison Ave, New York, NY 10016

Routledge is an imprint of the Taylor & Francis Group, an informa business

© 2008 Four Arrows, aka Don Trent Jacobs

Typeset in Garamond by
Florence Production Ltd, Stoodleigh, Devon
Printed and bound in Great Britain by
CPI Antony Rowe, Chippenham, Wiltshire

Every effort has been made to ensure that the advice and information in
this book is true and accurate at the time of going to press. However,
neither the publisher nor the authors can accept any legal responsibility
or liability for any errors or omissions that may be made. In the case of
drug administration, any medical procedure or the use of technical
equipment mentioned within this book, you are strongly advised to
consult the manufacturer's guidelines.

British Library Cataloguing in Publication Data
A catalogue record for this book is available from the British Library

Library of Congress Cataloging in Publication Data
Jacobs, Donald Trent, 1946–
    The authentic dissertation: alternative ways of knowing, research
    and representation/Four Arrows, AKA Don Trent Jacobs.
        p. cm.
    Includes bibliographical references and index.
    1. Dissertations, Academic.   2. Research – Methodology.
    3. Qualitative research.   I. Title.
    LB2369.J33 2008
    001.4 – dc22   2007049641

ISBN10: 0–415–44222–2 (hbk)
ISBN10: 0–415–44223–0 (pbk)

ISBN13: 978–0–415–44222–0 (hbk)
ISBN13: 978–0–415–44223–7 (pbk)

I dedicate this work to my two grandsons,
Sage and Kaien;
and to all of the children and grandchildren
of and beyond the seventh generation;
and to all the creatures, large and small,
with whom we share the air, land, and
water; and to all the plants;
and to the rocks, rivers, and mountains
and the wisdom they contain;
and to great mysteriousness that
surrounds and informs;
and to the spirits of the invisible world;
and finally,
to life itself and its continuation into
and through death.

Contents

Introduction

> So, please dear boy, not so many notations in your essay on the thoughts of men long dead. Profundity is seldom achieved by misquoting the opinions of those who cannot return to defend themselves. It is an unfortunate habit cultivated by the more modest minds at Oxford who can only impress their peers by building on a bulwark of old ideas. It disguises, of course, the absence of any new ones of their own. By all means, use the quotes of the dead to clear the known ground, and then dare to walk the wildest unknown path. In this way we can look forward to some intellectual progress.
>
> (From Bryce Courtenay's novel, *Tandia*, Toronto: McArthur and Company, 1992, p. 304)

The concept of formal education is universally acknowledged as a major resource for maintaining and improving the social, economic, physical, and spiritual health of our world. Doctoral programs represent the highest level of such education, and dissertation work is the pinnacle event in them. Many educators, however, are not satisfied that this culminating product is really doing all that much to solve the challenges facing us in the twenty-first century. In fact, a number of us believe that in many ways, directly or indirectly, the "academy" may be partially responsible for our collective inability to significantly mitigate warfare, global warming, social and ecological injustices, domestic violence, loss of habitat, racism, economic despair, loss of the commons, etc. The dissertation authors featured in this text recognize how tapping into more diverse perspectives, more authentic experience and reflection, and more creative abilities can address the problems.

The brief dissertation stories that follow, as diverse as they are, have one thing in common. They are authentic. They are, in essence, spiritual undertakings and reflections that honor the centrality of the researcher's voice, experience, creativity, and authority. As such, these researchers created dissertations that:

- focus more on important questions than on research methodologies per se;
- seek to make the world a better place;

- move away from an over-emphasis on academic writing if it tends to stifle creativity or one's true voice;
- are aware of shortcomings in the English language;
- tend to be interdisciplinary;
- do not fall for the "myth of objectivity";
- do not rely on external authorities;
- reveal virtues (generosity, patience, courage, respect, humility, fortitude, etc.);
- align with sustainability priorities;
- are not overly anthropocentric in nature;
- remember that art, music, and story telling are living information systems;
- are situated in experience;
- respect multiple culturally determined ways of thinking and living;
- care about and contribute to social and ecological justice;
- comprehend the true value of diversity;
- regard the *people's* version of reality;
- challenge all forms of oppression;
- are critical of cultural and educational hegemony;
- appreciate dreaming and visions as potentially valid resources for knowledge;
- recognize the pitfalls of a male-dominated, white-Western world;
- see service to others as a component of research;
- honor traditional Indigenous ways of knowing;
- integrate knowledge, scholarship, research, reflection, and practice;
- understand the power of stories, music, and other forms of art as a source of wisdom;
- reveal mindfulness each step of the way;
- appreciate the role of sacrifice in the journey;
- pay attention to perennial cycles and wisdom in nature;
- remember to look for life's beauty and joy.

The goal of this book is not to replace the historical values of academic research in the Western tradition, but only to challenge some of these values and offer alternative ideas that stem from different, sometimes opposing values. Some scholars are concerned that such an effort may result in less rigor, quality, and excellence than seems to be associated with the status quo ideas about dissertation work. I submit that such work may actually be more likely to reach standards of excellence than those projects whose authors are stifled by the confines of academic rules and habits. In the journal *Academe*, published by the American Association of University Professors, Lovitts' 2005 article, "How to Grade a Dissertation," described the conclusions of 276 faculty members at ten research universities who collectively had sat on nearly 10,000 dissertation committees, across the sciences, social sciences, and humanities. I highlight their conclusions about dissertations that the faculty rated as "excellent." Keep in mind that the research revealed that outstanding dissertations "were very rare," a problem I hope will be rectified when more scholars begin to reach the goals stated above and express them in their work. These findings are relevant to legitimate concerns about the rigor of work that is arts-informed, storied, autobiographical, critical, anti-oppressive, ecologically situated, or Indigenous-oriented. In fact, my reading of their determinations leads me to conclude that a dissertation has more potential to be rated as "excellent" if it moves in the directions that the stories described in this book reveal.

- There is *no set formula* that leads to excellence.
- Outstanding dissertations *defy explication*.
- Faculty "said such dissertations display a richness of thought and insight and make an important breakthrough."
- Such dissertations are a *pleasure to read*.
- "The faculty members [describe] students who produce outstanding dissertations as *very creative and intellectually adventurous*."
- The dissertations "leap into new territory and transfer ideas from place to place."
- The dissertation writer "used or developed new tools."
- The dissertation pushes the discipline's boundaries and opens new areas for research.
- Outstanding students typically *think and work independently*.

There already exist a number of excellent books that explore the ontological and epistemological bases for alternative dissertations and/or provide guidelines for how to proceed (see Bibliography). However, this book contributes something different to the alternative dissertation movement (and a movement it is). Authors of unique, "out of the box," and "authentic" dissertations, some that have received international awards, tell brief stories about their dissertation journeys. They share their reasons for challenging the status quo and the special value of their subsequent scholarship. These stories are presented as a transcript of an imaginary conference on alternative ways of knowing, research, and representation. In addition to the presentations, other scholars "in the audience" add to the conference dialogue. These individuals include such notable thinkers as Patrick Slattery, Elliot Eisner, Robert Kaplan, Howard Gardner, Manulani Aluli Meyer, Thomas Barone, Gregory Cajete, Rita L. Irwin, and many others.

In addition to these real-life scholars, I have invented two fictional characters for the dialogue. The protagonist is an American Indian woman and esteemed Indigenous scholar named "Runner." The antagonist, Dr. Samson, is a Western gatekeeper steeped in traditional academic assumptions about research. These two will help stimulate a meaningful dialogue that will help readers assess the merits and challenges surrounding the various topics.

The contributors to this book have broken new trails. Some have done so with research approaches that understand and challenge hegemonic beliefs that objectivity is an essential aspect of legitimate research. Others have done so with forms of representation that demonstrate that presenting research is as much a part of research as exploring "data." Noreen Barman and Maria Piantanida, in their 2007 text, *The Authority to Imagine: The Struggle Toward Presentation in Dissertation Writing,* speak about a dissertation author's freedom to create forms of representation that are in harmony with the author's own histories and unique sensibilities. Linda Tuhiwai Smith says in her book, *Decolonizing Methodologies: Research and Indigenous Peoples*, that representation is important because it leaves an imprint of what is true, and that presentation form can be central to the achievement of research goals.

Of course, many of our "presenters" have used unorthodox processes for both research and its presentation. These pioneers and others like them have already had an impact on research methods and forms of representation. Names have been given to many approaches such as:

- Qualitative Research
- Phenomenology
- Hermeneutics
- Symbolic Interaction
- Historical Research
- Interpretative Phenomenological Analysis
- Grounded Theory
- Conversation Analysis
- Observational Research
- Q Methodology
- New Paradigm Research
- Critical Methodology
- Anti-oppressive Research (Decolonizing Methodologies)
- Indigenous Research
- Narrative Inquiry
- Difference Centered
- Action Research
- Participatory Action Research
- Mindful Inquiry
- Ethnomethodology
- Evaluation Research
- Theoretical Inquiry
- Autoethnography or Autobiographical Research
- Arts-based or Informed Research, including documentary video, drama-turgy, music, collage, dialogue, story telling, poetry, fiction, lyrical inquiry, etc.

Whether or not a research approach or a means of representing it has been given a name, any format can be sufficiently "valid" if it makes a unique and substantial contribution to understanding the world better or to making it a better place to live, and our dissertation stories have proven this so. Labeling "methods" may even get in the way of more creative ways to answer important questions. Nonetheless, as difficult as it is to categorize the dissertations represented in this text, I have attempted to do so according to the basic form of representation that was used. Then, before each presentation, I offer a bulleted list of "methods" and descriptors for other strategic concepts that are illustrated by the presenter. Perhaps doing this will enhance the usability of this text as a reference.

Our imaginary conference is divided into seven "days." The first day's session, "Indigenous Ways of Knowing," opens with Indigenous scholars and their alternative dissertation stories. We begin with this group because Indigenous ways of learning have always been about the inner journey that respects intuition, spirituality, artfulness, interconnectedness, Mother Earth, and situated experience as the ultimate "primary resources" for "data." Academic habits that fragment and isolate and measure things have, it seems, caused us to lose touch with what is really important (and authentic.) To paraphrase Bill McKibben's ideas in his classic book, *The Age of Missing Information*, the more money, sophistication, and technology we accumulate the more happily stupid we have become. Indigenous research and its long history of resistance to colonizing research methods may offer an antidote to this problem.

I also open with Indigenous stories because I believe most of the alternative ways of knowing, research, and representation illustrated in this text originate from Indigenous principles about the sacredness of space and place; the purpose of research to benefit the community; and the spiritual awareness that everything is connected; and that knowledge must incorporate the mysterious. Evo Morales, the first Indigenous president of Bolivia, has stated that he is convinced that Indigenous Peoples are the "moral reserve of humanity." An assumption revealed in the stories that follow is that good research must be a moral endeavor. One way or the other, the Indigenous perspectives on education include:

- the importance of trusting personal experience and the relative distrust of experience practiced in dominant Western approaches to education;
- attention to the larger cosmic rhythms and connections, rather than a reductionist view of the world;
- recognizing the problem of anthropocentrism in American education;
- asking the question "What does it mean?" instead of just "How does it work and what use is it for me?";
- accepting secrets and mysteries from Nature instead of trying to force them out;

- recognizing the value of diversity;
- realizing that technology will likely be destructive if it does not relate positively to community, communication and culture in ways that emphasize balance;
- remembering the importance of one's sense of place and self-determination;
- viewing character education as the focus for education and skills as the context, with the virtues taught being represented in Nature;
- seeing conflict resolution as emphasizing putting relationships back in order;
- seeing the world as dynamic, not static;
- recognizing the rights and "personalities" of non-human entities;
- understanding that the natural world is more cooperative than competitive;
- frustration with fragmented curriculum;
- seeing the problems of organized religion, especially fundamentalism, while respecting the value of spirituality in all aspects of life;
- the importance of humor, especially in addressing cognitive dissonance and harmful stereotypes;
- seeing art as a living process for communicating and understanding.

Day Two offers the second series of "presentations" that are referred to as dissertations that tell "creative stories." Here our authors tell about their dissertations that were actually fictional novels or short stories.

Day Three illustrates dissertations that emphasize "poetic inquiry" and visual arts such as collages.

Day Four combines a group of presentations that illustrate dissertations that used film and/or photography as a main approach to research or representation.

Day Five presenters tell about the dissertation journeys that emphasized drama and dialogue in the work.

Day Six discusses autoethnographic and autobiographical dissertations.

Day Seven focuses on the voices of research participants, ending with an example of a Web-based dissertation. The day closes with commentary from some pioneers whose experience summarizes the importance of this work.

I want to reiterate that these categories have very loose boundaries and many dissertations incorporated mixed methods, cultures of inquiry, and forms of representation. If the reader is to truly understand his or her own creative urge to write an "authentic dissertation," he or she will be best served by reading this entire book as if attending the conference. I do not mean for it to be a "how to" book by any means.

I conclude this introduction with some wisdom I just now received in an email from one of the students in Fielding Graduate University's doctoral program in Educational Leadership and Change. Her name is Amy Scatlif. She is an artist living in Philadelphia and just beginning her alternative doctoral dissertation, which will consist of personal narratives as well as filmed interviews with friends and colleagues who represent people who operate within a creative paradigm. By applying appreciative inquiry and creative research methodologies—such as usability and human-factor design, creative-thinking techniques, and visualization applications—she intends to use such creative exchanges to "increase sensitivity to available opportunities of invention and social harmony." Proving that I continue to learn more from my students than they learn from me, I conclude this preface with her important observation.

From: amyscatlif
Sent: Tuesday, May 08, 2007 7:57 PM
To: Four Arrows
Subject: your new book

Hello,

It is good to hear that you have received so many submissions from so many countries. You're right, it has to be tough to choose from so many in order to comply with the publishers 100,000 word requirement.

I see an important point to get across to your audience of faculty and graduate students is that an alternative model for a dissertation starts with the first graduate course. I find that the students who follow the conventional rules early on in their coursework rarely imagine a more innovative dissertation. Growing a shared framework with faculty, building courage, making workable community/professional connections, as well as having the valuable time to experiment with impractical visions and then start over again begins in early course work and not just with the dissertation plan.

I think many students' valuable and innovative ideas collapse because students and faculty revert to the 'just get it done' traditional formats when the necessary groundwork or important faculty shared understanding has not been established.

I do hope this point can be mentioned to help students learn how to experiment early on with alternative models.

Thanks!

Amy

Part I

Day one

Indigenous ways of knowing

It is our opinion that one of the most fundamental principles of Aboriginal research methodology is the necessity for the research to locate him or herself . . . We resist colonial models of writing by talking about ourselves first and then relating pieces of our stories and ideas to the research topic.

(Kathy Absolon and Cam Willet in *Research as Resistance*, edited by Leslie Brown and Susan Strega, 2005, p. 99)

"Brilliant or bullshit!"

Four Arrows' story

with Manulani Aluli Meyers, Warren Linds, and Gregory Cajete

- Autobiographical (relating one's own life story or a portion of it)
- Phenomenology (the study of consciousness)
- Critical methodology (being critical of dominant assumptions that lead toward oppression)
- Auto-ethnography (about the self as part of a different culture to help explain differences)
- Theoretical inquiry (an attempt to explain and organize so as to draw assumptions and predictions for future benefit)
- Story telling (a narrative of events, real or imagined, that conveys meaning)
- Ethno-methodology (the study of how people understand their daily lives)
- Indigenous approach (valuing visions)

(Editor's note: Transcript begins at 08:30, after opening prayer and sage ceremony)

Runner: Mitakuye pi. Mi chante ata wo wogala ke, na nape chiusu pelo. My relatives, I speak from my heart and offer each of you a warm handshake. For the rest of our time together, I will go by my nickname, Runner, although my full name translates in English to "Fast Runner Who Comes from the Water." I am Oglala Lakota from the Tetuwan Oyate. I am a mother and a grandmother. I grew up on the Pine Ridge Reservation near the town of Porcupine. I am also a retired university professor, so I think I understand a little of the world most of you live in now.

Before I introduce my respected friend and colleague, Dr. Samson, someone asked if I would translate the opening prayer I offered in the Lakota language this morning, before the transcribing of our sessions together began. In essence I was saying that each of us, as well as all of those in our communities, have important contributions to make in putting our world back into balance. I said that we have come to a time and place of great urgency. The global environment is being destroyed by the ignorance of human misdirection. I offered that the fate of future generations is in our hands. I said that we must use our minds, our hearts, our intuitions, and our spiritual awareness all together. I explained that it is expected that what we were given in life we can use in positive ways for the health of all the People, which includes not only us two-legged, but all of that which exists with spirit, from the rocks on Mother Earth to the birds in Father Sky. I talked about seeing ourselves as part of the universe, both the visible and the invisible universe, and that we as humans are not better or not worse than the trees, the grasses, the animals, or the stars. I ended by reminding us that we are all related.

Now it is my honor to introduce Dr. Carl Samson, a distinguished professor and author of numerous texts on research methodologies. Carl will serve with me during our week together as sort of a co-facilitator. His perspectives, which are based on traditional "Western" academic values, are sure to challenge those of us with different views to defend the validity of our ideas.

Dr. Samson: Thanks Runner for sharing with us the meaning of the beautiful Lakota words you spoke to us this morning. I must say though, that I am not all that comfortable with prayers in this or any other academic setting. I also want to say to everyone, and I think it may be relevant to our reasons for being here, that I do not think things are quite as dismal as Runner's prayer seems to imply. Frankly, and I know I am to be frank in these dialogues, I also resent the idea that a rock is as "important" as a human. I hope talking to rocks will not be part of the alternative dissertation agenda (*laughing*).

Runner: It is not the talking to the rock so much but the listening that would be important for dissertations (*laughing*). Anyway folks, as you can see, it won't take much to get the two of us arguing, but I do want to remind everyone that our arguments in these sessions are not competitive, but cooperative. In other words, we hope they will be dialogical and open for continued learning as opposed to attempting to win a particular position. Oh, and I will be the first to admit, not all of the rocks can talk, only some (*smiling*).

Dr. Samson: (*Laughing with the audience*) OK. Well, let's move on. For the sake of readers who will want to use this transcript as a resource, we have tried to organize the presentations according to some kind of logical structure. We will begin with a number of Indigenous presenters.

Runner: We will open each presentation with the presenter's name and the title selected for the talk. We'll make available a brief list of concepts, approaches, or methodologies (established or new) that may be applicable to the particular dissertation. So let's get started with our first presenter, who also happens to be the organizer of this event. Please give Wahinkpe Topa, Four Arrows, a welcome.

Four Arrows: Thank you and welcome to everyone! I want to talk to you a little about my own dissertation for the Curriculum and Instruction doctorate, with a cognate in American Indian worldviews, which I received from Boise State University in 1999. I believe it is a good example of how Indigenous scholars see personal experience and introspection as a major source of authentic authority.

This is also why it is important for me to say a little about my personal experience and ancestry as a beginning. Although I now go by my Lakota name, "Four Arrows," *Wahinkpe Topa* in Lakota, I have no Lakota blood. On my mother's side, I am Creek and Cherokee, related to the Stewart and Bumpass Cherokee lines from the Southeast territory of the U.S. On my father's side I come from the Wallace line, located on the border of Scotland and Ireland. Any pride in my Native heritage was largely suppressed by my family, apparently for my own protection, but after a stint in the Marine Corps during Vietnam, I began to question the wisdom of my anti-Indian prejudice. I wound up living and working on the Pine Ridge Reservation eventually. I became a Lakota Sun Dancer and during a vision quest I saw the things that ultimately resulted in my being given my Lakota name. Years later, on the day the U.S. invaded Iraq, another vision guided me to start going by this name publicly. This has not been an easy journey nor very good for my "career," but that is a story for another time. However, I think the reason I was guided to do so is because my "Indian" name offers opportunities to begin relevant discussions about the importance of Indigenous ways of knowing for our times. In any case, I wanted to mention the relevance of the vision in connection to my name because the vision is considered to be a legitimate source for new knowledge in Indigenous cultures and a vision was the centerpiece of my own dissertation.

Before telling my story, I want to say that, in one sense, I believe all people are all ultimately "Indigenous." We come from ancestors who once lived according to the rhythms of a particular place. We have in our DNA the potential to recall the harmony and balance of life that we understood from living and observing in that space. We can tap into this knowing to again bring about right relationships with all of creation. I do not intend that we should not pay special attention to contemporary Indigenous peoples or that we should not try to stop genocide and oppression and injustice against them. Nor do I want to suggest that anyone can easily access Indigenous wisdom. I only suggest that to be "Indigenous" goes beyond race, tribal affiliation or even the teachings that stem from observing a specific geographical place. All of us can learn, and I believe it would be in all of our best interests to learn as much as we can, from the Indigenous worldviews practiced by today's Indigenous Peoples who still are able to remember and act according to them.

I've titled my short presentation "Brilliant or Bullshit," because these were the actual words that my dissertation committee chair wrote on the bottom of my cover page after he finished reading it. Although disappointed and a bit confused about what would happen next, I was not really surprised. I was fifty-four years of age and pursuing my second doctoral degree, the first obtained more than twenty years previously. I was not a stranger to the "ivory tower." I would have been the first to admit that my dissertation might have been difficult for a Western academic to accept right off.

I was also not surprised because my dissertation proposal had not prepared anyone for the final product, including myself! It had merely explained that I would return to live with and research the Raramuri Indians of Mexico (also known as the Tarahumara). The proposal was also supposed to be an ethnographic study about how the cultural wisdom of their shamans can be a model for transformative learning and for the kind of critical thinking and situated action that can overcome educational hegemony in schools.

My proposal was not completely forthcoming, however. I did not mention the two most important reasons I wanted to return to the remote Raramuri lands. One was that I wanted to do something to help stop the Fontes drug cartel's murderous treatment of the Raramuris. The second related to my wanting to better understand a powerful vision I had fifteen years earlier, several days after Mexico's Rio Urique had nearly drowned me during an attempt to be the first to successfully kayak down it. The Raramuri Indians had saved my life and the life of my companion. During our incredible climb out of the eight-thousand-foot steep canyon, I had a vision that I had been reflecting on for many years. It related to a mountain lion and a fawn and it had been life transforming for me. It led me to ideas about the role of trance states, fear, authority, language, and nature in the process of transformative learning, although framing it in these ways was a result of my new dissertation studies. At the time of my dissertation work, I wanted to better understand the vision and how it had seemed to affect my life and what could be gleaned from it that would have an application in the field of education.

I said nothing about my vision in my dissertation proposal for two reasons. First, I did not know for sure if it would actually play a role in my final dissertation or not. Second, even if I thought it might play significantly into my dissertation, I knew that my committee would not have accepted a vision as a basis for my research hypothesis. Somehow, I thought, I would just deal with the information that related to the vision, without mentioning this source for it. I guess I was guided by the old saw that says it is better to ask for forgiveness than to ask for permission.

Of course, the vision wound up being the mainstay of my dissertation. I wrote partially as autobiographical story of how the vision and my life subsequent to it had helped me learn a new theory of learning. From the vision of a dead fawn, and the letters in the word, I explored how the constructs of fear, authority, words, and nature are understood differently in traditional Indigenous cultures than in traditional Western ones.

In spite of my chair's initial reaction, I managed to convince him and others on my committee that the work was not "bullshit." Ultimately, I successfully defended my research in front of a formidable audience. The next year, my dissertation was published in book form by Inner Traditions International with the title, *Primal Awareness: A True Story of Survival, Awakening and Transformation with the Raramuri Shamans of Mexico*. I have collected many letters from people who say it impacted their lives in good ways. I continue to grow and learn from the work and just last year was invited to present on it, more than ten years after its publication, at the University of Arizona's Center for Consciousness Studies.

I hope my short dissertation story will give new doctoral students the confidence to use their own dreams and visions as a "valid" source of knowledge. Conclusions can still be triangulated for validity with more traditional research of course, but until scholars are allowed to give credibility to their dreams and visions, the academy will continue to stifle possible solutions to the many problems that face our world.

Thank you.

Dr. Samson: Well, Four Arrows, you have asked me to be bold and forthright in these proceedings so I may as well start now. What concerns me is, well, that you may be advocating that people not be clear about the research during the proposal stage, or worse, that they be deceptive.

Four Arrows: If one is unsure of what will emerge during a research project, it seems that attempting to predetermine the structure or focus can block the emergence of creative material. Also, although visions and dreams are well established in Indigenous cultural research, they are not seen as appropriate sources of knowledge in the academy. The academic research on dreams and visions at the time that would have supported them as sources of knowledge was mostly anecdotal. So what choice did I really have? I do not want people to be deceptive, of course. The purpose of this conference is to create a climate whereby doctoral candidates can be forthcoming about things such as basing a dissertation on a vision or dream. Finally, there is a cultural or a worldview issue here. Although the Western academy may not put much stock in visions, from my Indigenous perspective it makes more sense for me to rely on a vision than to rely on, say, factor analysis.

Dr. Samson: I think, since we have a little extra time before the next presenter, that it would be good at this point to talk a little about what "research" is and is not. Runner, do we have time?

Runner: We do.

Dr. Samson: The best definition I have found comes from Chris L.S. Coryn of Western Michigan University's Evaluation Center. He says that research is a "truth-seeking activity which contributes to knowledge, aimed at describing or explaining the world, conducted and governed by those with a high level of proficiency or expertise." (For those of you who would like to read his entire article or who need to cite this reference, his online piece is entitled, "The Fundamental Characteristics of Research." I'll write the Web site on the board. It is:

http://evaluation.wmich.edu/jmde/content/JMDE005content/Definitions %20of%20Research.htm.)

I'm sure we will all agree with this definition and that we should proceed to evaluate the dissertation examples you all have brought to share with us in the light of it. And I would ask you to consider whether talking about a personal vision meets the idea of conducting research with such expertise.

Runner: I can see by the expressions on many faces that there is some disagreement with the definition. I'm also a bit uncomfortable with the use of the word "expertise." I know, I know, a "doctorate" is about being an expert, you will say. It is about giving authority to a person's knowledge in a particular field. In my culture we do have medicine persons who have special gifts that are recognized by the community. Still, there is something about the term "expert" that does not resonate. I can't help but think of the definition I once heard that an expert is anyone who has a slide show and travels further than twenty miles from his or her house. There is also the one about an expert being anyone who knows enough in their field to be scared. And I also remember a bumper sticker that read, "There is one person in every organization who really knows what is going on. That person must be fired," meaning that even the person with the most knowledge if not "officially" deemed the expert will be dismissed.

I think there is a system in place that prevents a certain kind of knower from being accepted as an "expert," and this kind of knowing might have much to offer the world. Kuhn and others have argued that the scientific community is comprised of people whose common beliefs and values create a uniformity that can prevent such new ideas from coming forth. This is why paradigm shifts often come from people outside of the area of research. For example, did you know that a mortician invented the direct dial telephone upon learning that his competitor's wife was the local telephone operator?

Dr. Samson: We are talking about doctoral level research. Are you saying we should just give doctorates to anyone who has proficiency in something or comes up with a new invention or wants to tell a story about a dream they had? Look, can we at least agree that research should contribute to new knowledge?

Runner: Unless you believe there is "nothing new under the sun." My culture believes that we were placed on earth last so we could learn from those put on it before us. So maybe it is not so much "new knowledge," but new ways of understanding and applying existing knowledge. But I'll go along with your definition if there is no one in this group who wants to jump in and challenge it, then let's proceed.

Dr. Samson: OK. Then can we also agree that it is about describing or explaining the world?

Runner: I would want to include, no, emphasize, the concept of interpreting the world instead of explaining it. Actually, I think that is all we can do.

Four Arrows: I would like to ask one of our honored guests to say a few words about Runner's point here. Many of you know Manulani Aluli Meyer of the University of Hawaii at Hilo and her wonderful work in education, sustainability, transformation, and Indigenous epistemology. Manulani?

Manulani: Runner's idea about interpreting rather than explaining is important. It is about moving from intelligence to interpretation. From fragmentation to wholeness. From status-quo objectivity to radical/conscious subjectivity. This work helps lead us toward a different way to approach literacy, research, energy, ideas, data collection, sustainability, and *all* collaborations.

Dr. Samson: Are you saying we should move away from epistemology, away from a solid basis for what counts as knowledge or truth?

Manulani: When I talk about moving from epistemology to hermeneutics I don't mean we are saying that epistemology is not still important. To the contrary. Talking about what knowledge is or isn't and debating about what may be the difference between knowledge, information, and understanding, is vital. All Indigenous Peoples I have met know this discussion is inevitable. We know that intelligence is far more complex than what a poor SAT score tells us. *We know this.* We know that facts and truth are not one and the same. *We know this.* We know that objectivity found in measurement is only part of the picture we are looking at. *We know this.* And because these times call for courage in our truth-telling, we are now able to express ourselves *through* our intelligence into our interpretation. Understanding occurs in interpretation— the i'ini of a word, the ea of ideas. Our own interpretation will change everything. Understandings will shift. It is indeed a time of 'ike kai hohonu: of searing and deep knowing. Now comes the telling. And as we all know: *It is in the telling.* It is not about labels that we give such as "action research" so much as it is about respecting the telling of stories and the ability for this group of previously helpless people to realize their ability to INTERPRET what is going on. Your research is sacred. How does the interpretation of knowledge as spirit affect your research? It doesn't. *You do.* It merely points to a frequency that if heard will synergize with your courage when you write without fear after asking questions that search for deeper meaning to an act, an idea, a moment. An epistemology of spirit encourages us all to be of service, to not get drawn into the ego nurtured in academia, and to keep diving into the wellspring of our own awe. In that way our research is bound in meaning and inspired by service to others or to our natural environment. This is not objectivity we are discussing, it is fully conscious *subjectivity* and it holds the promise of being effective in a radically different way if you understand its meaning and prioritize it at all levels of your research. It is called meta-consciousness, and it is really what Dr. Jacobs' (Four Arrows) dissertation and book is all about.

Dr. Samson: Well, for now I'll not argue with that, if the interpretations are scholarly, of course.

Unnamed Person: Excuse me, but I was looking up the definition of "research" in the *Concise Oxford English Dictionary*, published in 2004. It offers this definition for "research" and I think it definitely allows for the interpretation component: "studious inquiry or examination, or investigation or experimentation aimed at the discovery and interpretation of facts, revision of accepted theories or laws in the light of new facts, or practical application of such new or revised theories or laws."

Dr. Samson: Hmm. Does this mean that a musical composition or some form of interpretive art could qualify as research?

Runner: I think when you hear about what our dissertation authors and other guest scholars have to say in the coming days you will have your answer!

Dr. Samson: Dr. Linds, it looks like you wanted to interject something?

Warren Linds: I thought I would share that the French word for research, "rechercher," comes from the root word "recerchier"— "parcourir en cherchant", which means "to travel through while searching." I think it is therefore important to realize that research, especially as it relates to discovery and interpretation, is a dynamic process. I think Dr. Samson's idea of knowledge is too rigid. I take a more holistic view . . . that research is about "knowing emerging into being." In other words, "knowledge is not a thing," but constantly becoming.

Runner: Thanks, Warren. By the way everyone, Dr. Linds is with us from Corcordia University in Quebec. He will be talking about his alternative dissertation later on and is well known with his work relating to the role of theater in the development of youth leadership around social justice issues.

Dr. Samson: Even if I wound up conceding to your arguments, this certainly would not apply beyond the soft sciences. Such subjectivity and certainly such research based on art forms could not play a scholarly role in mathematics or physical sciences.

Unnamed Person: Actually, I have recently come across some literature from an organization that refers to itself as the "Qualitative Research in Geography Speciality Group." They promote the use of hermeneutics and phenomenology or constructionist research in teaching and research on this topic.

Runner: Thank you. Geography would especially lend itself to the alternative format, I would think. The power of place is a major aspect of Indigenous culture. I also know a number of Indigenous scientists from around the world who have referred to research definitions given by the United States Committee on Science, Engineering, and Public Policy to try to get support for their approach to science. Their definition definitely embodies alternative research designs, even recognizing crossover relationships between basic and applied research. Keep in mind that this is a joint committee consisting of the National Academy of Sciences, National Academy of Engineering, and Institute of Medicine. They conclude that research is a "search for the unknown whose outcomes are virtually unlimited." Because of this, they conclude that research defies exact definition. By the way, if anyone wants to quote their definition, you can look them up on the Internet or you can get a 2001 government publication entitled *Implementing the Government Performance and Results Act for Research: A Status Report* from National Academy Press in Washington, D.C.

Dr. Samson: You also know that very few Indigenous research projects in the sciences have been funded by the U.S. government. It tends to support only what it calls, "evidence-based research," implying that what you may be wanting to promote is not evidence-based. So I'm afraid you are up against it in the real world with all of this alternative business, whatever merits it may have.

Besides, there is a vast ocean between the ways of thinking relating to what you are referring to as Indigenous and the kind of Western research that has brought us to the moon and back.

Gregory Cajete: If I can briefly butt in here, respectfully, I would like to say a few words.

Runner: Ladies and gentlemen, please let me first introduce Dr. Gregory Cajete who has stopped by to join us. Greg, I hope you can stay long enough to hear about some of the dissertation stories?

Colleagues, Greg is a Tewa from Santa Clara Pueblo and is director of the University of New Mexico Native American Studies Program. He has authored a number of wonderful publications including *Look to the Mountain: An Ecology of Indigenous Education*. Go ahead Greg.

Gregory: Thank you. First, it is important to note that we are making some progress here with reference to Dr. Samson's concern. The American Association for the Advancement of Science has begun to recognize the potential contributions that Indigenous people can make to our understanding of the world around us. More and more folks understand that Native science evolved from a different creative journey and a different cultural history from that of Western science. But it is past time for a dialogue like this one so both Native cultures and the world at large can benefit from their understandings of the natural world. Our science comes from a core set of beliefs relating to personal and community relationships to the natural world. Indigenous science reflects the unfolding story of a creative universe in which we are active and creative participants. So science itself evolves through the creative process of insight, immersion, creation, and reflection. And, yes, from personal visions, especially those that come from immersion in nature. It is about metaphors relating to a creative engagement with nature. It reflects the sensual capacities of humans. It is tied to spirit and is both ecological and integrative. But the mysterious part of the definitions you were mentioning is important because ultimately the universe is a creative expression at a magnitude beyond human recognition. So I'm interested in seeing how these dissertations will—even if they are focused on the social sciences—focus on the subtle, inner natures wherein lie the rich textures and nuances of life and for life. Western science, or perhaps research in general, seems committed to increasing human mastery over nature. This is different than tuning in to the idea of receiving gifts of information FROM nature, which is how we see the goal of research.

"A facilitated journey"

Veronica Arbon's story

- Ularaka—the "rationality of essence, identity and consciousness"
- Inside-out process to research
- Descriptive, reflexive, cyclical
- Colonialism and hegemony in curriculum and employment practices
- Yanhirnda arratya—speaking in consciousness to make correct

Runner: Over the past sixty years Indigenous scholars the world over have challenged facets of Western knowledge and knowledge acquisition. We have attempted to understand research from our own perspectives. This next presentation does this and more as it moves beyond Western philosophical positions to the Ularaka—the philosophical knowledge and practices—of the Arabana people. This morning I have the pleasure of introducing a person who has traveled a great distance to present on her dissertation which exemplifies a:

- passionate naming of "assimilative intent";
- use of Indigenous philosophy, ontologies, metaphor, and language within research;
- complex and detailed discussion of "expert"-led resistance to change; and
- vigilant demonstration of the multi-faceted and parallel nature of existence.

Dr. Arbon graduated from Deakin University with a Doctor of Philosophy, in 2007. Ms. Arbon's dissertation is titled "Thirnda Ngurkarnda Ityrnda: Ontologies in Indigenous Tertiary Education." Focused on change in curriculum and employment in an Indigenous tertiary institution it is a complex study. Veronica, I am anxious to hear more. Welcome.

Veronica: Thank you. I acknowledge the wadlhu Nharla—the people belonging to this country—I am privileged and honored to be on your land. As an Udyurla Arabana, I also acknowledge my Mathapurda and Udyurla urriya parda—my Elders. Kudlha anthuna naninda.

As indicated by Runner, my dissertation is centrally focussed on understanding resistance to Indigenous-led change within a tertiary institution in Australia. This institution offers award studies across both the higher education and the vocational education and training sectors. The institution has responded to Aboriginal and Torres Strait Islander peoples learning aspirations from across Australia for over thirty years. Many of the students come from northern Australia where educational opportunities are limited and Indigenous knowledge, including cultures and languages, are very visible and resilient.

My dissertation is grown from within my people's worldview. I engaged, interpreted, and understood the Ularaka at deeper and, much more complex levels with the support and wisdom of Elders. Key features emerged. These features signified, for me, core meanings to being, knowing and doing as an Arabana Udyurla. I saw these key features as ontology, in a paradoxical and changing world. My Elders were a bit perplexed by this word when I brought it and the related words of epistemology and axiology home for discussion. The word ontology emerged in Western philosophical thought back in the fourth century, but it is useful in describing how the vastness of the Ularaka (Arabana philosophy), the wadlhu (land to which we relate), and the wibma (ancestral stories) can be drawn on for more complex understandings within my dissertation. Therefore, the concept of ontologies allowed for both a journeying back—right back—to Arabana history and a drawing from this knowledge system.

This greater knowing of the Ularaka was achieved by traversing "experiencing, engaging, and interpreting"—this knowledge system and Western philosophies. In turn I was able to articulate my understanding of what it is to be, know, and do as an Arabana Udyurla.

My dissertation holds many journeys—recordings of what has occurred for millennia in the Arabana wadlhu and surrounding areas—telling of the past and the present. And in the dissertation other scholars and, in particular, Indigenous writers are invited into the telling of the overall dissertation. For the Arabana the words "story" and "journey" have both metaphorical and temporal meanings and are critically important to knowledge transfer through the generations. Thus, the use of these words within this thesis took me to both the temporal and, at times, the sacred world.

The first stages of the journey to complete my dissertation were often deeply personal. This journey required numerous visits to the country and discussions with Elders. There were also visits to libraries and archives, often with Elders. A number of Elders also provided writings or comments on their experiences of the colonial process fifty or sixty years ago. This was a delving into the Ularaka and the history of colonial impact on Arabana and other Indigenous peoples lives in Australia. There was a need to capture all this information in some storied form and I turned to a metaphor.

This was the Yalka, a small onion that grows in our country, which has a fine brown skin and porous layers. The Yalka was drawn on as the central metaphor to articulate key features of the Ularaka. The use of the Yalka as metaphor facilitated a coherent representation of the complexity of Arabana philosophy. The Ularaka and the Yuwa (common law) therefore came to form a loosely integrated framework to my doctoral study. The metaphor of Yalka captured beautifully the complexity of not only the Arabana Ularaka but, also later in my studies, the vagaries of colonialism that continue to impact.

Importantly, the metaphor of Yalka facilitated the representation of the rationality of "essence, identity, and consciousness" tied in relatedness at the very core of each entity. Moreover, the fundamental imperative of the relatedness of the Ularaka itself could be raised. The metaphor also allowed representation of a vertical and horizontal, as well as a close and a not-so-close relatedness within the temporal and sacred Arabana world.

I must state that taking up this metaphorically represented ontological position from within the philosophy of the Arabana was not a "creation of a minority space within western thought but a marking out of the validity and strength of Indigenous knowledge and ontologies as read from within the Ularaka" of my people. This position allowed a complex multi-faceted understanding and 'right doing' as is my obligation. Finally, the metaphor allowed understandings from within the Ularaka that went beyond the capacities of many Western philosophical positions and the ideological hegemony of Australian society.

Clearly this approach to my dissertation was not achieved easily. I made several attempts to develop an initial proposal. In the end as my colloquium was planned I submitted a proposal. I had thrown the draft out and in several weeks re-written the whole document. At the time I was anxious to be moved from enrolment in an EdD (doctorate by coursework and portfolio) to a research dissertation. Was I caught up in the definitions of others? Or was I struggling to break free of the concerns raised by one of the gentlemen who dropped in earlier today?

The colloquia eventuated with nine academics making up the panel. I faced the colloquia with great trepidation but, also, with relief as I learned two members were Aboriginal. I continued to worry, however, as the approach I had attempted to articulate was somewhat exploratory and un-formed. But after a couple of hours of intense questioning and insightful responses from both sides of the table, I felt comfortable. Then a critical question was posed. This came from an Aboriginal member of the panel who had honed in on the fact that I was moving to what could be considered a "double degree." This panel member could see I planned to work from an Arabana knowledge position and, then, intended to apply this position to the analysis of "data."

I responded that this was basically what I was doing. He smiled. I knew my struggle had just begun.

At this colloquium meeting I asked for an Arabana Elder to be engaged as a supervisor and that an Elder be permitted to graduate with an honorary PhD at the time I received my award. Sadly, this Elder was never officially engaged on a salary. However, Thanthi (my great grandfather) continued as an educator, carefully mentoring my journey. Other family members also played this role to a lesser degree. Thanthi was an examiner commenting on the philosophical/cultural aspects of my dissertation for which he received a payment. I was pleased with this eventual outcome but none of my relatives agreed to graduate with me earlier this year.

Going back to the early phases of my doctoral studies I read and attempted to engage and to understand the philosophy of the Arabana in greater detail while working through Western science and philosophy. I often came up against a monolithic wall within Western philosophy. What was a dissertation? How could I articulate the dissertation in English? This was a language I struggled with continually in my life. Eighty-thousand words, how was I to do that? More taxing was the fact that many articles and books were written from within the Western philosophical position and were often skewed, or skewed the reality that I understood. How could I work from relatedness in this fractured Western world of domination and subjugation? A major question was also how to articulate the Arabana philosophy in ways that I could draw from it without revealing the secret and sacred aspects of this knowledge position. I went into avoidance. I could not "see" a way forward.

Eventually a supervisor suggested I place myself at the core of my study. I was, for the first time, embodied. This embodiment was a new freedom. Clearly, I was now located in the complex issues of life, of work, and of my studies. I was engaged from within the Ularaka. I went to the Elders for advice. I decided, with the support of Elders, to write from the "inside out." I drew the Ularaka close around me and began to write from within this secure place. Now the hard work seriously started.

In Australia, as in many other parts of the world, education, including tertiary education, became a transformational tool of colonial practice. This tool replaced the central Indigenous learning mechanisms of ceremony, family, and life. This form of colonialism denies or subjugates Indigenous aspirations for ongoing sustainability in philosophical, social, physical, and economic areas of their lives. I encountered these aspects of this transformational education tool often in my doctoral work. As a result of the "assimilative intent" in society, writing the dissertation was often complex. The "path to knowing from within an Arabana cosmology and the continuity of knowledge . . . was . . . subject to dominating power" and change in Australian history. Therefore, I found a need to clearly articulate the wimpa, or track, that I was to follow.

I stumbled on the writings of Manulani Aluli Meyer, who just spoke with us, and I must say it was worth my traveling all this distance just to meet her again! I highly recommend any and all of the books and articles she has written! She taught me that the best way to honor spiritual beliefs is to first be led by them. This wisdom added to the strength and wisdom offered from a number of Elders to bring new insights and great clarity to my study. I learned to "See . . . hear . . . feel and smell (take it in) our *Ularaka* and *Yuwa* (common law)" in much more complex Arabana ways. The wimpa I needed to follow, became clearer. A new consciousness emerged as I entered Indigenous knowledge and, in particular, the Ularaka, powerfully.

I understood all animate entities embody and, are embodied. I understood each entity, in fact, all entities, exist as located and have a presence. I understood this holistic worldview at one level has a complexity and instability of the most fundamental kind while at another is organized and controlled through the kinship system. I understood this system of relatedness mapped over all of life. I understood that dialogue, responsibility and mentoring were central to experience, engagement, and interpretation in this Arabana knowledge system. I understood that other Indigenous groups around the world also held within their philosophies some similar aspects such as relatedness, locatedness.

The above clarity that the ontological features captured within metaphor brought me to "bear witness" on the data, another idea I extracted from Manulani's work. I wrote vigilantly. However, I often worked in isolation of my supervisors at this stage of my dissertation, as the knowledge being experienced, engaged, and interpreted by me was foreign. I was fortunate, though, as one of my supervisors was Aboriginal. This isolation then led to stops and starts and, at times, long discussions with both my supervisors and family. Silences were also present as I resisted suggestions. These supervisors, with our support, recently published a paper about supervising Aboriginal doctoral candidates who had successfully completed, in which they state that trusting Indigenous judgment was critical.

As I moved forward in completing my dissertation, a chapter on the failures of tertiary education in Australia and how "assimilative intent" in these systems brutalized and subjugated Arabana and other Indigenous knowledge positions was included. An additional chapter explored the growth of tertiary education in the Northern Territory, which offered an alternative model while highlighting the fact that this model was being undermined and erased through limited policy formulation and funding cuts. These chapters highlighted the broader context of, and inability to understand Indigenous tertiary education and the visions of Indigenous people within this system over many years.

This information then led to two Yanhirnda arratya. This is a process of speaking consciously (in this case writing) about an issue or issues for all to hear in order to correct a situation through dialogue. In the past this method would have been used early in the morning and no one could respond until after midday or until all members of the community had returned to the camp. This approach therefore included an invitation to comment on the position outlined by the speaker. The Yanhirnda arratya process is an important knowledge affirmation and generation method that has the capacity to bring to discussion difficult matters. In my dissertation, the content, forms, and essence of resistance to curriculum and employment changes were documented.

I then take up the invitation for response to the "data" captured within the Yanhirnda arratya. This process revealed the complexity of the situation within the institute. One of the critical factors revealed was the undermining and temporary loss of Indigenous-led vision. I argued within my dissertation that Indigenous vision concerning our sustainability must not waver as it can be manipulated easily by "experts" in such a situation. These "experts," the politicians and practitioners constructed as hegemonic agents who "speak" solutions for Indigenous people in Australia, are not necessarily concerned with such a vision. It was clearly shown that the focus of the "experts," those leading the resistance to change at the institute, was aiming to maintain an accepted status quo. Is this what we want? Indigenous vision is critical to change for Indigenous futures. However, numerous complexities can emerge in change situations. In the Institute the "benevolent" dominations of history surfaced to powerfully subvert Indigenous vision.

Notably, recent Australian history informs Indigenous people they can be named as the "stirrer" when situations of conflict occur. This is a derogative term that comes with practices to pacify or remove the behavior or voice of an Indigenous individual threatening the accepted status quo. At the institute, certain staff who worked for the required changes to achieve the endorsed vision, were named in this way. In the end these named Aboriginal staff members were removed. In this instance the agendas of others—the "experts" —asserted the accepted status quo. Planned changes were therefore blocked and Indigenous vision temporarily thwarted.

A "new old" way is necessary in such circumstances. This is argued in my dissertation. I argued, drawing on the ontological features of the Indigenous past and reading these from within the Arabana philosophy (in my case) can bring powerful learning and hard-hitting critiques. I argued such a position can 'grow' the critical mass of Indigenous thinkers who have knowledge of both worlds. These individuals are critical to making the necessary and complex changes important for Indigenous sustainability. Moreover, I argued, to *do* in full *knowing* of what it is to *be* as an Arabana person—an Indigenous person— would be critical to this "new old" way.

My dissertation contributes, as it is a statement on Arabana existence. My dissertation also contributes as it outlines the importance of content, processes, and practices, defined from within the Ularaka, to sustainability. Importantly, this notion of sustainability is linked to the criticality of Indigenous-led vision within my doctoral study.

My dissertation also highlights the fact that "benevolence" operates as an "assimilative intent" demanding conformity within Australian society.

A further contribution of my dissertation, I believe, is its ability to open dialogues on Indigenous-led change in complex tertiary education contexts. Furthermore, my dissertation placed for discussion resistance to change. Importantly, it is here that the dissertation becomes critically important as it documents the forms of resistance and activities that emerge as shifts to the status quo occurred at the local level.

My dissertation also contributes through drawing on metaphor, dialogue, reflexivity, and cyclical approaches in research. These are approaches that allow for a stronger dialogue in a complex and paradoxical world. My thesis is also important as it operates from a fundamental premise of relatedness, locatedness, and mentorship and the balance constantly sought within Arabana philosophy.

Ultimately, my work *Thirnda Ngurkarnda Ityrnda: Ontologies in Indigenous Tertiary Education* is important as it reveals many aspects of an Arabana way— an Indigenous way—and articulates issues for improved understanding. And in this Indigenous way the role of Elders and important peers are defined as critical to Indigenous knowledge generation and transfer.

Completion of my dissertation was a difficult but highly rewarding journey. There were many pitfalls and false starts as I struggled to find the right track and leave behind a story that will transfer through the generations. The study was personally rewarding as it forced me to consider my responsibilities as an Arabana Udyurla. Finally, undertaking the dissertation required me to expand my consciousness in the presence of Elders and 'new old' understanding.

"Tin-can bear fat"

Sandi Warren's story

with Trudy Sable and Angayuqaq Oscar Kawagley

- Tin-can bear fat methodology
- Familiarity with the broader world as a prerequisite for specific research

---

Runner: Thank you Veronica. Our next presenter is Sandi M. Warren, a Seneca woman and PhD candidate at Trent University's Indigenous Studies program. She holds a Master's degree in Continuing Education, specializing in workplace learning and a Bachelor degree in Women's Studies. She is an organizational and human resource strategist when she is not dedicating herself to family and community. Please welcome Sandi.

Sandi: Thank you Runner and thanks for inviting me to speak at this important gathering. I am so inspired to see so many of my Native brothers and sisters who have been able to successfully complete their dissertations without selling their souls and you have all given me even more courage to continue my journey.

My father was a hunter and fisherman. He passed away in 2005 at the age of ninety-one years.

He would sit for hours, watching, listening, basking in the sun or freezing in the rain. Tin-Can Bear Fat is a methodology that is reflective of my father's approach to the land, the creatures, the seasons, and all relations. I would like to dedicate my little talk here today to his memory and acknowledge his inspiration to my work.

The late and great Vine Deloria, Jr., a Lakota educator who also has inspired my work, told us that separating knowledge into categories is a major barrier for many Indian students who understand that there is no separation from the rest of creation. My dissertation "methodology" recognizes this. Tin-Can Bear Fat situates an Indigenous method of inquiry that relates to a story of harvesting fish and the angler's relationship to the environment. The environment is represented by the tin can. The experience fits an Indigenous worldview, in which a new angler [*sic*: researcher] works with Elders and community knowledge keepers, who have "harvested the waters" before her.

The methodology, the name which comes from a story my Cree friend Michael Thrasher once told me, serves as a contrast to hermeneutics and phenomenology, which originated and resides in a Eurocentric worldview (in terms of the language associated with these inquiries) since "tin-can bear fat" utilizes oral traditions and narratives as text.

The concept of a "tin-can bear fat" research methodology was envisioned as a process that articulates interpretative inquiry from a mindset that is reflective of Indigenous community livelihoods, without separation. Envisioning "tin-can bear fat", one must think in terms of stories and experience. We begin with the quest of a new angler and her desire to learn how to fish [or hunt]. In the past, when someone approached a skilled angler and asked "show me how to fish," the skilled one would answer "I will show you the water, the land, the seasons, and all the relations that connect you and the fish. When you understand these things, you will understand how to harvest fish."

To acquire this knowledge, the angler must become familiar with the broader world around her/him, as well as the unseen landscape experienced by the fish. To understand the specifics of the fish's world, the angler extracts a small sampling of the environment below the water's surface. To enter this world, "skilled" anglers fasten a tin can, lined with bear fat, to the end of a line, which is lowered to the bed of the river or lake. The cooler temperatures cause the bear fat to congeal, which allows the plant and earth material from the lower depths to be sucked into the container and pulled to the surface. The angler utilizes her knowledge of the broader landscape and the localized information collected in the tin can [gathered from specific targeted areas] to interpret the "patterns" influencing her relationship with her surroundings and the fish.

When Michael shared his story with me, I envisioned the landscape and surrounding areas as the history and contemporary narratives, which provide situational or environmental factors that contribute to policy, structural or identity "attitudes and conditions" impacting our communities. In this manner, the life lesson of harvesting fish creates a discourse that is relevant to the community, who routinely traverse the waterways impacting their existence. By dropping our "tin-can bear fat" the approach provides a means of understanding the whole story, through small and focused samplings. To successfully navigate this approach, the researcher undertakes an intellectual activity that is reflective of what is going on in the community and the various factors impacting its livelihood.

As an Indigenous theorist, I rely on a position that is relevant to Indigenous communities. The interpretative methodologies of hermeneutics and phenomenology offer a vocabulary for contemporary research methodologies by employing tactics "as if" you were there, but I want to write about actually being there. I want to experience and interpret the depth of my communities as a participant or co-author of events. This way I can more authentically uncover the values embedded in the community's language that I am studying. Furthermore, "Tin-can bear fat" sustains the purpose of the interpretative methodologies and navigates "hidden treasures" by drawing from lived experiences, which are embedded in an Indigenous worldview.

The vocabulary of exchange shared between "tin-can bear fat" and the community is more than symbolic replacement of the term hermeneutics. These applications operate from an objective that participants understand their environment and function together to disseminate knowledge and build group cohesion through shared stories, narratives, and actions. The exchange is a conscious interloping and tactical expression of Indigenous ways of knowing and being, and serves as essential criteria for conducting experiential, interpretative, and applied methods of research about "doing," within an Indigenous worldview. The research strategy reflects the goals and questions, not just posed by the literature, but the goals and questions initiated by community conversations. The outcome is a collaborative conversation between researcher and the community, as a means to reflect on ideas and surface concepts both informally and formally, within the group.

By applying a "tin-can bear fat" methodology, the research community engages a process that understands the whole story, through small and focused samplings, while remaining connected to the larger environment and relationships. Tin-Can Bear Fat provides for interpretative inquiry a vocabulary that weaves contemporary Indian history together with the contradictions that have previously excluded the Indigenous ways of learning and teaching. By articulating a methodology relevant to the ontology of Indigenous people, we can affirm the validity of Indigenous knowledge and, hopefully, this knowledge will be honored and used to solve our world's problems before it is too late.

Dr. Samson: Thanks Sandi and good luck with your dissertation. I don't know if the tin-can and bear-fat research will make it into a research text in the near future, but I suppose it is not that far of a stretch from some of the methods now being introduced. Look everyone, I understand the experientialist paradigm for curriculum and research, but scientific research is what ultimately creates cultures, at least those that last. Science and technology have brought us into a world where their wise use will determine the vitality or the end of a society. Relying on the community culture exclusively and on a sort of self-discovery journey will seldom bring forth solid, scientific conclusions.

Dr. Trudy Sable: What you are saying, Dr. Samson, tends to ignore the fact that knowledge, including science, may be a cultural product.

Runner: Excuse me Trudy, let me just introduce you to everyone. Dr. Sable is the Director of the Office of Aboriginal and Northern Research at the

Gorsebrook Research Institute at Saint Mary's University, Halifax, Nova Scotia. She is investigating Innu and Western scientific perspectives into research. Go ahead Trudy.

Trudy: Taking this cultural view of scientific knowledge allows us to view learning as a process of identity formation, and culture as a system of symbols including language itself. This identity is based on personal, cultural, historical, and social factors that come to bear on each student's definition of who they are and what knowledge is pertinent to survival and well-being. (*Turning to the person sitting on her left*) Oscar, would you share something about Indigenous scientific knowledge that you said to me a few minutes ago?

Oscar: Well, I am enjoying this talk very much. I am Angayuqaq Oscar Kawagley and I entered school in Bethel, Alaska, knowing only the Yupiaq language. My grandmother would not let anyone take me to a boarding school. I am now an Associate Professor at the University of Alaska and the Co-director of the Alaska Rural Systemic. I want to say that the depth of Indigenous knowledge that is rooted in the long inhabitation of a particular place offers lessons that can benefit everyone, from educator to scientist, as we search for a more satisfying and sustainable way to live on this planet. The tendency in the earlier literature on Indigenous education, most of which was written from a non-Indigenous perspective, was to focus on how to get Native people to acquire the appurtenances of the Western/scientific view of the world.

Until recently there was very little literature that addressed how to get Western scientists and educators to understand Native worldviews and ways of knowing as constituting knowledge systems in their own right, and even less on what it means for participants when such divergent systems coexist in the same person, organization, or community. It is imperative, therefore, that we come at these issues on a two-way street, rather than view them as a one-way challenge to get Native people to buy into the Western system. Native people may need to understand Western society, but not at the expense of what they already know and the way they have come to know it. Non-Native people, too, need to recognize the co-existence of multiple worldviews and knowledge systems, and find ways to understand and relate to the world in its multiple dimensions and varied perspectives.

While Western science and education tend to emphasize compartmentalized knowledge, which is often de-contextualized and taught in the detached setting of a classroom or laboratory, Indigenous people have traditionally acquired their knowledge through direct experience in the natural world. For them, the particulars come to be understood in relation to the whole, and the "laws" are continually tested in the context of everyday survival. Western thought also differs from Indigenous thought in its notion of competency. In Western terms, competency is often assessed based on predetermined ideas of what a person should know, which is then measured indirectly through various forms of "objective" tests. Such an approach does not address whether that person is actually capable of putting that knowledge into practice. In the traditional Native sense, competency has an unequivocal relationship to survival or extinction—if you fail as a caribou hunter, your whole family may be in jeopardy.

Runner: Thank you Sandi. I can't help but feel our whole world is in jeopardy now for survival or extinction and our work is thusly important!

"Whispering the circle back"
Joyce Schneider's story

with Suzanne Stewart and Carole LeClair

- Interpersonal interviews
- Oral transmission of knowledge participation
- Listening with the heart
- Mixed media
- Drumming
- Community

Runner: It is my pleasure to introduce another First Nation's scholar, Joyce Schneider, who received her Master's degree from the University of Northern British Columbia. She is one of the few people who were invited who has not completed a doctoral dissertation, but we felt her story was important since our ideas about alternative research apply to all academic research, not just doctoral level and because her story says much about doctoral level research as well.

Joyce: At first I did not understand why I was invited to attend this conference because I did not have a doctoral degree, but as I read about the reasons for this conference, I immediately understood. The topic, methodology, and work of my thesis have been a lived experience for me that have impacted my, as well as my children's, life paths. So I have come here to whisper ways of being that have come to live within my heart as I journeyed towards obtaining a mainstream education through participation in the oral transmission of knowledge.

As a member of the *St'at'imx* Nation, I needed to honor the ways of knowing that are traditional to my people in the fulfillment of the requirements for my Master's degree in First Nations Studies. In doing so, I have recorded on my heart the teachings so gently shared with me by my Uncle Ray Peters, Aunties Laura Purcell and Rose Smith of the *Samahquam* Band, my Aunty Toni Archie of the *Tsq'escen* Band, and by Tina Fraser and Leona Neilson from the First Nations Studies department at UNBC. Through blending the understandings I have gained from both the academic and Indigenous worlds, my thesis represents the possibilities that await us when we seek to honor and value diverse ways of knowing.

As I completed the course work for my Master's degree, I became increasingly aware of my propensities to utilize the methodologies of a system foreign to *our* own ways of knowing. As a *St'at'imicw* person, I will use the term *our* to indicate my belonging to the *St'at'imx* Nation, to the collective, and to the common underlying principles of the Indigenous peoples of Turtle Island. I realized that I was no longer comfortable with the idea of learning the stories of my nation to fulfill the requirements of academia. It began to feel inappropriate for me to choose this path of discovery to gain the knowledge that was of such personal importance to the continued remembering of who I am as a *St'at'imicw* woman. I became concerned about the implications of setting to paper the knowledge that would be shared with me, and I questioned the integrity of my taking this *fast track* to heightening my cultural awareness without honoring the value of our own ways of learning and knowing by experiencing and practicing them. I came to realize that the lack of publications on the *St'at'imicw* people was in fact a blessing, for it inspired me to take the time to travel to my community on a number of occasions, establishing a crucial connection that might not have been made had there been an abundance of information readily available in the university library. I was not only exposed to *St'at'imx* ways and knowledge while connecting with family and community, I also came to understand my responsibilities to these connections.

This enlightenment led me to the realization that I needed to learn and honor the ways of my people in the manner they were meant to be learned and was the driving force behind everything, from the oral tradition methodologies I chose to complete the thesis to the eventual title of the work. By conducting fourteen short, un-recorded open-format interviews with my Uncle Ray Peters (*Samahquam*), my Aunty Toni Archie (*Tsq'escen*), my aunties Laura Purcell and Rose Smith (*Samahquam*), and with Tina Fraser and Leona Neilson of the First Nations Studies Department at the University of Northern British Columbia, I experienced learning by listening to, reflecting upon, and retelling the conversations of the interviews. The sessions were not recorded because I wished to experience gaining knowledge through the natural processes of the relationships I have with each of the participants. I wanted to see how I listened and what I heard when I knew there were no recordings or notes to rely on—I had only my remembering of the session and personal reflections (both important components of the oral tradition), to consider and document in writing after the session was over. I wished to do as I heard a Maori Elder said the Maori once did, listen not only with the ears but with the heart—in effect doubling, and changing, the attention I gave to the person so kindly sharing his or her thoughts with me.

It was my first intention to conduct interviews with nine different people; an Elder, Teacher, and Storyteller from each of the two First Nations' communities, and three First Nations' people from the academic community of UNBC, for a total of nine separate interview sessions. However, upon careful consideration of what my main goals and hopes for this study were, I came to realize that it would be more beneficial to my understanding of traditional ways of knowing, to interview, without recording, two people from each community on three separate occasions. In this way I might experience different levels, or stages, of participating in the sharing of knowledge and move through the various levels of knowing, mapping, and considering the traditional methodologies of passing on and receiving knowledge. With this approach, I practiced transmitting back what I heard or understood on each successive visit after I had had the time to reflect and internalize what had been shared with me. The questions in the Interview Guide focussed on the participant's experiences with learning from both mainstream institutions and the oral tradition. I chose this methodology because I was not comfortable with the mainstream practice of analyzing what the participants shared, I preferred to reflect upon the impacts their words had on me and the path I would take because of what they shared with me.

To demonstrate the valuing of different ways of knowing, I chose to blend academic and oral-tradition methods of learning both in the final dissemination paper as well as in the defense presentation.

Thanks to the wisdom of my Aunties who assisted me with this work, I learned the importance of taking the time to reflect, pray, remember, and share what I learn, doing so takes vast amounts of time and it was a struggle to allow this process to take as long as it did (four years, seven months). It was difficult to reveal the personal and spiritual impacts this journey had on me, on my life, in an *academic and professional* manner. It is not easy to trust mainstream institutions with such personal revelations, but I was blessed with an amazing and supportive academic committee that always encouraged me to share what I needed to share, they made it safe to do so. I also came to understand that this *professionalism* is what keeps us from connecting in real ways and connection is crucial to understanding, learning, healing, etc.

The benefits of this work have been many. The understandings about responsibility to community, nation, and around truly valuing diversity, have been instilled in me forever and all have been passed on to my children. I look forward to teaching courses at the college and university level that inspire students to value connections and each other's ways of being to the extent that we begin to share a world view that sees all life valued, respected, and celebrated.

My final presentation was a mixture of media to demonstrate the valuing of numerous ways of sharing knowledge. I began with a recording of our *St'at'imx* language, speaking about the importance of the hand drum and the songs we sing. My children and visiting family members helped me drum our

Welcome song to welcome all those who had traveled and/or taken the time to witness my thesis celebration. The audience was invited to enjoy coffee, bannock, *tswan* (dried salmon my Auntie Rose brought from Mt. Currie), and freshly made berry compote. My daughter told me I presented like I was talking to a group of friends; it was comfortable, with food, drumming, and laughter. My presentation went over the time limit by ten minutes and although the chair, Dr. Robert Tait made it clear it could not be more than twenty minutes long, he later indicated it was fine and good to allow me to tell my story the way it needed to be told.

I shared with the audience the Story Stick I had made, to remember all that I had learned strictly through the oral tradition by participating in my community, and I also used a PowerPoint presentation with photographs to trigger the oral presentation portion of my defense. All but two of the six knowledge sharers witnessed my defense, and tobacco was given to the committee members and to an audience member from each area represented in the room. Gifts were offered to each of the knowledge sharers, the members of my academic committee, and to each of my children for standing to drum with me on this important and special day. My family and I drummed the "Woman's Warrior Song" after hearing I had received a clear pass and we spent some time introducing my *St'at'imx* family to my university family. It was a real blessing to see the two worlds in which I live and learn come together in such a good way that day.

The impacts of this journey have been poignant and life changing. As I internalized the importance of connections and responsibilities to my community and Elders I struggled to cope with the loss of many Elders and Youth suffered by our community. As I was learning about the significance of our relationships, about watching and listening carefully to our Elders, I was hearing of their journeys to the Spirit World. I questioned many times whether I was where I was supposed to be, and often fought to see through the tears as I wrote my way through the realization that I would never have the opportunity to learn from these loving people again. I carry the words and aspirations that many of them have shared with me in my heart and I in turn share them with my children with the hopes that they will learn at an age far younger than I, their role in the community and their responsibilities to family, community, the oral tradition, and our ways of being.

This work and the course work that is growing from it is all about tearing down the walls that separate us, it is about changing the norms and moving us back to a more natural way of being, a return to a sense of community that would never allow its children, Elders, and youth to feel anything but strong, important, and happy. My work seeks to dismantle the conventional state of individualism society adheres to because it really does not work. Promoting a sense of belonging and community in the classroom has the potential to grow out into the larger community and beyond because it is in the classroom that our mainstream worldviews originate. This work represents a potential catalyst for change, because it is in shifting the way that graduating students think that change becomes reality, for this is where all actions begin, in the way we see the world and ways of being in our minds.

Runner: Wopila, thanks for sharing your story. We have some time left before our next presenter and I see some hands waving out there. Suzanne, go ahead.

Suzanne Stewart: I just want to thank Joyce for the way she honored her culture in her research and for her courage to do so in the academic setting. I am finishing up my PhD at the University of Victory and am of the Yellowknife Dene First Nation. I know what she means when she talks about the personal and spiritual impacts of her journey. Many of us from Indigenous communities feel emotions of self-doubt and fear in today's academic environment. We feel that we must prove not only our research but also ourselves as Indigenous people, as legitimate.

My own university, like most, was rightfully concerned with the rigor of my research, and this I anticipate. I often even enjoy the challenge of meeting this demand. Yet I have always felt somewhat emotional about justifying my identity as a Native person in the context of my research projects. Again, perhaps these feelings come from my personal history, particularly in childhood that is amply littered with experiences of racism, prejudice, and exclusion from the dominant Western society. But I overcame that, didn't I? I left that place and found my own niche where I was accepted when I quit my Aunt's suburban home and grade nine and made a life on the street with people who were like me—battered (in various ways), ostracised, looking for a sense of belonging, looking for something we didn't have in former homes. However, it is also true that some of these oppressive experiences have occurred more recently in my life, within the context of "modern" post-secondary education. What has been positive for me in my current research experience is the support and encourage-ment of my doctoral committee members, each of whom has inspired me to stay true to my voice as a Native person, and has fostered a sense of ability to incorporate this into my research in a way that is both systematic and true. Carrying out research that is beneficial to both scholarship and to the community in which the research has occurred is satisfying. There have been times when my faith in the goodness of research has wavered (many times, in fact), and this has disconcerted me, as I have been committed to seeking out and conducting ethical and successful scholarship since I began graduate studies. Having participants and other community members experience benefit from each stage of the research gives me a sense of pride and accomplishment in the work, and myself. I have not simply fulfilled part of the doctoral requirements but I have done something that was of greater good for people within the context of the greater society. Anyway, thank you. Thanks to all of the Indigenous researchers. Being here to listen to these stories of Indigenous scholars has given me even more inspiration and courage. Thank you.

Runner: Carole. We would be honored to hear from you. Would you introduce yourself to everyone?

Carole Leclair: Boojoo everyone. Well, I did my doctoral dissertation at York's Faculty of Environmental Studies, in a story-telling way consistent with my Saulteau/Metis cultural perspective, in 2002. It was a challenge, both for me and for my committee, because my work was a total departure from the usual dissertation gymnastics, but it can be done! I am now a tenured faculty at Wilfrid Laurier University in Brantford, Ontario.

I just wanted to underscore what all of the previous First Nations speakers have emphasized, and that is this idea about research participants and other community members experiencing benefit from each stage of the research. If only more people in the dominant culture would understand what this emphasis has to offer the world. In my own work as a Metis, for example, I continually asked throughout my research, "What principles and practices of traditional Metis cultures are useful to those who search as we do, for answers and hopeful directions away from the misery of permanent organic pollutants, toxic waste, depleting ozone, melting polar caps?" The answer is that we *begin* by remembering and keeping alive ideas about the meanings of land that are older than the idea of real estate. Our ways of remembering are through story, song, ceremony, dance, feast, tears, and celebration. Many layered messages are contained in our stories, messages that express the usefulness and wisdom of a way of life. When we remember Aboriginal stories about frogs, we learn that we have a long and reciprocal relationship to them. We know that a part of oneself is lost when a local developer paves over the earth where the peepers sing in springtime. We mourn that loss. Through our stories and our choices, we bring our Metis consciousness into urban realities, countering the common attitude, "It's his property, he can do as he likes." Like those spring peepers, our voices can still be heard by those who know how to listen.

Runner: Carole, I know you brought an outline of your dissertation today. Would you give people in the audience a more concrete sense of what your dissertation actually looked like?

Carole: Sure. Chapter One "Issues in Defining Metis Identity," explores issues in defining and resisting definitions of Metis identity. In this and subsequent chapters, I draw on and write about my own life experience and that of my family members. To do this is to take risks. Is this practice "ecology," or strictly the province of personal narrative? Is it autoethnography, or merely anecdotes? Are these terms not legitimately ecological? Our personal narratives do reflect our relationships in the world, and yet I refuse to describe my writing in these terms. To use such descriptors is to look at Metis identity through a squared circle. I remember and recount as a child of the old ways. Clearly remembered facts form only a part of the whole story. In the spaces of silence, those spaces where memory fails, the spirit of truth may also be visible. Questions of race, religious belief, and political organizational strategies are only touched upon in this chapter, as each of these elements of Metis identity deserve their own lengthy treatment.

Chapter Two, "Talk to Text," rehearses the writings and conversations of selected contemporary Metis writers who have contributed to the development of my own critical approach to Aboriginal writing, an approach so aptly described by Rick Monture as, "a non-approach, involving much word play, a few inside jokes, self-deprecation, humour, anger, sadness and elation—all in equal amounts in order to bring about a balance of literary voice that speaks to, and for, all people."

Chapter Three, "Metis Models of Enquiry" explores interpretive research strategies from within Metis perspectives. Borrowing a term from Metis Elmer Ghostkeeper, I reflect on ways to engage in what he calls *wechewehtowin*, or working in partnership with Euro-Canadian researchers and their strategies that respect our differences and fulfill the requirements of both traditions. In the past, Euro-Canadian researchers have used Metis as informants to their projects, fitting their information into predetermined models of academic disciplinary traditions. I review David Burley, Gayel Horsfell, and John Brandon's archeological study *Structural Considerations of Métis Ethnicity* and demonstrate how *Métis* oral tradition can enhance the project's findings. Following a discussion of Metis traditional values, I use the research project, *Song of Métis Women*, to illustrate how a research project designed and implemented by the Métis Women's Circle reflects Métis values while using an adapted form of Action Research.

Chapter Four, "Metis Ecology: Some Practices and Beliefs," presents a fine-grained study of selected portions of interviews with Eugène Serré, Arthur Bottineau, and Christina Agawa in which they discuss their relationship with *bush ways* and the cultural elements that both connect and separate Métis and *mixed-blood* heritages.

Chapter Five, "A Return to the Grandmothers," links together the contested identity Métis/Metis, traditional, community, and bush values in an urban environment. Using the Métis Women's Circle, Inc. as illustration, I discuss ways of enacting Metis identity and community in urban settings.

My work demonstrated the power of story as a form of knowledge. Our remembering is not merely nostalgia. As I neared the end of my study I understood even more clearly that Metis can speak from within a center of consciousness that is uniquely Metis. Finding one's footing here is difficult. From the beginning this must be confronted. There seems to be no solid place on which to stand, but we must stand, no clear forum from which to speak, but we speak here about doctoral-level research addressing our current world's problems, we might all well start thinking about this subject in terms of survival or extinction, like Oscar mentioned earlier.

"Double wampum"

Barbara Mann's story

with Bruce Johansen, Susan Deercloud, and Robert B. Kaplan

- Double wampum as a spiritual principle and a "dual delivery" system
- Use of humor in research and representation
- Native thinking as different from Euro-centric
- The problem of "one-thinking"
- Critical race theory (supports the contention that the ways of knowing of racial or ethnic people have not been fairly acknowledged)

Runner: Although a number of the arts-based dissertations that are going to be talked about later might be seen as somehow stemming from Indigenous perspectives on the value of what is called "art" in the English language, our next presenter will be the last of our Indigenous dissertation authors to share their specific dissertation stories with us.

Barbara is currently a lecturer in the English Department at the University of Toledo. Her books, book chapters, and journal articles have made a significant contribution to Indigenous studies and I strongly recommend everyone read her chapter, "Where are Your Women?: Missing in Action," published in Four Arrow's book, *Unlearning the Language of Conquest*. Barbara, it's all yours.

Barbara: Thank you. It is an honor to be with all of you at this important conference. My name is really The Barbara, inherited from the original La Barbara of my family, a Grey-Eyes, Snake Clan Wyandot who escaped the nuns around 1835 when she was sixteen. Stealing a canoe, she paddled alone around Lake Erie from Ontario down to the Maumee River, where she knew Seneca hold-outs were hiding. Joining them, she was adopted into the Bear Clan of the Ohio Senecas and married to Hetoh, the leader of the longhairs there. She decided to keep the name La Barbara (The Barbarian), feeling that she had damned well *earned* it. It passed down in the family to the current The Barbara.

The modern holder of the name honors her ancestors, feeds the spirits, and keeps the Old Things as well as she can for the people in Ohio.

My difficulty with dissertation motifs actually began with my Master's thesis back in 1994. When I received back the all-important preceptor's comments on my finished draft, I was shocked to see that he obviously had not had a clue as to what I had been doing. I should thank him, however, since he forced into conscious articulation something that I had been doing unthinkingly throughout my educational career: using the double-wampum format of formal discourse. This fairly ancient method based on character-writing knotted into wampum belts, was once widely employed throughout the woodlands.

Double-wampum is a dual delivery system deliberately replicating a spiritual principle. Because the cosmos exists by halves for us (Mother Earth/ Brother Sky), it is impossible to have one of anything before we first have two of something. That is, the One Good Mind of Consensus can emerge only after the two cosmic halves of Earth (Turtle/Water/Blood) and Sky (Wolf/Air/ Breath) have joined in common discourse. In other words, the whole community needs to get its two cents' worth in before any decisions can be made. This way, the cosmos is respected by being reproduced in human interactions. Incidentally, just about everything of importance will be canvassed in the process.

To represent this principle in civic affairs, double-wampum messages were constructed. Wampum belts had messages knotted into both sides. Since there were two messages—from each of the clan halves if women, or from each of the national halves if men—there had to be two speakers, one from each half reading her or his side of the belt. Moreover, each messenger addressed the clan or national half *opposite* her or his own, in crisscross (X) fashion. Thus, there were four required and equal parties to every address, two in delivering the message and two in receiving it. This only looks like a base number of four to the uninitiated. In fact, each half formed a whole unit, one of earth (\) and one of sky (/). Meanwhile, forcing each half to address the half opposite ensured the full and equal participation of everyone at the meeting (X). This is, by the way, is binary math, which underpins our economic gifting systems, too.

Getting back to my Master's thesis, my preceptor rather haughtily tossed it at me, announcing that it was disjoined: it consisted of two separate theses with a shifting audience. I was jolted by his displeasure. It had never occurred to me to set it up in any other way. Since he had caught me flat-footed with his critique, I was not immediately able to tell him *why* I had set it up that way. Indeed, the reasons were still pretty invisible to me at that point, as most deeply laid cultural approaches are to their practitioners.

This experience did rouse me to dedicated thought on the subject, however, so that by the time I reached my dissertation in 1997, I had become fairly militant on the subject of formats and was able to articulate what I was doing. Turning my mental searchlight on the "problem" of my thesis, I started to understand comments on much of my graduate writing that, till then, had been inscrutable to me. I recalled my final, in-class exam on Henry James, which consisted of two theses concerning his interminable *Daisy Miller*, each argued equally. That professor had been quite flummoxed but decided only to grade the first thesis and regard the second as "a mistake" I had made, presumably under the pressure of the exam. I recalled a Master's paper on Martin Delaney's *Blake, or the Huts of America*, likewise set up in double-wampum format and likewise puzzling to the professor. I recalled a class presentation on James Fenimore Cooper that looked at Natty from both a Native and a settler vantage point—that one leading, traumatically enough, to attempts to wash me out of the graduate program.

It finally dawned on me that Euro-Americans cannot see two of anything without immediately assuming that one of them must be the deadly enemy of the other. Only one can be legitimate for them; the other is flawed, an impostor that must be rooted out. This "ONE-thinking," as I call it, is a direct reflection of the Manicheanism rampant in European and Euro-derived monotheisms. It is in profound conflict with the cooperative binaries of Native American cultures, a point I made at illustrated length in *Native Americans, Archaeologists, and the Mounds*. The dissonance between Native and European ways of seeing is only compounded by the very unilinear Puritan sermon format shoved down the throats of American academics as the one, true form of discourse, a point I canvassed in *Iroquoian Women: The Gantowisas*.

By the time I got to my dissertation in 1997, I was loaded for bear. (A pun. I'm Bear Clan.) I had already included references to the two-pronged approach in "Euro-forming the Data," a published critique of European ethnology, included in *Debating Democracy*. Emboldened by the publication, I made a point of informing my dissertation committee members that I was using the double-wampum format, describing how it would work out in my text, and basically letting them know that they could like it or leave the committee. Largely because I had a wonderfully open-minded scholar, Geoffrey Rans, sitting influentially on the committee, I got away with it. Since that success in carrying my point, I went ahead and used the format again in my first solo book, *Iroquoian Women*. Since then, I have used it regularly, even in such a trenchantly Westernized "inquiry" as history. It may be embedded more subtly in such texts, but I do ensure that a Native voice can be heard, as in *George Washington's War on Native America*.

I want now to jump to set two of my story. Apparently, I have to learn the hard way. By the end of the dissertation ordeal, I realized that there were endemic DIFFERENCES between Native and European discourse styles, but somehow, it did not occur to me that they might include anything as innocuous as joking. The often scatalogical humor and sheer playfulness of Native American discourse—and particularly the sacred clowning that deflates pomposity—is something else that Europeans and their descendants shake disapproving fingers at. There is a sign somewhere in the constipated bowels of academia that reads: NO LAUGHING ALLOWED. It probably has a little brother somewhere bawling, ALL DISCUSSIONS OF SEX MUST BE MEDICAL.

Unbelievably to me, I was treading on dangerous ground in *Iroquoian Women* when I went to recount the raucous point in the tradition of the Great Law at which the Peacemaker sought to cut the overgrown penis of Adodaroh down to peaceable size. In tradition, Adodaroh's kill power, as denoted by the length of his penis, was so great, that he wore it wrapped around his waist three times before tucking its head into the coils, to keep it securely in place. The Peacemaker wanted the penis down to resting (peace) size, or six thumb-widths in length. Taking out his hunting knife, he uncoiled it and sawed it off at six thumbs, only to see the danged thing immediately surge back to its former size. Three times, the Peacemaker hacked it off to thumbable size, and three times, it grew right back, with Adodaroh wrapping and tucking each time. Of course, the sober point is that neither Earth nor Sky could rule the other, but that both must work in tandem. Nevertheless, the amount of waxing, waning, thumbing, and tucking going on in this tradition is pretty darned funny, yet I was cautioned not to push its unseemly humor in that section. Later in the text, I had to fight to retain my jocular reference to rejected husbands, sent home to Mother with their six-thumb penis tucked between their legs, because it might be too much for undergraduates to, um, handle.

In another instance, both in the dissertation and later as pulled out for publication in a freestanding book chapter, I gleefully recounted the unintentionally hilarious theology of the Moravian adherent, Count Nicholas Ludwig Zinzendorf. As practiced by the Moravians in America, Zinzendorfian Christianity was blindly erotic, and sometimes, homoerotic. First, all souls were depicted as female, whereas the creator was emphatically male. Next, Zinzendorf described spirituality as a sex act, with the female souls as the "playmates" of God, cavorting about in a sort of cosmic marital bed. Of course, God remained male throughout. The plot thickened, of course, when one realized that at least half the playmates in God's bed were physically male. It gets better. Zinzendorf's cockamamie "wounds theology" was quite fond of the wound to Jesus's penis made during circumcision. That got to remain male, but the wound in his side transformed into a vagina, shoving out newborn converts apace. Adherents were to lick and taste the wounds, presented as "succulent" and "juicy." Now, let's all think about that. (*Audience laughter.*)

Alas, I appear to have a highly reprehensible funny bone. Critics (all Western) have drubbed me more than once on my "sophomoric" humor, as did several pre-publication readers of "A Sign in the Sky: Dating the League of the Haudenosaunee." All seemed distraught at my mention of what I termed the "naked insult" of 1524, when New England Natives mooned Giovanni di Verrazano and his crew. None of these prudish readers looked twice to wonder whether I was indulging in traditional humor; they just assumed that I was a potty mouth. Readers of another offending article that became "The Lynx in Time," primly informed my editor that I was "a snot." By the time the *Mounds* book hit, with my unreconstructed Indian humor still on the loose, one stuffy reviewer intoned that "fans of Barbara Mann's work" might like my lunacy, but proper intellectuals would eschew it (at which I thought, "Fans? I have *fans*?").

As with double-wampum formatting, I have decided to continue throwing in humor, and maybe even, to accelerate its use. Watching Euro-academics gasp for air is actually a lot of fun. Anyway, I'm happy to be here and hope that you all will continue to challenge those things in Western education that are doing violence to us all.

Dr. Samson: Dr. Mann, I truly have great respect for your work, and at the same time—notice I am not falling into the "one-thinking" trap—at the same time it seems that your strong words about what you call "Euro-academics" seem to do exactly what you are criticizing. It seems you are making Indigenous approaches to research "legitimate" and Eurocentric ones found in the traditional academy, "flawed."

Barbara: There you go, assuming that two of anything—say, methods—must mean that one is WRONG, because only one can be RIGHT. That is the very description of ONE-thinking. Look, just because I'm advocating that Euro-academics move over to make room for Other ways of seeing does not mean that I refuse to allow the Euro-way of thinking. Now, think about this: in a world where the Indigenous voice has all but been stomped upon, and where Indigenous People have entered into higher education to make contributions to new knowledge only to face suppression, I think that offering a critique of one so as to allow for the voice of the other is anything but "one-thinking." Bruce, I see you smiling and know that means you want to say something. Friends, this is Bruce Johansen. Bruce is neither "Indian" nor is he "one-thinking," but he is a brilliant and prolific Indian studies scholar and the Kayser Research Professor in Communication and Native American Studies at the University of Nebraska. His dissertation, which established that The Iroquois Confederacy was a major influence on the concept of democracy and the form of government established in these United States, was the beginning of a long series of important books, with the most recent being the *Encyclopedia of American Indian History* from ABC-CLIO.

Bruce Johansen: I just wanted to underscore Barbara's response. Even being a non-Indian, when I asserted in my dissertation that Native American politics had influenced those of Anglo-Americans, I found myself swimming upstream. First, many of my advisors had no idea that Indigenous Americans had even possessed political structures. In the 1970s, the wild man of the woods was the common intellectual currency, even in academia. Secondly, I was studying in a history department at the University of Washington in which what later was rather blandly labeled "the encounter" (e.g. the displacement of Indigenous

Peoples by European-descended immigrants) was called "the history of the Western movement," as if movement had occurred in only one direction—e.g. the Europeans brought civilization to "the other." I found myself positing communication theory that led me to believe that ideas are shared in any contact going both ways. "Westward movement" allowed no space for the "eastward movement" of ideas. I have never lost my sense of awe at how the reactions have varied, from absolute denial to avid support. At one point during the debates over "political correctness" and the validity of multicultural education in the 1990s, the idea seemed to have blazed through the right-wing cocktail party circuit in silly, truncated form, causing all sorts of household names, from George Will to Rush Limbaugh, to Dinesh D'Souza, to pounce on it with a degree of gut-level discourse that I never would have used. Behold this mild-mannered Midwestern college professor peddling alleged "fiction" (Will) that "is worse than facts," (Limbaugh), pushed on innocent students by a "Visigoth in Tweed" (D'Souza). There were many, many more like this. I was told time and again that "no reputable scholar" would entertain such ideas.

Robert B. Kaplan (Bob): I don't think anyone is arguing that Native American views have not been suppressed. There's no question that traditional scholarship has done irreparable harm to Indigenous people—but not only to Indigenous people; e.g. the young folks dying in Iraq right now, some of whom are Indigenous people but some aren't. Years ago, I wrote a paper urging speakers of standard English to be a bit more tolerant and to recognize that speakers of what is now called African American Vernacular English (AAVE) weren't from some other planet; the article got no takers, but it did earn me a few kicks in the head. What I'm trying to suggest—obviously not very successfully—is that you might wish to consider some compromises—a bit of sugar—to increase the number of listeners. I guess I'm not a very good model for a revolutionary—I tend to favor evolution over revolution at least in the sense that evolution is a bit less bloody.

This said, I believe what Dr. Samson is saying is that while Barbara's story is interesting, she seems to be doing exactly what she properly objects to. She may not want to do "one thinking" per se by shutting out Western ways of thinking as practiced in the academy, but she does nonetheless cut herself off from communication by using a device that the audience doesn't understand. The English language scholarly dissertation is considered successful if it moves from introduction to conclusion in a straight line; tangential material is not acceptable. Spanish, for example, welcomes tangential material—indeed, the writer is expected to demonstrate the full scope of his/her knowledge. "Double-wampum formatting" would be anathema to the scholarly article. That is not to say one is "better" than the other; rather, if you turn on the radio expecting to hear Kiri Tekanowa and you get a blues singer or a country singer there will be a moment (a period) of suspended attention because the expected isn't there, not because one is better than the other.

Dr. Samson: Everyone, allow me to introduce Bob Kaplan. His seminal work in the 1960s is largely responsible for the field of study known as contrastive rhetoric and its younger sister, comparative rhetoric. Bob is Professor Emeritus in Applied Linguistics at the University of Southern California, and founder of the Annual Review of Applied Linguistics. His expertise in discourse analysis is legendary and his publication record is a mile long.

Bob: Please don't get me wrong. I've tried all my professional life to make the point that buying into the academic style does indeed constrain communication and creativity. In 1660, Robert Boyle invented the scientific article, and he and his colleagues in the Royal Society created the overriding code of the gentleman in science—a code that has persisted into the twenty-first century. Thus, the scientific (i.e. academic) article was free of humor, was serious, was polite, and was scholarly; none of these characteristics contributes much to creativity or to fascinating communication. I think Dr. Samson's view, and it is just one valid perspective, is that student writers must learn to participate effectively in a particular discourse community and are obligated to do so as doctoral candidates. On the other hand, I could also support the idea that the students renovate this particular genre. Genres are not static structures; they evolve (and I do mean evolve) changing over time and environment. That's why chemists can talk to chemists but may find it difficult to talk to sociologists. I anticipate that the academic article will be significantly different in 2050 largely, perhaps, because of the kind of work all of you are doing here.

Runner: Dr. Kaplan, excuse me, Bob, I truly understand the wisdom in your perspective. And perhaps you are right that evolution, not revolution, is what works best. Still, I remember the words of Martin Luther King, Jr. when he said "Damn the tranquility drug of graduality!" My own people "evolved" for tens of thousands of years only to have our cultures wiped out in a matter of a few decades. If education is our salvation, and if our world is truly facing the kind of serious challenges many of us feel it is facing, then something revolutionary must happen in education it seems to me. And returning to that which *did* evolve in my cultures, that is, the use of the arts and story telling to teach, then, maybe this is not so revolutionary after all!

Dr. Samson: I think it was our academic institutions and the rigor of the scientific method and the use of empirical research methods that has brought us to a place where the world is much better off than it ever was—better medicine, better communication, more food, longer life, etc.

Susan Deercloud: Could I interrupt here? I feel that we are, and the academic world seems to do this often, you know, getting all caught up in what we think is so important and imagining that we are solid and have boundaries and solidity and mechanical time and even absolutes. What I love though is how even in science more and more of the scientists speak as traditional Indians, poets, mystics, and other people of "crazy wisdom." More and more they speak in terms of a vast web of universe, of mystery and trickster surprises (although they may use different language for it). Of course, many scientists still will not speak of any of this as sacred . . . but I feel it to be so. I feel that "sacred" every time I write a poem or story or laugh with another human being or see light like fire opals on the snow.

Barbara was not talking so much about European people versus Indian people. She was talking about how people from early on are forced into using language in a certain way so that their very minds/hearts/bodies are put into lifelong lockdown. I have talked to students at college level, both in community colleges and university. Many of them hate writing because of what teachers insisted was good writing . . . a series of carefully laid out coffins all leading to a proved point in the end . . . with a lot of insistence on using pared-down sentences, on not taking chances with the eagles of words, on not soaring and feeling the sun and the moon on one's language wings. For such students, writing is nothing but piling word-corpses on a set number of pages.

Such use of language lends itself to a competitive, argumentative, angry, and depressed society, to people who can better be controlled through their confusion and hungering, and to other people who are brutal enough to do the controlling.

I have never understood why rhetoric can't be of poetry and real eloquence. Our great chiefs soared in their language, and some of them still soar. Their persuasions mingled with poetry. Clan mothers, too, one being Frieda Jaques from Iroquois Confederacy, continue this beauty that was originally responsible, as Bruce said, for the ideals of American democracy. As for dissertations, it is nice that they reflect a human being's learning, studies, but I have read enough conventional dissertations to think I would not wish to read any more. I would rather read a poem!

Part 2

Day two

Creative story telling

Story telling and Truth were interconnected and it was with the utmost trust that The People received the tales of those who had gone before . . . [Eventually], the stories became words in books, but the subtle nuances, understandings and beliefs were lost. [They] became "stand alone" narratives and the connections to the culture from which they came were irretrievably severed.

(Shannon Thunderbird, from *Art and the Magic of Indigenous Story Telling*)

"Seeing red"

Pauline Sameshima's story

with Patrick Slattery, Howard Gardner, Elliot Eisner, Rebecca Carmi, and Gregory Cajete

---

- Critical reflexive inquiry
- The dissertation as an epistolary novel
- Embracing contradictions and multiple perspectives
- Parallax (the apparent change of location of an object against a background due to a change in observer position or perspective shift)

Dr. Samson: Good morning. This morning we have some presenters whose dissertations include creative writing in the form of fictionalized stories written to convey research data and interpretations. As some of you know, some great debates have occurred regarding the merits of a fiction in writing a dissertation, and one of the most famous was between two distinguished educators, Howard Gardner and Elliot Eisner, who, by the way, I've been told will make an appearance today.

It is my pleasure to introduce Dr. Pauline Sameshima. Pauline is an Assistant Professor in the Department of Teaching and Learning at Washington State University, where she specializes in alternative forms of knowledge production and art-based curriculum. She received her doctorate in Curriculum Studies from the University of British Columbia in 2006. Her dissertation, which was recently published by Cambria Press with the title, *Seeing Red— A Pedagogy of Parallax: An Epistolary Bildungsroman on Artful Scholarly Inquiry*, is the recipient of numerous awards, including:

- The 2007 Outstanding Dissertation Award by Arts Based Educational Research (ABER), the special interest group of the American Educational Research Association (AERA). This award is for the best dissertation that explores, is an exemplar of, and pushes the boundaries of arts-based educational research.

- The 2007 Graduate Research Award from the Arts Researchers and Teachers Society (ARTS) in the Canadian Society for the Study of Education (CSSE).
- A 2007 Dissertation Recognition of Excellence Award from the Canadian Association for Teacher Education (CATE).
- The 2007 Ted T. Aoki Prize for an Outstanding Dissertation in Curriculum Inquiry.

She also won the Gordon and Marion Smith Prize from the University of British Columbia. It was not for the dissertation directly, but is given to a student who shows most promise as an artist and educator.

Pauline: Thank you Dr. Samson and good morning to everyone. It is a thrill for me to be a part of a conference such as this. I'm also happy to know that Rishma Dunlop is here and will talk a little about her pioneering work because her dissertation was a major inspiration for me.

My intentions in writing a novel for my doctoral research project were multi-fold. I wanted to tie themes and characters together so that my stories would bind theory and practice. I wanted to encourage the viewer/reader to integrate self into multiple perspectives and become, in a sense, a co-author with multiple interpretations of each of the fictional letters that are part of this work. Using fiction in an autobiographical format as I did offers powerful opportunities for dialogue, especially between dominant and marginalized cultures.

This dissertation was purposefully written as a novel in an effort to provoke the reader. I wanted to challenge the form of the traditional dissertation, which often gets left on a shelf in the library. The work is an epistolary bildungsroman. Epistolary, in that it is a collection of letters from a graduate student to the mentor she is in love with. Bildungsroman, in that it is a story of developmental journeying, education, and metamorphosis. Bildungsroman, a narrative genre originating in the late eighteenth century, also describes either an actual or metaphorical journey in which the protagonist seeks reconciliation between the desire for individuation (self fulfillment) and the demands of socialization (adaptation to the given social reality). Etymologically, the term means the relationship between man and God in the composite sense of *imago dei* (image of God)—so the main character works through a quest for wholeness through her journeying. Further, the term bildungsroman is related to *entfaltung*, which is a creative broadening of acquired skills or qualities without external restriction and assimilation.

This work makes three claims, that:

- The sharing of stories encourages reflexive inquiries in ethical self-consciousness, enlarges paradigms of the "normative," and develops pedagogical practices of liberation and acceptance of diversity.

- Form determines possibilities for content and function thus the use of an alternate format can significantly open new spaces for inquiry.
- Transformational learning may be significantly deepened in pedagogical practice through the intentional development of *embodied aesthetic wholeness* and of eros in the dynamic space between teacher and learner. *Embodied aesthetic wholeness* attends to teaching and learning holistically through the body with consideration to: increasing receptivity and openness to learning; fostering skills of relationality; modeling wholeness-in-process in explicit reflexive texts; layering multiple strategies of inquiry, research experiences, and presentation; and acknowledging ecological and intuitive resonances.

The story line: a fictional editor, Georgia, puts together letters written by Julia. Julia has disappeared and Georgia believes that in publishing the letters, and working through the letters, an understanding of what has happened to Julia will be found. The letters are all from Julia to Red, one of Julia's dissertation advisors.

The title, *Seeing Red* refers to the reader "creating" the character of Red solely by reading Julia's letters even when it seems that Julia has lost herself. There is also a reference to the Red Scare period during McCarthy history when people were incarcerated for being subversive. As well, *seeing red* when watching recording levels on an equalizer is to achieve the optimum recording levels. There is great benefit to researching, learning, and living in the liminal edge.

A central theme of the book is based on the word *parallax*. Parallax is the apparent change of location of an object against a background due to a change in observer position or perspective shift. The concept of parallax encourages researchers and teachers to acknowledge and value the power of their own and their readers' and students' shifting subjectivities and situatedness, which directly influence the constructs of perception, interpretation, and learning.

By changing the form of the dissertation, the "shape of the box," the contents were given tremendous freedom. Fiction allowed me to write a fusion of autobiographical experiences, embellished "truths," and the experiences of others as one character's voice. I was also able to challenge audience expectations and acculturated perspectives. For example, most readers will assume that the loved advisor is a white male. Although Red has blue eyes, the astute reader could notice that of the main character's three mentors, she speaks of two of them in her letters, pointing to the fact that Red could possibly be the female advisor.

Likely the most challenging aspect of writing this dissertation in this particular form was juggling the various aspects and levels. The work follows the seasons that correspond to the Chinese elements (wood, fire, earth, metal, water), which in turn correspond to Asian levels of awareness (hun, shen, yi, po, zhi). These layers are connected to the unfolding love relationship as well as the art that was created as part of this project. Further, in order to allow the reader to "See Red" or develop Red's character based on Julia's letters, I had to "open" all the potential avenues for multiple endings to be possible. At one point, the dissertation was very lengthy and to shorten a novel like this is not simply a matter of cutting out a chapter or two. The epistolary genre was useful in reiterating my belief that learning takes time and cannot be presented whole, but rather in pieces that the reader individually puts together. So in shortening the book, I had to create a complicated schematic of where particular themes were appearing and what layers could be removed.

One of the reviewers, Norman Denzin, described this work as "bold, innovative, a wild, transformative text . . . almost unruly; a new vision for critical reflexive inquiry." The Director of Cambria Press, Toni Tan, suggests that this book opens windows for others where they did not know windows existed. It is my hope that examples of reflexive inquiry, writing about the process of thinking through experience-based understanding, arts-informed perspectives, and a/r/tographic ways of being, are instrumental in contemplating, conceptualizing, and challenging elements of research. I am hopeful that sharing stories of process encourages subjectivity, opens windows into alternate spaces, disrupts conceptions of form, heartens lived experiences as theory and knowledge, decolonizes writing, and broadens the richness of living the research of *currere*. In fact, a proposed EdD. program at my university for evaluating arts-based research is currently waiting for state approval, and my work has been an inspiration, I think, for this opportunity for future educators. Thank you.

Dr. Samson: Rebecca, I know you have asked to say a few words that relate to Pauline's dissertation story. Everyone, Rebecca Carmi is a cantor and a doctoral student at Fielding Graduate University's School for Educational Leadership and Change. Four Arrows is her dissertation chair in fact. She is the author of two children's science books and several prize-winning works of short science fiction that have appeared in periodicals and anthologies.

Rebecca Carmi: Although I am just beginning to learn about the possibilities for using fiction in academic research, I am fully supportive of it. Fiction is the language of vision—why shouldn't it also constitute research? If we truly want to create new realities, we have to imagine them before we can move into them. Imaging is a powerful tool of empowerment—it is used extensively in sports coaching and in the performance arts. By employing one's imagination to simulate positive outcomes, it has been proven they are more likely to occur. Likewise, by imagining new forms of expression and interaction as a society, we bring ourselves one step closer to actualizing them.

How do new paradigms of thought come into being? It is not simply a matter of pouring isotopes into different test tubes and applying vacuum distillation to measure their rates of precipitation. The only vacuum distillation that exists for the human mind is the imagination, and nowhere do we pursue more strands of possibility than in our fiction. Every tradition has its own use of story. We use stories to teach children values, to understand our etiology, to work out ethical issues of humanity in multiple realities—to bridge the gap between loss and belief. It stands to reason that in the pursuit of new methodologies of "being," of education, of leadership, that fictional narrative in the hands of writers can explore more outcomes than any practitioner could possibly develop and document.

In human organizational science, in organizational psychology and in educational leadership and change we seek to understand and posit new ways of structuring our interactions to create greater outcomes for ourselves and for our society. Imagine, if you would, a series of fictional journeys that explore different interventions, organizational cultures, and coaching techniques, and follows them through to the outcomes that exist as possibilities in all of our futures. Like the proverbial monkeys in front of an infinite number of type-writers, somewhere along the way we would create Shakespeare. We ourselves, in our innermost collection of experience, connection, and potential, contain the knowledge of humanity better than any limited test application can. If it can be imagined . . . it can be created! By limiting ourselves to the known and provable physical outcome, we hobble our ability to create new paradigms of being.

Furthermore, if dissertation is truly about bringing new information into circulation, a well written, compelling authoring of "truth," based on exploring new methods of interaction in the multiplicity of venues that a fictional world offers, stands far more chance of actually being read than more dry, citation-laden research that reaches a limited number of scholars, most of them on a review committee. How much have we learned from Tolstoy, from Faulkner and Proust? Within the story, be it oral or written, lies the kernel of our human experience. By melding the research to which we expose ourselves with our own embedded archetypes of process, the writers amongst us can unravel from their core a narrative thread of connection that can point to a new way of being: grounded in theory and ignited by the creative genius that needs not the laboratory to explore—only the Mind, the Soul, and the Word.

Dr. Samson: Thank you Ms. Carmi. I'm sure your colleagues here appreciate the eloquence with which you have addressed this topic. I remain, however, worried that this path needs more rigor, and is too ripe for dysfunctional consequences. I know it has been a long time since Dr. Gardner and Dr. Eisner debated on this topic and many universities, especially in Canada, have embraced such things as fictional novels like Pauline's. Nonetheless, I hope they show up and want to learn if Dr. Gardner has changed his mind any since 1999 when he argued against the idea of a novel serving as a doctoral dissertation.

Runner: Until they arrive, we also have the distinct honor of having Dr. Patrick Slattery with us. Patrick, I think you were at the AERA debate were you not?

Patrick Slattery: Yes, I remember it well. It created quite a stir. The question on the table was whether or not a work of fiction, a novel specifically, could be considered as legitimate research.

Runner: Patrick, before you go on, allow me introduce you in case someone here is not familiar with your work, which I doubt! Your most recent book, published in 2006 by Routledge, is actually a much longer second edition of your text *Curriculum Development in the Postmodern Era*. This updated edition provides the current thinking on alternative forms of research and holistic philosophy. Your article "The Educational Researcher as Artist Working Within," which appeared in the journal *Qualitative Research*, provides an excellent example of autoethnographic methodologies. And, of course, all of your books for the past fifteen years have been committed to justice, compassion, and ecological sustainability.

Patrick Slattery: Thanks Runner. I'm so happy about what is going on here. Actually, you all are not the only group exploring alternative forms of data representation. We have in many ways as a culture lost faith in the theory of language on which scientific inquiry has been based. I have, in my own writing, questioned the usefulness of rigid disciplinary boundaries that separate the humanities, social sciences, natural sciences, and the arts.

I believe that multiple approaches in the realm of the visual, musical, and theatrical must be encouraged and legitimated. Traditional social science research in either quantitative or qualitative form is no more rigorous or insightful than informed eclectic postmodern alternatives. Painting, musical compositions, film documentaries, readers' theater, art installations, or multi-media projects are valid forms of data representation. They have validity. Certainly the Indigenous ways of knowing have validity as well, and I am especially happy to see the many scholars from First Nations who are part of this conference. I think it will become apparent that our current explanations of reality have contributed to the absurd dream of a complete, unique, and closed explanatory system fueled by binary oppositions. Indigenous ways of thinking can help us re-create a holistic, just, and ecologically sustainable educational culture. I believe this is not only possible but essential to the survival of human life, and I share the same sense of urgency revealed in Runner's opening prayer.

I honestly think that postmodern philosophies—especially when interfacing with complexity theory, critical theory, poststructural psychology, phenomeno-logical aesthetics, and proleptic eschatology—are emerging as a viable and exciting alternative form of representation in educational research that move well beyond progressive education and social reconstruction. These new forms, like those you are addressing here, can dramatically affect not only doctoral level research but also teacher training programs, Master's-level courses, and elementary and secondary classroom practices.

I think that we should all understand the gravity of this dialogue and although Dr. Samson seems to be greatly outnumbered, I think we owe him a round of applause for not only his courage in being here, but also for his insightful arguments that we truly need to hear so we do not become a part of the rigidity to which I referred early. (*Applause*)

As we explore the idea of an "authentic dissertation," hear the dissertation stories and discuss these issues, a paradigm may emerge that offers hope for a global community that has endured the tragedies of the modern pathos—the holocaust, slavery, genocide, environmental degradation, racism, apartheid, homophobia, nuclear destruction, religious persecution, colonialization, economic class warfare, ecological destruction, and the other tragedies of the modern era that are all too obvious today. Many scholars, not just those in this meeting place, have a vision for research that can lead to a just, caring, and ecologically sustainable global culture.

(*At this point, in the back of the room, there is a noticeable buzzing of voices as two men enter the room. The two men are no other than Harvard's Dr. Howard Gardner who pioneered the work in "multiple intelligences," and Stanford's Dr. Elliot Eisner, whose work in reflective practice and arts-based research is widely known.*)

Patrick: Well, speak of the devils!

Runner: How wonderful that both of you could be here.

Dr. Gardner: We really can only stay for a short while. We are both speaking in town this week and Four Arrows was very persuasive!

Dr. Eisner: Yes, his constructive persistence also brought me here. I had turned him down several times in fact. In any case, I am happy to see a conference such as this.

Runner: Well, having the two of you together in the same room is such an honor and an opportunity for this group. I want to jump right in and ask you, Dr. Gardner, a question. Those of us who believe in arts-based research believe what Dr. Eisner says about it—that such research is not just about applying a variety of loose methods, but it is about artistically crafting the description of a situation or subject so it can be seen from another angle. What, in your estimation, is wrong with this idea? Your position seems to be that the arts do not have a role to play in scholarly discourse.

Dr. Gardner: I stand by my position, as I framed it in our 1999 debate, perhaps with some minor modifications. I love novels and paintings and music, but people who want to produce such works should become artists. If they want to have doctoral degrees in education, they should use the symbol systems and criteria that have been established by the several scholarly disciplines. Of course, these will change over time, but I don't see any way in which novels (or other works of art) can or should substitute for a work of psychology, philosophy, history, etc.

Runner: In Indigenous communities, art is actually an expression of life, of cultural lessons that lead to unique realizations about life, and even transformation.

Greg Cajete: Yes, and art has the kind of rigor attached to it that seems to be missing from your perception of art, Dr. Gardner. Art has an orientation stage, an incubation and an evaluation time where one stands in defense of one's creation against critics. There is much attention to the sources of art materials for example, and how they relate specifically to current needs (such as social problems) of the community. You speak of the dissertation as a symbolic product. Wow, symbol and symbolization are the essence of art in every form! I write about this in my book, *Look to the Mountain*.

Runner: Dr. Gardner, where I remain vexed relates to what seems to be a contradiction between your work on multiple intelligences and your position about art-based research. Why does not the concept of multiple intelligences play into wanting to see other "intelligences" exercised during the doctoral journey in ways that might include art-based work?

Dr. Gardner: I think that you are confusing the use of an intelligence, which can be used for anything, with the characteristics of a certain kind of symbolic product, in this case a written dissertation. I don't care what intelligences you use, or don't use, in researching and writing the thesis; I care enormously that the thesis has the signs of scholarship, as developed over time by the community (and of course these standards will change, as I've already pointed out).

   Nonetheless, Four Arrow's comments during our communication together caused me to think of something; I could certainly see someone including a work of art, or part of a work of art, in a thesis. And in including or making sense of that work of art, the author and reader would be using various intelligences. But the work of art (or science, or magic, or whatever) would be illustrative; it would not substitute for the argument, conceptualization, and evidence that are needed in a scholarly work.

Runner: I am hearing two ideas from you. One makes sense to me, not the other. What works for me is how nice it would be if multiple intelligences were used in research and in preparing a scholarly product. What does not work is that "in the end" dissertations cannot directly reflect these other intelligences. I find this to be a bit insincere. If one finds an authentic way to use an "intelligence" to convey important work; or if one places authentic value on the ability of a story or image or poem or work of historical fiction to convey "new knowledge," but they are prohibited from allowing the value or the intelligence from being expressed per se in the scholarly product, then, well, I see a contradiction.

Dr. Gardner: I think my point did not come across. To put a doctoral dissertation—a sign that one has entered the fraternity of scholars—in the same category as a work of art is to commit a category error. The same category error is committed, in reverse, if an art gallery were to display doctoral dissertations. No one says that a work of fiction can't tell us something important about education, but so, for that matter, can a joke on late night television. It is great if you use any and all intelligences in your thinking about and preparation of a scholarly product. But in the end, dissertations contain words, equations, diagrams, and not pictorial caricatures, invented dialogue, or catchy tunes. I wonder whether publishers of fiction, or gallery owners, should be asked to include doctoral dissertations in their offerings.

Pauline Sameshima: I stubbornly disagree with you Dr. Gardner. You seem to be advocating that doctoral candidates should create a blueprint for "mastering education as a discipline" and then once in the academy, reproduce this mastery through mentorship of graduate students. This is the same greatest problem in our teacher education programs. We cannot continue to imagine that student teachers will become fine practitioners if we provide blueprints of mastery. First, mastery is a myth and an excuse for those who have lost passion and desire, and second, to imagine that we can clone teachers or reproduce lessons and knowledge is to envision that the teacher identity, instructional proficiency, and learners in context are blank slates of conformity.

Dr. Eisner: If I may, for I really have to run, let me just say this: research is a generic term that describes an activity intended to enlarge human understanding. Human understanding is, in a certain sense, embodied in the symbol systems or forms of representation that culture makes available. The broadest and deepest conception of research reflects an understanding that each form promotes and restricts particular ways of knowing. What we refer to as the arts are ways of addressing the world and revealing its features. Education is, in part, a way to awaken us to the complexities and subtleties of the world in which we live. To restrict the concept of research to what is quantifiable or scientific is to pay too heavy a price for securing a *certain* amount of precision.

Cutting-edge inquiry in research has come a long way from addressing the merely measurable. Today, film, narratives, poetry, computer- based images, are all resources for researching the world. We don't need artificial constraints. We need, I think, to find new seas on which to sail rather than old ports at which to dock.

Runner: I know you both have to go now. Thank you so much. Although you are heavily outnumbered here Dr. Gardner, know that we respect your position and your work and appreciate that your concerns must be addressed to prevent arts-based and anti-oppressive research from becoming less than it has the potential to be. Thank you so much for being here.

All: *Applause (as Dr. Eisner and Dr. Gardner exit).*

Runner: And please let's give Dr. Slattery a round of applause as well for his words of wisdom earlier, before the wonderful interruption by two scholars who might not ever have got together were it not for us being here to do the work we are about to do.

All: *Applause.*

Dr. Samson: I realize there is much excitement about moving the academy in a different direction, with the story telling and arts and all, but I hope as we discuss the stories of those who have experimented with these approaches, that Dr. Gardner's remarks will ground us to the value of academic research and how it has served our world during the past century or more.

Barbara Mann: Dr. Samson, with all due respect, I want to challenge your words about the value of Dr. Gardner's remarks rather than allow the session to end with them unchallenged! As a Native scholar, I resent the insinuation that our stories cannot tell us "something important." Maybe this is true for Western art forms that merely entertain or are for, as you say, hanging on walls. But our art deserves more respect. From our stories, for example, we know that co-planting is a vital agricultural technique; we know how to germinate seeds, how far apart to space them, how deeply each goes into the earth, how to watch the motion of the stars and moon to determine the plant-date; we know when to hoe and when to hold the little green corn tasting. How is our "invented dialogue" about our worldly observations less significant than a bio-chemistry course that achieved its dead data without even asking the plants whether it was all right to use their energy to test their make-up? Seems to me that, using our stories, we created two-thirds of the world's current crops, and about 60 percent of its "medicines," in the allopathic sense of the term. How, then, is our way of knowing inferior to Europe's?

Runner: I wish Howard did not have to leave so early. I would like to have asked him if it is the "entertainment" aspect of Western art that most informs his reasons for not seeing art as an implicit part of higher education research. Anyway, I think it is time for a break. See you back in about thirty minutes.

Dr. Samson: And thank you Dr. Mann for reminding us that we will be bumping into different paradigms along the way in this conference!

"Boundaries"
Rishma Dunlop's story

- *Bildungsroman*, the novel of education and formation of the individual
- *Künstlerroman*, the novel of formation of the artist
- Hybrid genres
- Post-structural open texts
- Arts-based research

Dr. Samson: Thanks so much, Pauline, and now I want to introduce the person you told us was an inspiration for your work. Of course, I'm referring to Dr. Rishma Dunlop, who is an Associate Professor at York University, Toronto. She is jointly appointed to the Department of Education and the Department of English where she is the Coordinator of the Creative Writing Program in English. Dr. Dunlop is an award-winning poet, playwright, and essayist.

Rishma earned her PhD at The University of British Columbia in 1999 and her dissertation, a novel titled *Boundary Bay* was the first novel to be accepted as a doctoral dissertation in a Faculty of Education in Canada. *Boundary Bay* was a hybrid form, moving between texts of theory, fiction, autobiography, stream of consciousness fragments, poetry, and epistolary forms. The novel, prior to defense at UBC, was a semi-finalist for the Chapters-Robertson Davies Prize for fiction in 1998, and a manuscript of poetry from the dissertation was a finalist for the CBC Literary Prize in poetry. And if you did not know it, it was *her* dissertation that created the now famous debate between Howard and Elliot we just heard about.

Dr. Dunlop's work created a precedent both at the University of British Columbia and internationally for vast changes in the ways in which dissertations are written and in the possible forms of research representation. This work received much attention in educational circles in the late 1990s and over the past few years, resulting in keynote speaking engagements and teaching at numerous universities.

Rishma, thank you for joining us here. Can you say a few words about your career path and your current thinking about arts-based dissertations and research?

Rishma Dunlop: Thank you for your kind introduction. It has been a fascinating journey since those years of doctoral work. I am pleased to see new researchers like Pauline Sameshema have been able to develop innovative work as a result of a legacy that I think I am part of at the University of British Columbia. My sincere congratulations, Pauline, on your wonderful accomplishments.

As Pauline and other researchers are aware, my dissertation resulted in some drastic changes in the rules and regulations of graduate studies at the University of British Columbia and at other institutions. My career path was strongly influenced by the April 1999 American Educational Research Association's annual conference in Montreal, where I was involved in an Invited Key Session that resulted in a debate between Howard Gardner, Elliot Eisner, and other panel members. The debate occurred prior to my doctoral defense and the discussion was about the merit of a novel as an acceptable form for a dissertation and, yes, my novel/dissertation in progress was at the center of this debate. It was very interesting to see the two of them and to hear them speak on this subject after all these years. Elliot Eisner of Stanford University and Tom Barone of Arizona State University offered strong endorsements and support for the directions of my dissertation, as did my supervisor Stephen Carey, and committee members Rita L. Irwin, Carl Leggo, and Laurie Ricou. Dr. Barone and Dr. Eisner have continued to be valued mentors throughout my academic career. However, in 1999, the fictional form, indeed all "alternative" forms of dissertation, was still suspect in educational research. Of course, Howard Gardner clearly represented the dissenting factions, arguing that there might not be any dispute about the quality of the novel as literary work, but that it was not an appropriate form for a dissertation, a position, we have just learned, he still largely holds.

The three-hour panel session was called "Shaking the Ivory Tower: Writing, Advising and Critiquing the Postmodern Dissertation" and it included papers by several doctoral candidates and their supervisory committees. My paper was titled "The Novel as Educational Research." There is an AERA audiotape of this session, by the way, that may be very interesting to researchers, especially doctoral candidates and supervisory committee members. At AERA in 2001 and 2002, I also presented panels, along with Tom Barone and Lorri Neilsen, on the topics of fiction, artistic practices, and research.

Boundary Bay included an introduction in which the work is situated within literary and aesthetic theory and in the genre of the female Bildungsroman, more specifically the *Erziehungsroman*, which focuses on training and formal education, and the *Künstlerroman*, the novel of education and formation of the artist. The main character, Evelyn, is a poet, academic, and Professor in a Faculty of Education, and the work explores the embodied nature of engagements with art, poetry, education, the natural world, sexuality, diasporic, gendered, and sexual identity, feminist theory, and the visceral and intellectual nature of reading and interacting with art and literary texts. In *Boundary Bay*, and in many of my later creative and scholarly works, the color red is a central thread in the narrative, as it is in Pauline's work. In my works, red is linked to artistic creativity, South Asian and female identity, and to an artist–researcher collective.

As I have continued my academic career at York University, I have continued to envision scholarship as creative practice and have written in nontraditional forms. My work includes a wide range of experimental practices, poststructural open texts, lyric essays, essays in verse, creative non-fiction, non-linear narratives, even a radio play, and also works that include visual art and photography. Some of these works include excerpts from *Boundary Bay*, my novel/dissertation. The contribution the novel made to my own work and to the field of scholarship was to support my convictions that scholarly writing should be creative practice, and I have built my career on producing works that are hybrid genres in the belief that these texts are "open texts" in a poststructural sense. Open texts become what Roland Barthes called "readerly" and "writerly" texts. They are open texts that admit the imagination of the reader, as opposed to the traditional, closed texts of traditional academic prose. In turn, this is the type of work I have encouraged and fostered in my graduate students with courses I have developed such as Research and Artistic Creation and The Act of Writing. As Dr. Samson mentioned, I have now had the opportunity to teach workshops and offer guest lectures and courses to researchers at many universities in Canada, the United States, Finland, and, along with the supervisory work I do at my own university, I have had opportunities to work with international graduate students and serve as an external examiner for graduate theses from Pakistan, New Zealand, Canada, Finland, and the United States.

Over the past decade, my goal has been to continue with creative research in ways that abide by the guidelines from the Social Science and Humanities Research Council of Canada: 1) the research activity or approach to research forms an essential part of a creative process or artistic discipline and directly fosters the creation of literary/artistic works; 2) the research must address research questions, offer theoretical contextualization within the relevant field or fields of literary/artistic inquiry, and present a methodological approach; 3) both the research and the resulting literary/artistic works must meet peer standards of excellence and be suitable for publication, public performance or viewing. With these criteria in mind, it is my view that the evolution of what began anchored in experiments in arts-based research must move towards high standards of artistic creation and that the study of contemporary art practices and the development of skills in professional art practices must be attended to. As my thinking has shifted in this direction, the course I offer now to researchers is called Research and Artistic Creation. The focus includes components of apprenticeship and extensive training in contemporary arts practices with an aim of developing professional levels of artistic skills, craft, and production in order to improve the quality of artistic work integrated into research inquiry. My current advocacy is that educational researchers interested in artistic forms of inquiry would benefit from intensive and long-term study of the humanities and fine arts disciplines they are using in their research. These types of commitments to training and education need to be built into our graduate programs and our evaluation and assessment criteria with attention to standards of professional arts practices.

The French root of the word "research" is to see again, seek again. If we are creating strong, compelling, and significant research, we are in the process of making something new, a *poiesis*, or making. In a world that is constantly barraged with material violence, we create art and tell stories in order to live and survive. The work of the arts provides us with ways to move across disciplines and differences and, if our research reflects such aesthetic impulses, we can move our scholarship out of the confines of universities in order to speak in more compelling ways to the public sphere. We can perceive scholarship as *Viva Voce*, the traditional name for doctoral defense, meaning "in the living voice." This is the vital function of education, to be a living voice.

To new researchers, I say tell your own stories and the stories of others with artistic power and skill. Accept the responsibility attached to writing stories.

I'll leave you with a brief excerpt from the introduction I wrote to *Boundary Bay*, lines that I still offer to graduate researchers today:

> My novel *Boundary Bay* is a form of epistemological work, an exploration of ways of knowing that attempts a politics of transformation. The novel as research provides me with a form to say what I could not say otherwise. As a teacher–educator, a poet, and a fiction writer who teaches about reading and writing practices, I wanted my research to embody and perform the beliefs about knowledge and education that I try to embed into my teaching practice. This is my research, my act of fiction, an act of passion.
>
> And the novel unfolds, written between the gaps between reading, teaching and the imagination, the fashioning of art and inquiry, not as reproduction furniture, but as an extension of the notion of literary anthropology. The nature of the discourse is not to replicate art but to imply, through language, qualities of life that are often ineffable, what cannot be said, particularly in conventional perceptions of schooling and educational life.
>
> The reader fills the gaps with imagination, as does the writer. Writing and reading become acts of performance, intertwined acts of inquiry. The writer becomes the books she frequents, journeying through books and creating literature as a primary source for speaking about human experiences. The novel as research paradigm allows a questioning of conventions

and the literary text holds these conventions up to the light for close inspection. Fiction becomes exploratory, explanatory, hopeful, and generative in its premises for epistemological positionings. The fictional text constitutes boundary crossings transgressing over referential fields of thought and textual systems of representation.

The novel's narrative begins with language—the writing/reading of things that haunt us. It begins with reading. Our books, magazines, newspapers, our sea of texts, the infinite scripts of language, glossy pages, textured papers, woven bindings, true stories and fiction, fingere, texere, threaded through the breathing texts of living bodies. In the inscriptions, encryptions, decodings of lives as texts, we read our lives as books. We read cultures within the multiplicity of texts and cultures read us. We write ourselves as we read. Within these perceptions of reading and writing lies an aperture of hope. The lens opens us to the complexities, the richness, and multiplicities of human nature and its possibilities, the infinitely diverse ways of knowing the world.

The novel intertwines fictions through an assemblage of facts, tangled through the language of bones. The writer wants to write of men and women, real or invented, offering them open destinies. She wants her voice to be like a modern painting, voice and story like the colors of a Mark Rothko canvas. This is how she wants the story to be, written in an alphabet of bones and blood, trembling with light and vibrant hues, spiraling with winds, rooted in earth, breathing with tides.

"Breaking silences"
Douglas Gosse's story

with Tom Barone and Robert B. Kaplan

- *Bildungsroman* (educational novel)
- Arts-based and arts-informed research
- Social criticism/activism
- Homophobia
- Importance of multiple interpretations

Runner: Welcome back everyone. Our next presenter is Dr. Douglas Gosse who is an Assistant Professor in the College of Education at Nipissing University in Ontario, Canada. He is also the Director of the Northern Canadian Center for Research in Education and the Arts. He earned his PhD from the Ontario Institute for Studies in Education at the University of Toronto (OISE-UT). His dissertation was an entirely fictional educational novel that won the Arts Based Educational Research (ABER) special interest group's Outstanding Thesis/Dissertation Award of the American Educational Research Association (AERA) for 2004–2005, for the best doctoral dissertation that explores, is an exemplar of, and pushes the boundaries of arts-based educational research. He was also one of three finalists in 2007 for AERA's Narrative and Research Special Interests Group for a Narrative Research Article that stemmed from his work and was entitled, "My Arts-Informed Narrative Inquiry into Homophobia in Elementary Schools," published in the *International Journal of Education and the Arts*. His doctoral research was funded by the Social Sciences and Humanities Research Council of Canada. He also wanted me to tell you that he has a wonderful schipperke dog named Sebbi.

Douglas Gosse: Runner, thanks for that introduction and Sebbi thanks you too. I want to start out by telling everyone that the word "jackytar," the title of the novel that stemmed from this dissertation, is a derogatory term associated with laziness and moral decrepitude. It designates Newfoundlanders from the Port-au-Port peninsula who are White/Native and Francophone, as is the protagonist's mother, and himself, too, therefore. Some people still use this racist term today.

In this work, Alex, the protagonist, receives a phone call that his mother is dying, and returns to rural Newfoundland, where confrontation with people and events from his past are the catalyst for self- and social (re)examination. Alex drifts in and out of sites of power and marginality in provocative ways, as do the other characters, including his parents, grandfather, brother, sister-in-law, a childhood friend, and the local Anglican priest. I explore this phenomenon through the implicit and explicit lens of sexuality, using literary devices such as symbolism, metaphor, atmosphere and mood, and via examination of the overlapping identity markers of race, class, gender, sexual orientation, disability, geographical location, and language and culture.

My dissertation, entitled, "Breaking Silences, an Inquiry into Identity and the Creative Research Process," is in two parts. One part is the Bildungsroman or educational novel, *Jackytar*, and the second is an appendix on the creative research process. Some commonly known Bildungsromans are *Catcher in the Rye* by J.D. Salinger, *Tess of the D'Urbervilles* by Thomas Hardy, and *The Pearl* by John Steinbeck, all of which were favorite books of mine. Basically, they recount an individual's progress or apprenticeship through the obstacles of life and towards greater consciousness. When I was a teacher in the 1990s, I worked in a junior high school and taught literature and language in English and French. Literature was just a way of life for me. Story telling is a very powerful way that we learn from each other and exchange and build knowledge. It never occurred to me that creating a novel for my dissertation might be a problem! Little did I know that this wasn't de rigueur, that this wasn't necessarily standard. Because I had been teaching literature for so long and had an undergraduate degree in Francophone literature, for me storytelling and creative writing were as natural as breathing. I hadn't fully realized that by *breaking silences*, I also had to break with academic traditions, which can be rigid and, in my view, contrary to true academic curiosity and inquiry.

I did of course face some barriers as many people who embrace the arts in research do. Upon starting my doctorate, I began working as a research assistant right away. I worked with some very strong, qualitative researchers on several projects, and they were very supportive. I'm grateful for the training I received, and the sense of community. For one of the major projects, the principal investigator would have allowed me to use the data for my own dissertation, and that was the plan for about two years. This potential supervisor knew that I would be creating a novel as a major part of my dissertation. However, once we formed the thesis committee and held our first meeting, I knew this was doomed. They had more of a positivist approach, whereas I was definitely postmodern and even poststructural in my theoretical persuasions. They couldn't quite get their minds around how I would take data from interviews and translate that into a novel, even though I had a 100-page proposal, and had brought along samples of fictionalized research.

One of the committee members said, "Well, what do you do with everything that ends up on the cutting room floor? You have to answer to that." My response was, "Well, what do YOU do when you conduct qualitative research with what ends up on the cutting room floor?" It went downhill from there.

Ultimately, there was a conflicting theoretical paradigm. They were looking more at being able to ascertain truths and aiming for uncertainty reduction whereas I was striving towards knowledge (de)construction, fluidity of meaning, and multiple truths. With my own research, I didn't want to engage in uncertainty reduction, I actually wanted to end up asking more questions than finding answers! I had to abolish that whole committee and, fortunately, I was eventually able to find support in the Center for Arts Informed Research (CAIR) at OISE-UT. After a few months of chatting back and forth in e-mails and so forth during the spring and summer, Dr. Ardra Cole, an inspiring arts-informed researcher, agreed to be my supervisor. Then we got a few more committee members involved, Gary Knowles, who's also a leading figure for arts-informed research, Peter Trifonas, who excels at postmodern and post-structuralist deconstruction, and Rinaldo Walcott, an eminent social activist and queer theorist. And I hadn't even known that CAIR existed up until that point! For over two years during my doctoral studies, they were literally above my head. I was on the sixth floor and they were on the seventh.

Four Arrows asked me to mention the idea of distribution as it relates to a published dissertation. I think this is important because I think that research ultimately requires an audience to be of any benefit. There's no question that my dissertation has been better distributed than most research. With the traditional dissertation, you have your committee members and maybe a dozen people or so who read the dissertation. Then the thesis tends to gather dust on the shelf in the university library, rarely to be checked out or consulted . . . With my dissertation, the novel section has actually been published through a Canadian publisher, Jesperson Publishing. The novel, *Jackytar*, was distributed across Canada in every province and territory. Thousands of people have read it as opposed to the small number who usually read a doctoral dissertation. It became the first novel written as part of a doctoral dissertation in education to be published in its entirety in Canada, the first arguably 'gay' novel (for it has gay characters) in Newfoundland's literary history, and the first educational novel I'm aware of that focuses on investigating masculinities. *Jackytar* has been reviewed provincially and nationally in a number of newspapers, and I've had several radio interviews. In addition to that, I was still able to present at academic conferences by, for example, the American Educational Research Association (AERA), the American Men's Studies Association (AMSA), and the Canadian Society for Studies in Education (CSSE). I've published articles in refereed journals and written some book chapters, all based on my dissertation work.

Most importantly, I've been able to establish contact with so many non-academics, and this creating of bridges between the academia and the larger public is crucial to my research. I've had multiple book signings and readings across Canada and received dozens of e-mails from people who've read *Jackytar*, the novel from my dissertation. Readers have related to *Jackytar* in countless ways, which is what I desired. The goal of much arts-informed and arts-based research is to shed light on the multiplicities of the human condition. There shouldn't be a solid theme or conclusion that the writer drives the reader towards, which is contradictory to much popular fiction, and upsetting to some readers, while others embrace the active meaning-making. With *Jackytar*, readers are actually encouraged to interpret the work according to their own life experiences. I welcome multiple interpretations. This became readily apparent through all the e-mails I've received. Some people have related to themes of alienation because they've been divorced, or they've been single mothers, or they were bullied as children, or they've encountered racism. A number of people have encountered heterosexism and homophobia, or are linguistic and cultural minorities. All of these themes and leitmotifs, people have been able to embrace in different ways.

In 2008, Jesperson Publishing will be publishing a supplement to the novel, *Jackytar*. We hope it may be used to explore masculinities in academic settings, but also the creative research process for arts-informed and arts-based researchers. We anticipate that *Jackytar*, coupled with the new supplement, will be particularly useful in university courses in education, sociology, social justice, and gender and equity studies. The supplement will contain an introduction to male studies, a core section on provocative theory and methodology germane to the study of masculinities, and a final section dealing with creative fiction writing as social research, all pertaining to *Jackytar*. We've tentatively entitled this supplementary publication, *Breaking Silences, a Creative Inquiry into Male Studies and Masculinities*. There's a desperate need in academia to better address the complexities of masculinities and power, and to provoke more meaningful debate around revisionist readings of commonly accepted 'knowledge' and ways of knowing as they pertain to males and society.

I'm still conducting arts-informed and arts-based educational research, and initiating some of my students and colleagues into it, too, through our new research center, the Northern Canadian Center for Research in Education & the Arts (NORCCREA), which has members from various departments and walks of life, from faculty, to staff, students, and broader community members. We offer monthly seminars using artistic means to explore life, such as collage, music, and cinema. We're not so concerned over whether people view our work as arts-informed or arts-based, but rather with challenging social norms, procedures, and beliefs.

However, if I may make a distinction between arts-informed and arts-based educational research, for they do overlap and people frequently use them interchangeably, most arts-informed research has a *strong* emancipatory agenda and is informed by, but not necessarily based in, the arts. A core element of arts-informed research is that your qualitative data collection can be from the traditional to the very avant-garde. So some people will engage in traditional qualitative research techniques, such as interviewing, observations, document analysis, and triangulation, but also perhaps engage in artistic processes of data collection, such as using collage or poetry writing with research participants. Then there may be further artistic interpretation of the so-called 'data,' such as using fiction writing to interpret and represent results, findings, or philosophical truths, as I do. Moreover, arts-informed or arts-based research has, in my view, an incredible propensity to induce people to be very reflective in their readings of the research. Some people, as I did with my dissertation, will have more avant-garde, postmodern and poststructuralist underpinnings in their work, whether they call themselves arts-informed or arts-based educational researchers. Personally, I used my own tacit knowledge throughout my life, in my career as an educator, as a gay, bilingual male, as someone who grew up working-class in a rural area of Newfoundland, as a person who has lived with and continues to live with physical disability, and so forth, in addition to a thorough literature review spanning pop culture and literary novels to traditional academic journal articles and books, to inspire, explore and (de)construct the ideas for my educational novel, *Jackytar*.

I'm still conducting new arts-informed and arts-based educational research. I have one current project with a colleague whereby we're investigating male primary school teachers and reasons why there is such a high attrition rate in many Bachelor of Education programs. We're also looking at the experiences of male primary school teachers already working in the field, and exploring public fears around pedophilia and homophobia, and notions that it may be somehow inappropriate for men to be working with children. We've recently presented a paper at the American Men's Studies Association in Kansas City, and my colleague will soon travel to Amsterdam to another international venue. In the AMSA, Kansas City paper, "Researching the Halted Paths of Male Primary School Teacher Candidates," we created a composite, plausible, and yet fictional character based upon several of our 'real-life' participants' interviews, and used fictionalized narrative inquiry as a platform for discussion. I consider this paper to be more arts-based, whereas, in another recent paper we just submitted to a journal, "An Arts-Informed Narrative Inquiry of a Gay Male Primary School Teacher Candidate," fiction-writing techniques are more enhanced than in much narrative inquiry and qualitative research, but there is no fictional, composite character, so I call this arts-informed. It is a type of *testimonial*-inspired case study of one of our participants who is disabled and gay, and therefore a minority within a minority. Here, we developed ideas around symbolic violence that have emotional and institutional impact upon male minorities yet to be adequately examined or understood. Of course, in discussing the degrees of fictionalization of results or representations in my research, or any research, I would argue that *all* writing is fictional! Ultimately, as a researcher, fiction writer, and storyteller, I hope to connect to the hearts, minds, and emotions of people and vice versa, as we engage in dialogue, both within and beyond the academy. This is what truly matters.

Thank you.

Dr. Samson: Thank you, Doug. And thanks for the clarification regarding arts-based and arts-informed research. We have with us today one of the pioneers in the promotion of these cultures of inquiry, Dr. Thomas Barone. He is currently a Professor at the College of Education at Arizona State University. He is far too prolific for me to list his many works, but it is especially relevant to note he is currently a member of the AERA Task Force on Criteria for Humanities-Oriented Research in AERA Publications. In 2000 Peter Lang published his book, *Aesthetics, Politics and Educational Inquiry: Essays and Examples*, and his chapter, "Creative nonfiction and social research" will soon be published in Sage Publication's *Handbook of the Arts in Social Science Research*, edited by Ardra Cole and Gary Knowles.

Tom Barone: Thank you Dr. Samson, and thank you for your being willing to serve here as the sort of chief protagonist amidst this group of incredible story tellers and other arts-based researchers. This kind of dialogue that has been occurring since I arrived yesterday is exactly what this movement needs and your concerns are in many ways the concerns of all of us, perhaps.

I have been exploring the usefulness of forms of social research that include design elements associated with the arts for several decades, ever since my dissertation work at Stanford in 1978. Over the years, I have considered issues related to the value of what some call arts-based research, even as I have offered up examples of such work for edification and/or critique. My dissertation—at the time considered avant-garde and controversial—like my later work, explored the potential of creative non-fiction for inquiring into and raising questions about various educational issues and practices.

In that spirit I would like to offer observations and questions about some of the topics and issues touched on in this interesting conversation. My first observation involves the issue of categorizing and labeling forms of research. Isn't it possible that such labels serve to provide conceptual handles for bringing order to the realm of social research even as they diminish its richness and complexity? Surely, if research into the human condition is rigidly categorized into the humanities, arts, natural science, etc., it can blind us to both the commonalities within and the work of those who toil in those fields. Still, certain qualitative differences that characterize the work of various scholars do exist. To completely ignore either those similarities or differences would not, it seems to me, serve us well.

Second: I use the term "arts-based" to describe forms of social research that emphasize design elements associated with artistic production. Elements of research design can be found in both the inquiry process as well as the cultural text (written or otherwise) that results from the research. For example, the rather fluid methods employed in gathering data as well as the choice of expressive language and aesthetic form or format employed in data representation may be selected to serve the intended purpose or desired effect of an arts-based research project. For much artistically oriented research, that purpose may be framed as Dr. Eisner has framed it: as "artistically crafting a description of a situation so that it can be seen [I might suggest 'experienced'] from another angle." Or it may be seen as an attempt to stimulate, contribute to, and/or redirect ongoing conversations within various communities of discourse (especially, but not only, scholarly ones) by provoking, illuminating, challenging, and otherwise critically engaging with, privileged cultural systems, social outlooks, worldviews, policies, or practices. In other words, arts-based social researchers (both disciplinary and trans-disciplinary) may choose to produce texts with the potential to offer fresh perspectives that raise questions about dominant meanings attached to educational concepts, discourses, and issues. As with other forms of poststructuralist social research, arts-based research may serve to promote *dis*equilibrium in the mind of readers by exposing and interrogating stale presumptions about social phenomena.

Of course, not all artistically sensitive research is designed toward such interrogative aims. Beautifully crafted works of propaganda can, of course, masquerade as art. These sorts of projects exude an air of authority and certainty; they serve, instead, to reinforce dominant perspectives and worldviews. They offer enhanced certainty rather than a disturbance of the taken-for-granted, commonsensical, or dominant way of viewing social phenomena. Such "authoritative" texts are, I would argue, not truly artistic. They thereby more closely resemble works of propaganda, and fail in terms of several of the tensions mentioned by Dr. Eisner. They do not proffer diversity in interpretation, or pursue new questions and puzzlements, but err on the side of soliloquy, of directly, authoritatively "telling it like it is." True works of art employ design elements that invite discourse about multiple possible meanings rather than (even temporarily) closing off the conversation.

In this regard, misguided examples of (pseudo-) arts-based research may promote a purpose sometimes associated with traditional forms of "hard science." This purpose is indeed the enhancement of certainty regarding a particular set of phenomena. The research must, that is, contribute in a convincing manner to an established body of knowledge (a "knowledge base"), a contribution that offers persuasive explanations of, predictions about, and/or the possibility of control over similar future events. Such research is, therefore, indeed meant to result in knowledge claims. Although it is generally conceded that absolute certainty may never be attained within any research study, the goal of research may nevertheless be the attainment of the highest possible degree of trustworthiness, objectivity, validity, and reliability, in order to more persuasively argue about how to think and/or act correctly. When researchers have traditionally addressed issues of research design they have focused on the importance of elements—think, for example of "experimental design"—aimed precisely at that outcome.

Of course there are times when a degree of equilibrium and stability in our lives is welcomed, and traditional forms of research may sometimes be useful for supplying it. Still, a wide array of tacit, underlying social and cultural conditions in which such research is conducted (and within which its findings are intended to be applied) may be avoided, neglected, and ignored in the process. The enormous power of arts-based inquiry rests in its unique capacity for doing what other forms of research cannot: inviting and enabling members of an audience to vicariously re-experience facets of the empirical world. Good arts-based research does not merely aim to bring them closer toward a singular version of the truth of that world, but enables them to see facets of it in a different light, and even to envision how it might indeed be made otherwise.

Finally: so arts-based research offers this powerful invitation to re-live, re-view, re-search the world in ways that have been long kept unavailable. Indeed, powerful cultural forces still operate to deny us that re-visioning of the world would refuse us the use of the appellation "research" for forms of inquiry that promote the disruptions required for that re-visioning. A continuance of this conversation might result in the naming of those forces and speculations about the nature of the interests in which they operate.

I want to say again how important I think this conference is and how happy I am to be here. I look forward myself to the continuing conversation.

Dr. Samson: Thank you very much Tom, and thanks for recognizing that I am the enemy here. I truly am trying to see how arts-based research can contribute authentically to new knowledge, but worry that moving away from sound academic research and writing has a great risk to the credibility and rigor of what the doctoral degree means. I mean, doctoral dissertations represent the highest standards in education and perhaps the major opportunity for new knowledge to emerge. I think a major concern of mine remains the same as Howard Gardner's. The academy represents a particular kind of community, a community of scholars with certain proven ways of discovering and affirming knowledge. Bob, can you say a few more words about what Tom means by a "community of discourse?"

Bob Kaplan: Well, it is true that text occurs within the phenomenological perception of the community of speakers; it is also constrained historically by the way text has been used in that community and by the kinds of genres available to that community. As Dr. Mann's story made clear yesterday, doctoral candidates must at the very least realize the tactical, modal, and ontological difficulties they will face. A writer may, intentionally or unintentionally, introduce difficulties into the text, by choosing to use arcane or technical vocabulary (contingent difficulty), or by allowing him/herself to be understood only up to a point (tactical difficulty). The reader may find the writer's representation of the human condition to be inaccessible or alien (modal difficulty). Or the writer may undertake to bend the language itself out of its conventional shape (ontological difficulty).

It might also be helpful to note that English is the language being used in the doctoral research being presented at this conference. In English, the default model presents given information before new information, perhaps on the presumption that it is easier for the reader to start with something known. The subject also comes before the predicate. This practice of "old information first" is by no means universal; other languages may employ other practices, but it says much about how traditional academic research is structured, and expected. Arts-based research seems to be challenging this default model but maybe it is the start of a new way of looking at things. Still, if one's audience fails to understand what one is saying, the audience is not likely to start thinking in a new way; rather, they are likely to walk away, uniformed and unchanged.

Runner: Thank you Bob. Tom, did you have any parting words before we close the session?

Tom Barone: In departing, I briefly reference a slice of the history of educational research, a history that gives arts-based researchers much hope. Indeed, if this discussion were being held in the first half of the twentieth century, cautions very similar to those issued by Drs. Samson and Kaplan would have been heard. But back then *all* of today's "mainstream" forms of qualitative research as well as *many* now-familiar sorts of *quantitative* research were disallowed by a tight-knit community of scholars (and therefore audience members) who had been professionally socialized into a very narrow conception of what should count as research.

I am presuming that it is clear that arts-based researchers, unlike traditionalists of an earlier age, *welcome all social science-based approaches that achieve their intended purposes* into the citadel of educational research. That is because educational research *done well*—whether arts-based, science-based, humanities-based—can contribute to the enhancement of educational policy and practice.

Again, most social science achieves this by contributing to a knowledge base, by providing, as Dr. Sampson puts it, "authentically to new knowledge." But arts-based researchers do not make *knowledge* claims, authentic or otherwise. By offering fresh ways of perceiving educational phenomena, we raise *questions* about assumptions hidden within dominant perspectives. My humble suggestion is that those who cannot grasp the significance of that epistemological shift—or who find other central features of arts-based research inscrutable—might consider doing what I would do if asked to review a manuscript for a special education journal, or to serve on a thesis committee for a student using advanced statistics, or to serve at a defense that is being held in, say, the Ukrainian language. I would take a pass—not because I find anything unpalatable or harmful, but because my interests lean in a different direction, and I would be ill-equipped for applying criteria appropriate for making sound judgments regarding quality. And because I would very likely, as an audience member, "walk away, uninformed and unchanged."

In summary, then, times change. Or more correctly, times are changed. The field of educational research—bless it!—has, for a very long time, been changed through the efforts of pioneers who have recognized great value in methodological diversity. Pioneers of arts-based research methods (including, no doubt, those whose examples are highlighted in this conference) would simply ask to have the quality and usefulness of their work judged with criteria that are appropriate to this research approach devoted to wondering about what education might mean.

"Stories as relationship"

Deborah Ceglowski's story

- Short stories
- Mentorship
- Interpretive interactionism
- Influencing policy

Dr. Samson: Our last presenter this morning is Dr. Deborah Ceglowski, an Associate Professor in the Department of Special Education and Child Development, Ball State University. In 1996, the American Educational Research Association's Division D (Research Methods) and Qualitative Research special interest group awarded her dissertation the Mary Catherine Ellwein Outstanding Qualitative Dissertation Award. Subsequently, Teachers College Press published a book version of her dissertation entitled *Inside a Head Start Center: Developing Policies from Practice*. This book that has received much acclaim as a literary ethnography joined with critical policy analysis. I believe you used short stories to accomplish your goals, right?

Deborah: Yes, and my tale about writing short stories began in the 1970s when I was a student at Johnson State College in Vermont. Located in the Green Mountains, the college served mainly students from Vermont and the greater New England area. It was situated in a small town far from most anywhere. A friend of mine, Elizabeth, described Hayden Carruth as a poet who met with students who wanted to write. I didn't know anything about Hayden Carruth and his reputation, but I did like to write. At Elizabeth's urging, I set up an appointment to meet Hayden. He came to the campus a couple of times a week to work one-on-one with students. He used a windowless room in the basement of one of the dorms. The first time I met him, I was intimidated by his quietness. He sat in this room lit only by a table lamp reading through some of the poems from my high school days. After some time, he looked up and told me that he would "work" with me. The requirements were simple: I wrote and brought what I wrote to him. He would read it and discuss it with me.

Thus began my two years of writing under Hayden's guidance. He was a critical though not a harsh reader. He pushed me to describe things accurately. After writing a piece about trees, he and I took a winter walk in the Vermont woods. He took off my mitten and put it on a tree limb. "Here," he said, "feel this fir tree. This is what you need to write about."

My writing improved and toward the end of two years, Hayden told me that I could become a writer but it would take more time. I had majored in elementary education and was heading off for two years with the Peace Corps. I thought I would have time to think about writing when I was away, and I did. Hayden kept in touch writing detailed letters in longhand. When I returned to the U.S., I entered the Harvard Graduate School of Education and put writing on the back burner. I visited Hayden and his family but perhaps because of my decision to continue in education, I felt a rift had developed between us. I still read poetry and short stories but didn't see how creative writing could fit into my life.

In the 1990s I entered the PhD program in the College of Education at the University of Illinois. By now education *was* my life and I didn't think about creative writing at all. I was here to get a degree and move into a different phase of my career in early childhood education. While enrolled in a curriculum research class during my first semester, Norm Denzin came to speak to the class when the professor was away at a conference. By that time, we had heard several speakers talk about methodology and I thought this would be just another presentation.

I am still unsure *what* it was about Norm that was so compelling. He was dressed, as usual, in some faded printed short-sleeved shirt, baggy shorts, and flip-flops. It didn't look like his hair had been cut in some time. His loud booming voice filled the room as he talked about interpretive interactionism and viewing research as an interpretive act. His presentation was charismatic, similar to the style used by many high-profile preachers. Having little or no understanding about methodology, I was drawn by his fervor and decided that Norm could teach me something.

And he did. The first semester I took a class with him, the room was filled with graduate students from sociology, anthropology, education, cultural studies, nursing, and psychology. This was fall semester and the class met in an old building, a room on the second floor that had large windows. The windows were usually open and we could hear the leaves rustling against the trees. Norm came in late. He was always dressed the same and when he came into the classroom, he lit a Camel and began lecturing to us. He wrote notes on the board and I, like the others in the room, would try to keep up with writing and notes and with what he was saying. Most of the time I didn't have a clue what it was. We were always asking questions. One student, who was trying to understand a concept, started her question with "I understand my confusion differently." That became my slogan for this class with Norm, "I understand my confusion differently."

Norm had us read short stories written by Ray Bradbury. They were sad and tragic tales that after you read them, made you want to go out and have a strong drink. Norm also told us to write stories—well really, only one. We were to write a story about something that happened to us and then rewrite it two more times. The second time we situated the same story in the media surrounding the topic and the third time in the larger social/political context. I didn't understand the reason why we had to write the story three times, but I enjoyed the writing. More than that, I loved the writing—it was like finding a piece of me that had been dormant for a long time.

Norm wrote illegible comments on your work. He did tell me that he "liked my writing" and I continued to do another class with him that was mostly run by graduate students. Norm came occasionally and gave us some ideas of things to read. Norm agreed to sit on my dissertation committee and as part of the process, I conducted a preliminary study about Head Start teachers' salaries. At the end of defending this first project, my advisor asked Norm what he thought about the piece. Norm said "he liked my stories better." My advisor's response was to note that Norm was dressed in the same way as I described him in one of my stories!

I defended my dissertation proposal and head back to my part of the Midwest to spend two years as a volunteer at a Head Start program. I wasn't exactly sure what I was doing, but I had a vague idea that I would be figuring out how the staff made sense of policies. Like most novice researchers, I kept volumes of field notes about everything I saw, heard, and imaged. By the end of two weeks in the program, I had nearly thirty pages of single-spaced field notes. One day I was reading them over, and thought "boy, this is boring reading; they are so dry." As I was thinking about this, an image came to mind—that of a young boy who was part of the Head Start class. Several months before I began my volunteer work at Head Start, I walked by his farm with a friend. We saw this young boy, Steven, outside playing with his brothers, there were cows in the pasture, and his grandfather was working in the field. It was this image of Steven, once just another boy who lived along a country road, who now was a part of the children I worked with, that spurred me to write my first short story about Head Start.

I didn't give up keeping field notes but I continued to write the stories as well. My children, James 8, and Emily 6, would ask me every night, "Did you write another story? Can you read it to us?" The stories became part and parcel of what I did. I shared the short stories with the Head Start staff as I wrote them. During the year, one of the Head Start staff also wrote a story, about a young girl we learned was sexually assaulted by a neighbor.

At the end of my first year of volunteering at Head Start, I had 300 pages of field notes and fifteen or so stories. I didn't have a clue what to do with all this information. Fortunately my dissertation committee was willing to meet with me. Betty Merchant, a committee member, recommended I read McLaughlin's work on how policies are interpreted at the local level. Norm defined policy as "situational; it is open-ended; it is ambiguous; it is ad hoc." The combination of Norm's and Betty's help led me to thinking how I could write my dissertation around the short stories—using them as windows to understand how staff made sense of a myriad of policies.

During my second year at the Head Start program, that is what I did. I created my dissertation around the short stories. The stories are both the center of and conduit to my understanding of how Head Start staff made sense of policies. The stories included one told to me by the bus driver when we were picking up and then later dropping off children on the daily run. He told me about the donations that parents made to the program. Head Start has a policy that all programs need to produce so much " in-kind" service per year and one way that programs accumulate the in-kind is through donations. In this particular case, the bus driver told about a mother that kept giving him huge bags full of dirty plastic containers. He would haul them back to the center and the teacher would take one look at them and say, "trash." There was the story written by another staff member about Jasmine, who was sexually abused by a neighbor and how hard it was to imagine an adult treating a child in this way. That story paved the way to looking at how policies shape child abuse and neglect and how, in one circumstance, the Head Start staff were told not to pick up the child who was abused because of a policy that we might "hurt our backs."

With the help of a local English professor, I wrote my dissertation that included the stories and discussion about the policies at play. Most importantly, the Head Start staff I worked with read the dissertation as I wrote it and helped to clarify points and correct my mistakes. Finally, I had the draft ready. I sent it to Norm, who requires that you send your dissertation once it is completely written. I was in Florida at the time interviewing for a job. I remember getting an e-mail from him saying that it was a "good job" and I could contact the committee for the defense. I think that moment of hearing from him that it was a "good job" is a highlight of my graduate school experience.

So my dissertation defense went fine—a few changes were requested. And as I was meeting with the committee, I remembered back to a comment that Norm had made in the first class I ever took with him. He told us that if we chose to conduct research in the way that he described, it was a choice that would stay with us. You couldn't research and write in the way he advocated and produce a dissertation that resembled a standard model of writing up interviews and field notes. He was calling us to work with those we studied in new ways, to understand our work as entering into relationship with others, and writing in novel and inviting ways.

Well, that's all I have to say except I am delighted to see so many scholars who are here to cultivate the idea that people's stories and our creative ways of telling them should be given great value in doctoral research. Thank you. (*Applause*)

Dr. Samson: And thank you! Let's dismiss for lunch. When we return, we'll spend the rest of the day in our study groups and resume our presentations in the morning.

Part 3

Day three

Poetic inquiry and visual art

A democratic civilization will save itself only if it makes the language of the image into a stimulus for reflection, and not an invitation to hypnosis.

(Umberto Eco)

"Voices in the silence"
Dalene Swanson's story

with Jamie Moran and Eileen Honan

- Arts-based research
- Poetic inquiry
- Narrativity
- Critical rhizomatic reflection
- Social justice
- Hegemony in mathematics curriculum
- Interdisciplinarity
- Phenomenology

Runner: Good morning everyone. Say, did you hear the story about the senator who visited the Pine Ridge Indian reservation and made many promises to the people about better roads, schools, and job opportunities? After each promise, the crowd shouted enthusiastically, "Hooya!" The senator gained more confidence with each response. After his speech the senator was invited to tour one of the Oglala buffalo ranches, but first they had to walk through a cattle pasture that was owned by a non-Indian. The senator was about to step in a cow pie but his guide warned him just in time. "Be careful, you are about to step in the hooya," he said. (*Laughter*)

Our first presenter in this group of sessions we have described as relating to "poetic inquiry," is Dr. Dalene Swanson. Her arts-based dissertation exemplifies how creative work can broaden the socio-political dimensions within any arena, in this case the field of mathematics education, and can help us to consider issues of ideology and hegemony more closely.

Dr. Swanson graduated from the University of British Columbia in 2004 with a PhD in curriculum studies with a mathematics education emphasis. Her dissertation, "Voices in the Silence: Narratives of disadvantage, social context and school mathematics in post-apartheid South Africa," is a narrative, arts-based project that won four Canadian and international awards. These include the 2006 American Educational Research Association Outstanding Doctoral Dissertation Award for Curriculum Studies; the 2005 Canadian Association of Curriculum Studies Outstanding Doctoral Dissertation Award; the 2006 Illinois Qualitative Dissertation Award; and the 2005 Ted. T. Aoki Prize for the most Outstanding Doctoral Dissertation in Curriculum Studies at UBC. Dalene, it's all yours.

Dalene: Thank you; baie dankie; 'nkos' kakhulu [this is in English, Afrikaans, Xhosa, and Zulu respectively]. It is truly a pleasure to be here.

Runner referred to my dissertation as "arts-based" and it could well be described as such. I approached my research, most especially its representation, within an arts-based framework that emphasizes narrative and poetic inquiry. I drew on different literary sources and styles, South African and otherwise, so as to blur genres.

This said, when I describe my dissertation verbally I find myself calling it "critical reflexive narrative" or "critical rhizomatic narrative." The rhizome concept largely comes from the 1987 University of Minnesota text by Deleuze and Guattari called, *A Thousand Plateaus: Capitalism and Schizophrenia*. In essence, they use the term to convey the importance of replacing hierarchical structures and centralization of power with a system that recognizes and honors multiple dimensions and one that is always in motion. Because I refer to it often as "arts-based," presumptions are made, by some, about it and the "quality" of such work before it has even been read; a pre-engagement discourse of prejudice. This is a normative discourse that has arisen from the dominance of a hierarchy of discourses in the social domain that the academy actively invests in, rather than contests. The reification of the Scientific Method over other forms of knowing or being in the world, renders, from the academy's perspective, anything that does not conform to a Western historical construct of "scientifically-endorsed" knowledge, as lesser, inferior, inadequate, lacking. I was lucky enough to be able to do this kind of evocative and provocative work in a faculty at UBC that is a world leader in arts-based educational research. Nevertheless, not everyone was open to my taking a narrative approach to my work and dispensing with the more universally-accepted traditional approach that signals "academic rigour" to many. And, this is where the irony comes in: interestingly, the awards Runner mentioned were not only for my arts-based approach, but also for the dissertation's spoken-of "analytical and theoretical depth" and its "complexity," which ultimately were only possible because I *used* such an arts-based, rhizomatic, reflexive, narrative approach. Comments from awards committees were that my "dissertation particularly stood out because of its theoretical complexity, its interdisciplinary approach, its international positioning, and its use of arts-based methodology in a mathematics education context" the one committee noted that my work in the dissertation "presents—in very readable language—rich, compelling analyzes and themes, which have implications for theory, research, and practice." A further comment was that "*Voices in the Silence* is an academically sophisticated dissertation with a rich theoretical background that crosses difficult domains of knowledge and ways of knowing. Its uniqueness and strength is its challenge to existing interpretations of mathematics education research offering much potential."

I wrote my dissertation in four parts, using the metaphor and images of lunar phases that are in consonance with the Indigenous cyclicality of the pedagogy expressed in the work. This is also in keeping with a more "circular," or "elliptical," narrative-based approach synonymous with some African Indigenous epistemologies. My dissertation comprises sixteen pieces. I resisted calling them "chapters". Those pieces in the "full moon" phase make up the heart of the dissertation and contain its four major narratives.

> There is a moon within a half circle of light.
> Many choose not to see it.
> They look upon the soft smooth arc,
> the perfect curve,
> and see its boldness.

> But there are shadows between us,
> and a moon behind the arc we fear to see,
> for we have not yet learned the paths beyond the spaces we create,
> the contours of the unimagined.

A researcher can never be absolutely sure, only guided towards what she believes to be the way ahead. Making sense of the path depends on lunar changes in the forms of illumination.

My work strongly focuses on social justice issues, and attends deeply to hegemonic practices in mathematics education contexts. It is a critical exploration of the construction of disadvantage in school mathematics in social context. It provides a reflexive, narrative account of a pedagogic journey towards understanding the pedagogizing of difference in mathematics classrooms and its realizations as disadvantage in and across diverse socio-political, economic, cultural, and pedagogic contexts. The fieldwork mostly occurred within the Cape Province of South Africa, in schooling communities with socio-economic, cultural, and historical differences. Research took the form of interviews, discussions, and participant observation, in a recent post-apartheid context, but the product of this research—the dissertation—was rendered in narrative and poetic form. This shaped, developed, and contributed to the inquiry.

I believe the major contribution of my work is to open up spaces for dialogue with(in) silence through a reflexive narratizing. Ultimately, *Voices in the Silence* is an invitation to a dialogical journey that seeks to provide roots/ routes of engagement with the ideals of social justice and an egalitarian society. It attempts to find narrative moments within the difficult terrain of research work and lived experience where constructed disadvantage can be re-imagined and transformed into transcendent pedagogies of empowerment and hope.

The dissertation congregates around the idea that "silence" contributes to the social construction of disadvantage and the way it may be lived out in relation to school mathematics discourse in different contexts. While it interrogates the many slippery forms and interpretations of silence, it provides it with metaphorical significance through the theoretical feature of voice.

One of the narratives in my dissertation addresses the philosophy of Africanization, its incompatibility with the ideology of neo-liberalism, how Africanization can become subsumed within neo-liberalism, and how this plays out in a mathematics classroom in a context of "poverty." Issues of neo-colonialism, and how these inform poverty education and disempowerment within a mathematics education context, are at the fore. In this sense, the dissertation explores critical issues in mathematics education and highlights further contradictions and dilemmas within different research contexts.

The final section of my dissertation uses poetry to describe the many voices of silence as they infuse themselves within research texts. In Dewey's terms, from his 1934 contribution, *Art as Experience*, published by Capricorn Books, New York: "The poetic as distinct from the prosaic, esthetic art as distinct from scientific, expression as distinct from statement, does something different from leading to an experience. It constitutes one." (p. 75). I have used poetry in my research representation to bridge other styles of literary engagement, to provide another gaze on research issues that purposefully complicate meanings rather than reduce or simplify them through mainstream language use, and to express meanings in different, sensitive and creative ways that are both provocative and evocative. Poetic form has permitted me to provide a vivid, lyrical, perspectival, and engaging expression of research concerns that appeal to the emotional, sensual, intuitive, visceral, and philosophical, and that enhance meanings of critical issues, maintain their complexity, and raise them to a more insightful, spiritual, heart-felt and embodied dimension of human engagement.

> . . . Silence inheres in the dilemmas that create/are created by
>   disadvantage.
> It invests in conundrum,
> and manifests in contradiction.
> It plays a duplicitous game of duality,
> being both metaphorical and literal.
>
> Be cognizant! Silence metamorphoses and masquerades as counter-
>   narrative,
> and like a multi-headed Hydra, replicates its many other selves.
> It camouflages itself against the real,
> confusing the principles of the ethical, the moral, and the just.

From the beginning I avoided the traditional literature review and academic citation formats. I also theorized "voice" differently. I was not interested in peppering my dissertation with an array of diverse voices that correspond to the physical shells of bodies, as if this would grant the critical motivations behind my research automatic credibility, which is often advanced as a criterion for academic legitimacy within critical theory. Rather, I wanted to raise the level of discourse so as to interrogate more deeply and widely the investment of silence in the construction of disadvantage and the way it may be lived out in relation to school mathematics by viewing voice less literally, more metaphorically and somewhat more theoretically.

Traditional criteria of validity, verification, and generalizability were not my foremost concern, nor the emphases on frequency and consistency, criteria that were ever present for consideration in the relational sense to positions of hegemony within academic writing. I continuously deferred capturing "reality" or "truth," even as these criteria in themselves were not my research objectives. I have reflexively engaged with many of the tensions, contradictions, ambiguities, and paradoxes lived out in my fieldwork experiences. I have attempted to illuminate the ethical dilemmas of choice as they have informed broader discourses and debates. I have tried to engage with the underlying, often hidden, ideological premises of articulations and actions to make visible the innate silences and their agency these inform. I have not tried to reconcile the controversial and inconclusive, harmonize discord, and obfuscate innate discrepancies and disjunctions within discourses and positions. In this sense, I have embraced difficult issues and unanswerable questions with "rigor," or rather "vigor," through personal, spiritual, and theoretical engagement and a messy grappling. I have consequently resisted the traditionalist approach to social science research that modulates content as it regulates form by claiming greater "validity," and access to reality and objective truth.

I believe my dissertation contributes to new knowledge in its exploration of constructions of disadvantage, and their realizations across mathematics classroom contexts and communities of practice. The work opens up new spaces for dialogue that in turn breaks through the falsity and oppression of hegemonic assumptions that have stifled the potential for enabling mathematics education in disadvantaged contexts.

My work advances an arts-based approach in order to provide a broader base for interpretive possibilities, to challenge the existing interpretations of what Mathematics Education Research ought to look like, to contest the power principles that self-define and limit "the sayable" within Mathematics Education Research, and to deepen and extend its understandings and academic engagement beyond the usual, orthodox terrain of Scientific/Social Science research. An arts-based approach, therefore, is grounded in the belief that it can achieve the ends of greater critical focus and personal autonomy in mathematics education, and in education, research, and practice at large.

For those of you contemplating a similar journey, know that it is a dangerous one in many ways. Narrativity offers the possibility of flagrantly resisting formulation, and concerns itself with the human condition as lived and (re)imagined as its primary focus. It has the potential to lead toward a more democratic, egalitarian ideal of both citizenship and pedagogy. It embraces creative textural forms that produce pluralized meanings and it breathes life and feeling into storied human experiences. In these times, these goals themselves are somewhat dangerous. It is also a difficult journey because you are sure to be spun away from the safe confines of orthodoxy. You are left vulnerable in your openness. Narrative permits nuance, contingency, parallelism, and ambiguity. It permits the sensate, spiritual, mythological, and emotional domains of human experience, while valuing the aesthetic, literary/oral, intuitive, and interpretive dimensions that would honor lived experiences and explanations of the human condition. It, as I have said earlier, breaks from its anchor to safe harbors.

I want to conclude by reminding everyone that encouraging authentic narratives from research partners in itself cannot liberate communities without their being connected to further, collaborative activism and political action. The assumption that they can, reflects a naïve and privileged position. Academic researchers and narrative writers need to be careful about making claims to emancipation through research writing in itself, although it may well lead to emancipatory possibilities. These possibilities are worthy research objectives and academic goals in themselves, nonetheless. Nevertheless, narrative opens up a space for addressing responsibly the moral, political, and ethical paradoxes and dilemmas of the human experience through embracing pluralized perspectives in ways that give meaning and form to those experiences as lived.

Sala kakuhle (stay in peace)!

Dr. Samson: Thank you Dr. Swanson for a most impressive presentation. If I may, I would like to go back to your notion of rhizomatic narrative, a characterizing that would fit well with the terms put forth by Deleuze and Guattari. Turning my attention to Deleuze and Guattari, I am somewhat familiar with the writings of these authors and frankly find them to be full of nonsense. In their critique of capitalism and laws of science they deny the realities relating to how these have contributed to our world. They rationalize what is in my opinion an irresponsible approach to research. They seem to want to bring us to a new sense of ecology, for example, by ignoring scientific facts about the environment. Forgive me because I do not assign my concerns here with your work, but I just find that their ideas about rhizomes take us in no particular direction and give us no logical conclusions.

Dalene: Dr. Samson, I understand your frustration with their work and perhaps even with some of the ideas behind my own. Actually, I did not use Deleuze and Guattari's work anywhere in my dissertation. Perhaps some may see this as a "failure" that I did not cite such important work. Or perhaps one could see it as a "success" of alternative work like this in that I did not feel compelled to cite such work just because I was using a word used by them. It begs the question as to who owns the words we use. Throughout my dissertation I use words like rhizome, roots, and webs, to give a sense of the complex interrelated, pluralistic, holistically interconnected form of the work. In supporting a reticular or rhizomatic research, I refer to "moments of articulation" to support a particular methodological frame of reference, a philosophical gaze on inquiry that is organic and multiply informing, and that permits and supports complexity. Here, *moments of articulation* within fieldwork define utterances and somatic performances embedded within narrative contexts and their attending discourses, and instigate investigation, deliberation, and engagement in analyzing the multiple ways in which disadvantage takes root/route. These moments often occurred during fieldwork experiences that were invested in ambiguity and dilemma, so that my very body in that context often became a site of struggle between competing discourses. These narrative moments permitted me to stop and linger on the narratizability of the textual moment. These moments of articulation gave rise to rhizomatic engagement in narrative writing of the text that sought to be deeply reflective, reflexive, and robustly democratic.

In any case, with all due respect, your assertions about 'scientific facts' and the need for 'logical conclusions' have been a problem that I wanted to overcome. I used narrative and poetry as I did because I do not see research as an object that necessitates final closure. Narrative and poetic inquiry is a process of continuous *metaphoring* or *narratizing* that resists being temporally and spatially contained and formalized into a set of procedures or prescriptions. I have embraced narrative and other forms of arts-based inquiry to engage with sensitive research dilemmas, disjunctures, paradoxes, and controversies so as to grapple with, and hopefully sometimes grasp, nuance, subtlety, contingency, and complexity as they play out in often difficult narrative moments within the research contexts. Narrative offers the opportunity to broaden the horizon on these issues.

Runner: I am not at all familiar with the work of these two authors and honestly had never heard of a rhizome before today, except I think I came across the term in biology class long ago. But I see now how the idea of a rhizome as Dalene described it fits into Indigenous worldviews that tend to reject hierarchy as an organizing principle. The rhizome seems to be the opposite of hierarchy. Diversity, complexity, and mystery seem to us more appropriate in terms of trying to describe an organizing principle. Jamie, I see your eyes smiling. Would you save me from myself here and maybe get us back on track?

Folks, allow me to introduce Dr. Jamie Moran. He is a senior lecturer at Rohampton University and is one of the pioneers behind the use of qualitative research in psychology. I also know Jamie as a sub chief in the Cante Tinze. His Indian name is Poorwolf.

Jamie: No, no, you're doing fine! But I do think it is important for us to honor Dr. Samson's ideas in support of traditional academic or scientific research, but only as one option, and not the dominant option as a form of hegemony, one that silences other possibilities of ways of knowing. We should also talk about the role of phenomenology as an equally important, perhaps more vital, research approach in terms of the problems facing our world today, and although Dalene did not mention this in her brief presentation, and while she describes her research as interdisciplinary, I recognize features of phenomenology in her work.

Dr. Samson: Dr. Moran, would you be willing to give us more information about this from your perspective?

Jamie: Phenomenology, let's say "phi" for short, is about illuminating something so we know it better. It is looking, with as few presuppositions as possible, at something with enough light to reduce the need for preconceptions. So if artful renditions can bring in a form of "light" that can help reveal something in its "isness," then this form of light is a legitimate space for phi.

In Indigenous cultures, the sun served a metaphorical purpose of bringing balance to things. Spirits instructed the people not to have closed minds or to adhere so closely to a particular doctrine, but rather, to always take a genuine interest in *all* the phenomena that consciousness presents us with, including the very mysterious.

Ultimately, research at the doctoral level and beyond is about meaning-making. In terms of phi, meaning-making is a balance between the internal and the external. There is always a two-way back and forth, give and take. Therefore phenomenology does not accept any methods of study that ignore or abstract ways of knowing away from actual experience. It does not legitimize dividing experience up into secondary fabrications. So it asks the question, "what is it like for you or me or us to be here or there?" It does not work with variables defined by the research. It is more concerned with the meanings attributed to events by participants that matter, as with Dalene's work in South Africa.

These meanings therefore must be allowed to emerge in their own right, in their own "light," according to their own idiosyncratic perspective and agenda, but also according to their own potentialities and potencies of meaning-making—not constrained by a priori definitions and theories of the meaning phenomenon that would restrict it in a narrow way, by prescribing its nature and reach before it is even investigated. Meaning-making should be invited to show "what it has"—show what it is, and what it can do, and how it does it, and why. In this sense, it is meaning-making as an undiscovered continent, a terra incognita, until it is invited to come forth and reveal itself.

The kind of research Dr. Samson is thinking of is supposed to lead to predictions. Phi (phenomenology) aims to understand meanings that come through the research. This can happen, not by embracing "logical conclusions," but by struggling with complexity. Once you enter this struggle, things are not so neat, precise, and accurate, in control. The subject matter that is not so easily pinned down demands a more struggling, messy, provisional, and revisable, approach to research.

To make this point for my students, I used to use this metaphor: you can catch a shrimp in a certain finely laced fishing net; try to catch a whale in this same net, and one of two things happens: the net breaks, or the whale is shredded into small bits that lose its whole configuration. Here is another version of the same idea. Forty years ago I read of a scientist who proposed to study the human dream life. He was a "lab-type" scientist. Before beginning, he dreamed that his laboratory was under water and that he saw the most beautiful, multi-colored fish swimming around in that water. Then the laboratory was empty of water, and the fish were all laid out on a lab table, dead, and they had lost their color. And, the worst part about this was that the scientist puzzled about this dream and did not see the joke—and the warning —his own unconscious dream source was issuing to his conscious mind, with its lust for scientific conquest! It may be hard to research the living fish by swimming with them, but if you don't get your feet wet in researching something watery, you run the risk that the research act will distort and maybe even kill what you are researching. You end up with frozen fish—dead, and colorless!

As I started out saying, I think the mechanical aspect of reality exists and can be accessed by traditional quantitative research, although this is always merely a perspective on the truth about that "reality." But, when we confront other kinds of reality, the method must change to suit the other kind of reality. We need to ask other questions entirely about that "reality." Thus not only human creativity is at stake here, but the appropriate horse for the course. Nature's mystery, variety, levels, is at stake. If we insist everything must be like a shrimp to fit our net, then the bigger and deeper realities elude us. Aristotle had this right at least. Science should not be methods driven, it should be phenomena driven. Let the phenomena, when they are mysterious, supple, subtle, fluid, in flux, profound, dictate more tentative, yet deep, kinds of methods to do justice to the reality.

As with arts-based research that involves interviewing real people in real communities, phenomenology is one of the main foundational sources of all qualitative research. Phi is more of an attitude, or a perspective, than a method. It is fluid and subtle, not formulaic and rule-bound. Ultimately, I think it is about consciousness, meaning, experience, and action. These go together and cannot be separated and I saw them all operating in Dalene's dissertation.

Phenomenology then starts with consciousness. It is relational. It is a conversation on many levels at once, spoken and unspoken, explicit and implicit. Can you see how this fits Dalene's work and even the idea of the rhizome? Consciousness is an energy that interacts with other energies. This is different from mechanistic research that is predictable, therefore controllable, because it has no out-reach, no meeting with that which is "other," which could unsettle it, open it to the unexpected, and challenge it. We love mechanism because, like social convention, it provides handrails we can rely on. But it also leads to our abdicating control to some external impersonal force or social power. This leads to the kind of hegemony Dalene's project attempted to overshadow.

Consciousness also leads to the kind of creativity and love that seemed to drive Dalene's project. Creativity implies an ability to re-do things in a new manner, so the future is not dictated by the past, but can intrude upon it, and can welcome the strange and dangerous rather than getting fixed on the familiar and safe. As for love, I refer to what happens when we become truly involved in what consciousness presents to us. We worry about it, care about it, give ourselves to it. To love is to regard things, situations, persons, or creatures in the world, as "mattering," and allowing oneself to be bound to their fate; this rouses us to exceed the self, to rise above it, as nothing else can. This was most obvious in Dalene's work.

Finally, to be conscious is to be reflective. It is about our ability to raise fundamental questions about our life, its point, and to be honest and self-critical in all that we do. What is worth doing? This also implies that the world as conceived by modernist science is not "the real world." Modernist science too often is an abstraction away from authentic reflection because it is too concerned with making absolute a sense of the world under the name of "objectivity," a very dispassionate form of claimed objectivity—but it can only make sense of a certain aspect of the world, that aspect which is regular, predictable, explainable, and controllable. It creates a false sense of safety and security in this form of controllable knowing. Dalene knew this from the beginning and did not want to fall into the same kind of trap that she saw in the oppression of students caught in the hegemony of mathematics pedagogy. Dalene knows that this journey is dangerous because the real world is messy, ambiguous, paradoxical, fluid, in motion; the real world is specific and subtle, wonderful and terrifying, beautiful and ugly, familiar and strange.

Dr. Samson: Excuse me, but the idea of consciousness, which first of all would be difficult for us to define, seems to be an ending place, not a starting place. Research has to be conceived with a beginning, doesn't it?

Jamie: No it doesn't. At least not in research approaches such as grounded theory or phenomenology. In fact, consciousness is always about intentionality, directionality, agendas, positions, or, if you will, a hypothesis. This comes from the experiential aspect of consciousness. Experience registers in our conscious awareness the situation both *as we undergo it*, and *as we relate to it*. Dalene was conscious enough to realize the issues of oppression that related to the usual mathematics education and, with intentionality, was conscious enough to use the kind of approach she chose.

I would also guess that much of this intentionality stemmed from her life experience. Experience tells us how we are situated, because it tells us what it is like to be in that situation. It manifests an awareness that is not confined above the neck to the head, but is embodied in the whole living and breathing and moving body, and is not only embodied, but in fact reaches out into the surrounding field. Dalene told me in private about the experiences she had as a child in South Africa and how they informed her compassion for the people who were participants in her research.

Finally, we come to the idea of action. I was pleased to hear Dalene say in her concluding remarks that without follow-up action, the narratives themselves could not be truly liberating. And, like the journey she said was "dangerous," this part of phenomenology or the search for phi can be dangerous as well. Experience can open up, but action ventures more risk. Mathew King, the Lakota medicine man who followed Frank Fools Crow, spoke in an existential-phenomenological voice when he said, "Wisdom is not what we think, and wisdom is what we do."

Runner: Wopila—thanks Poorwolf. I also want to introduce one of our scholars from Australia, Dr. Eileen Honan, and ask her to say a few words about this Deleuzian concept of rhizomes that Dalene briefly describes. Eileen did her own doctoral dissertation with a rhyzomatic methodology and has published significantly on this since. She is currently a Senior Lecturer at the School of Education at the University of Queensland.

Eileen Honan: Thank you Dr. Samson. It is great to be here and to listen to the stimulating, creative, and pioneering research people are doing. I just want to say a very few words to clarify some misunderstandings. In brief, a rhizotextual analysis involves the exploration of the "middles" of these rhizomes. Rather than denying reality, the Deleuzian project is about expanding our understandings of divergent realities. Surely Dr Samson would agree, especially within this context of Indigenous research, that the "realities" of the contribution of capitalism to "our" world would look very different if one followed a discursive path exploring the growth of capitalism among new industrialists in the United States, or if one followed the discursive path exploring the impact of capitalism's drive for new markets on the colonisation of different Indigenous groups over the last 300 years.

Part of the excitement of coming to Deleuze is understanding that there is no one singular direction, no one method to follow and certainly no prescriptive recipe that would result in any "logical" ending. Deleuze and Guattari developed the understanding of knowledge as rhizomatic to disrupt taken-for-granted understandings in modernist philosophy of knowledge as "linear" and "logical," expressed most commonly in the use of the metaphor of the "tree of knowledge." It can help to understand rhizomatics by applying other horticultural metaphors to this postmodern understanding of knowledge.

Many types of grasses, bromeliads, and members of the ginger plant families are rhizomatic: rather than having a linear-type root system attached to a central trunk, they have complex networks of root systems. Plants can grow from any point in this network, and each plant is attached to the other through the network. I hope this helps a bit and that everyone can see how this concept relates to many of the methods (or should I say "anti-methods") that you all are introducing here.

Acknowledgment

This offering of my story is dedicated to Dr Karen Meyer, who deftly midwifed the birth of my Ph.D. dissertation with humanity, heart, and grace.

"A journey to praxis"
Patty Holmes's story

- Performativity
- Narrative representation
- Poetry
- Double-sided submission

Dr. Samson: Our next presenter is a professional classroom teacher of English Language Arts at John Norquay School in Vancouver, Canada. She is also the Vice President of City Stage New West. She came here with Dalene, who coached her through a narrative thesis. Patty asked if she could say a few words about why she has decided NOT to pursue a doctoral degree after having experienced the frustrations of the academic mandates during the acquisition of her Master's.

Patty: Thanks for letting me talk about my academic journey with all of you. Although I have been discouraged as a result of the process I went through, listening to all of you has, I must admit, been inspiring. Hopefully, it will inspire the academic gatekeepers and not just students who will have to suffer at their hands!

The critical philosophies of Mikhail Bakhtin, Judith Butler, Susan Miller, and Michel Foucault in regard to the intricacies of power relations, the hegemonic and exclusive nature of knowledge building within the academy, the problem of knowledge-compacting that occurs in the mere usage of academic linguistic practices, and the recent neo-liberal institutionalization and standardization of teaching practice have all convinced me to tell a story about my research rather than present it as a case to be argued and proven. True, these are many reasons, glibly given, and any one of these points could be a departure for a paper itself. However, it was not my purpose to engage solely in theoretical analysis and defense during my studies at the university.

I was more concerned with researching how I, an average teacher, given nothing but local materials in the form of a regular class and school in a working-class neighborhood, could put theory into practice, and then share that experience with other teachers in similar situations.

How best to represent the journey to praxis and then take that work experience beyond the academy? Simply, I would have to choose a medium that would be read by an audience wider than those engaged in work at the university. Working teachers, in my experience and myself included, are generally not interested in reading theory or a thesis during their busy teaching day. I have noticed, however, that teachers have strong and well-informed opinions about the best way to implement curriculum, and have regular daily meetings with colleagues to discuss this. These meetings take place in the morning before school, at recess, lunch, or after school, accompanied by food and coffee or tea. The information is usually passed on anecdotally, in a spirit of cooperation and community mindedness, with laughter, sharing, and empathy. The narrative style is employed to good effect by many, and a few become renowned on staffs for their story-telling skill.

This happens time and again in staffrooms, lunch halls, local cafés, and on the telephones and e-mail after teaching hours. Teachers do very much want to share their work, learn about what other educators are doing, and continually attempt curriculum innovations of their own. But, I believe they want to do so in their own voice and in their own discourse arena.

This is not to say that I think teachers are not interested in ideas in development at the academy or university, or that the work in classrooms is disconnected from the rigor of academic research work. Quite the contrary is true. However, I believe a common language is needed to connect those two research locations in reciprocal discourse. Insisting on using the academic paper as the only means of knowledge development alienates the very people who have the widest first-hand experience of the actualities of curriculum implementation, pedagogical practice, ontologies of learning, and epistemic and Indigenous ways of knowing. In the interest of widening the discourse arena, I think that if I choose narrative as a medium for representing my work, more people will join in the conversation about the research. After all, the narrative form of representation is rather more inclusive than the academic. And, as has been proven by master story tellers too numerous to mention, great and complex ideas can be conveyed within the shortest of stories.

I do not wish to judge my own writing, but I do know that those who have read the narrative of my research have been moved emotionally and, in some cases, pedagogically. I have had teachers challenge me about what I wrote, compliment me, commiserate with me, and laugh with me. Their reactions alone validate, for me, the use of narrative rather than the vocabulary-laden, noun-compounding, passive third-party voice of the academic research paper.

In truth, having a Master's paper read *at all, by anybody* is justification enough for the employment of narrative representation. All too many times have I heard the wry laughter accompanying a grad student's celebration of finally "publishing," knowing full well that the only people who *might* read it will be other people setting out to write Master's papers: *maybe*. Usually, the thesis sits on a shelf and gathers dust. Or, these days, it gets stored in a chip and is never read at all.

Not at all. My paper, in fact, is guaranteed not to be read by anybody who searches for it in the Canadian National Library database, or in the university graduate studies database. The reason it will not be read is because of the format it was required to be published in, completely at odds with its genre. The academic thesis paper formatting rendered my research story nonsensical, illogical, and impossible to read. Why? Because I was not allowed to submit it copied in the double-sided form narrative textual publication commonly employs. So, illustrations that go with particular vignettes do not sit side by side, poems and recipes that run across the bottom of every page cannot be seen in their true shape, and above all, the duality of viewpoints in the two main character's opposing voices describing events in the researcher's day is lost because they cannot be read in the comparative way that the performativity of facing pages affords. It is difficult to describe this problem in words but it is instantly knowable once the performativity of text is considered. To illustrate, imagine a picture book with only half the picture on each page, needing to have the other half on the facing page to get the whole idea. Without the whole picture, the reader must guess, predict, and infer meaning and be thwarted at every page turn.

On the day I handed in my paper, teeth clenched, sitting docilely at the desk at the dean's office, I wondered how much I should protest. The enforcement of the academic formatting on my narrative style was a clear power play against my researcher's voice. I felt like I was being pushed rather firmly into a location of anonymity and powerlessness, punished for using the narrative style with the special knowledge that my finished work would be made into nonsense. Regardless of my feelings, I only dared risk just one snide remark, asking the clerk petulantly if the page numbers were located in the correct corner of the page. After all, I'd put in a great deal of effort to create this story, and I knew there was very little chance that my one-person protest at this point was going to make any difference. Protesting about power politics and the performativity of text at that point would have only delayed the acceptance date, my graduation date, and also required that I enroll for another semester. What I needed then was to get that paper through the gate before the end of my August teaching "holiday" and get back to work the next week in the classroom to get a paycheck. I have a family to feed. And, I was woefully unprepared for the battle that I knew must follow. I couldn't change the system in a couple of days. That I knew for sure. Besides, I already knew nobody was likely to read the paper from this source, anyway. So, I had in my hands several copies I had printed at my friendly neighborhood printers: double-sided, color-illustrated copies that my teaching colleagues were happy to read. To this day, I am still printing more.

On that day, the graduate faculty clerk was diligently interested in all the matters of academic format. Not once was the meaning of the presentation of the text on the page beyond the margins, headers, footers, single-side copying rules, appropriate page numbers, referential practices, illustration decimal orderings, etc., even discussed. But then, I guess that's not really the clerk's job, is it, to question or examine the political intent of textual performativity?

That's our job, as researchers, I suppose. Up until a few weeks before the submission of my thesis, I had no idea how stringent the gate-keeping was, or how inflexible the rules were. My committee members had been most supportive: they had even warned me of the single-sided serpent, but I simply didn't take it as seriously as I should have. Carl Leggo and Dalene Swanson coached me tirelessly throughout the development of my work, and watched the story take shape. Carl showed me how to take a voice, how to express the moment in narrative and poetry, and how to reveal a story to engage an audience. Dalene, whose gripping narrative PhD thesis of mathematics education in a South African township context had won her the AERA dissertation award, was someone I had to get special permission to have on my committee, as she was not a full professor at the university. She taught me how to recognize the data within the student narratives I had collected, and how to represent that data in a narrative of my own. Karen Meyer, my third member, gave my work a final read and helped me to see that I was engaging in a living inquiry and that orienting myself within the discourse of the teaching community I was part of was the right thing to do. I was very fortunate to be able to select my own committee, and likely would not have finished the thesis had it not been for their brave guidance.

That said, I am not sure if I would pursue a doctoral degree in narrative style, or in any style. At this point in my life, with over twenty-five years of teaching behind me, I am beginning to reconsider the nature of data. Perhaps there is more meaning to be made, for myself and for the community of teachers, researchers, and students I am a part of, when I actually teach in classrooms. I have also joined a performance collective at the university, working with a group of graduate researchers to represent stories of education through performance. I find satisfaction in that, and in the small theater company I have started with a few friends in the suburb where I live. Our first performance event will include some stories of teachers, students, and schooling. Meaning and research, I have learned, does not always fit into academic discourse. Narrative, on the other hand, speaks to all.

"The creative potential of not knowing"

Robin Cox's story

with Lorri Neilsen Glenn

- Poetry
- Radical hermeneutics
- Lyric inquiry
- The folly of authorized knowing

Dr. Samson: Our next speaker, Robin Cox, received her PhD in Counselling Psychology from the University of British Columbia, Canada. She is doing some fascinating research and writing focused on further developing the work she began in her dissertation. This includes examining the disorientation of disasters as a potential site of creativity, and employing theatrical techniques, art, poetry and other multi-media forms of exploration in research and knowledge translation and dissemination strategies.

Robin Cox: Hello everyone and thank you for inviting me to be part of this remarkable conference. In keeping with the poetry theme of this session, I offer a poem to introduce myself to you:

> I am a traveler, an actor, and a journalist,
> Knowing we are all stories waiting to be told
> that in the telling we might know ourselves.
> I am a psychotherapist,
> sitting quietly with your panic,
> trusting the courage of even the smallest of steps.
> I am a scholar,
> weaving together the stitches of the disintegrated whole
> as I contemplate the opening in loss and suffering.
> I am a story teller, critical thinker, lover of complexity, artist, witness,
> healer,

discovering the creativity of my spirit
in the resonating depth of my compassion.
I am finding out
that if you put the circles together you get a woman,
no straight lines, just the curving possibility of what is around the
corner.

My dissertation, "Echoes, Transgressions, and Transformations: Identity Reorientation and the Discourse of Disaster Recovery," is based on a mix of methods integrated into an ethnographic study of disaster recovery. I included more or less traditional academic methods of analysis (e.g. grounded theory, discourse analysis) and less traditional methods (e.g. meditation and contemplative strategies and poetry writing). When I went to "write up" the research I wanted to reflect these different analytic methods with different narrative strategies. I used what I would call conventional academic prose to frame the text (intro, context—or literature review, findings), although even there I integrated some alternative narrative strategies to try to capture the felt sense of residents' descriptions of the forest fire that was the focus of the study.

At the same time, and throughout the research process, I had been employing mindfulness-based meditation and contemplation as a method of reflection and analysis of my embodied or enacted cognitive perceptions of my engagement with the participants and the content of the interviews with them. This process resulted in poetic expressions; findings that arose from my intuitive, contemplative engagement with my own uncertainty and from my mindful engagement with the uncertainty of affected community members as they navigated their personal and collective recovery process. I believe that the construction of new knowledge requires this kind of intentional blending of systematic, multimodal, data analyzes with a mindful, reflexive engagement with the process of research and its impact on the researcher and researched alike. As researchers, we must willingly step outside the safety of the certainty of authorized knowing into the groundlessness of not knowing, in order to open up other possibilities. These poems, in effect, are concrete representations of these other potentialities. The resultant series of poems documented my intuitive, embodied analysis of the ethnographic research data and process. They are woven through my dissertation, as prequels if you will, to each chapter. In this way they offer readers an additional entry point into the content of the dissertation while simultaneously offering a resting spot, or reflective pause between each of the chapters. Because the multiple focuses of the dissertation (the experiences and discourses of recovery) were complex, and because I used manifold analytic strategies, my dissertation (in addition to the requisite introductory chapters) includes four Findings Chapters—each reflecting a different aspect of the analysis.

I want to share just a little background to the writing of this dissertation. In the years working as a psychotherapist prior to entering the doctoral program in Counseling Psychology my work had focused on the emotional fallout of catastrophic transitions and violence. While working as a therapist I began volunteering as a psychosocial responder with the Canadian Red Cross Disaster Services. Then 9/11 happened. As a Canadian participant in the response to the collapse of the World Trade Center in New York, I met what felt like the heart of a disaster *at* the heart of a disaster. The city was alive with a vibrating vulnerability and the shattered naïvety of a culture thrust into a different vision of itself. In the staffing headquarters of the American Red Cross, in the bars and restaurants of Manhattan, and on the streets lined with people cheering the firefighters as they returned to the ongoing search of the "pile" that is the remains of the World Trade Center, people were reaching out to each other. There was a palpable and deep desire to connect in the midst of the vulnerability and sorrow that the 9/11 attacks had inspired.

Soon after returning from New York, I decided to return to academia to pursue my doctorate in Counseling Psychology. With my curiosity about what I had experienced in New York still pulling at me, and in the midst of responding to a devastating fire season in Canada that became known as Firestorm 2003, I decided to research the complex process known as disaster recovery. In particular, I was interested in the discourse of recovery, the language and social practices that shaped the practices of disaster recovery in North America.

Part of my interest in tracing the discourse of recovery reflected my long-standing suspicion that the dominant discourse of psychology is both a barrier to and an entry point into a new understanding of consciousness and our response to suffering. For a number of years, I had watched the emergence of traumatic stress as a disciplinary interest that was spawning a multitude of conferences, professional associations, journal articles, and clinical specializations. At the same time, I had watched trauma and stress research become a dominant site of inquiry within psychology into the mind–body connection. Trauma studies had become a place where neuroscience, cognitive psychology, and the practitioners of the mindfulness practices of Buddhism were in a dynamic intercourse. Research at the nexus of these interpenetrating discourses was challenging the classic Cartesian split that had defined modern psychology in North America. With the questions that had arisen in the context of 9/11 still reverberating within me, the proximity of the forest fire disaster presented me with the opportunity to immerse myself in an examination of psychology's engagement with/in the disaster recovery process. Thus, I situated my inquiry as a critical ethnographic study of the recovery process of individuals living in several rural Canadian communities devastated by one of the largest forest fires that season, the McLure Fire. The text of my dissertation wove the findings of a multi-pronged poststructural analysis combining the visceral methods of multi-sited ethnography, the constant comparative analytic strategies associated with the constructivist grounded theory, the deconstructive approach to knowledge arising within critical discourse analysis methods, and the embodied, intuitive knowing of mindfulness practices. In this multi-threaded mapping process, my goal was to produce a dis-closure rather than a closure, a text that opened space for new questions and possibilities in our understanding and experience of disasters and trauma.

In this weaving of methods, my voice became a presence in the text as an observer, interpreter, and commentator and, as in most good ethnographies, the voices of the participants were also present, albeit filtered through my interpretive lens. Grounded theory strategies shaped a text that presented an emerging mid-range theory of the psychological and social process of disaster recovery. The unpacking of the critical discourse analysis generated several bookend chapters that explored the constitutive aspects of the language and social practices of recovery evidenced in interviews and the media. Poetry, as a less linear, more kinetic narrative emerged as the vehicle for exploring and expressing my emergent theorizing and first person (i.e. visceral, reflexive, embodied) response to the research experience. My poetic representations were woven through the more conventional academic prose of my dissertation as invitations into a different relationship with the text and the knowledge claims I made.

I positioned my poetry as evocative prequels to other forms of analysis, a means of posing questions rather than suggesting answers. In form and content, poetry called upon my willingness to play with the patterns of language and knowing. It provoked an opening into my experience as a researcher and a doctoral student rather than a foreclosing around those experiences. To write poetry, I had to be willing to sit and reflect and allow. It was not a form to be forced. Rather, it was a way of being in the experience of the investigation of the research questions I posed, spiritually, intellectually, and physically.

The poems, which began every chapter of my dissertation, highlighted moments of free play in my analysis of the disaster recovery process and the dominant and alternate discursive practices of "suffering," "loss," and "trauma" in these collective events known as disasters. Written at various stages of the development of my research, the placement of each poem reflected the evolution of my process and, simultaneously, the relevance of each of the poems to the content of the prose that followed. Each poem emphasized the relational ground of the researcher to the research, and the interwoven and sometimes conflicting threads of my identities as a graduate student, disaster responder, Buddhist dabbling, quantum curious, qualitative researcher.

By using figurative language and a concentrated blend of sound and imagery, poetry also opened up the potential for multiple readings of the dissertation text. The construction of knowing was foregrounded in a way that was not as apparent when the academic prose stood alone. I, as the researcher/writer, was more evident in my poetic writing. No longer the detached author, speaking with the scientific authority of conventional academic prose, I offered my own intimate experience of the field, the data, and my emerging interpretation and theorizing of the disaster recovery process. Hence I offered this invocation to myself at the outset of my dissertation to trust the relevance of my intuitive knowing and the poetic representations I knew I wanted to bring to life, and I close my talk with it now:

I am,
We are,
Hermeneutically circling.
Questioning the existence of a stopping place
Intuitively understanding that below the binary,
Underneath the grasping at certainty,
Lies mystery, not mastery.

Looking back,
At the first stab
In this defrocking of discourse.
Like Dorothy's Lion, lacking in courage
My questions were assimilated and contained
My performance,
Standing perfectly still.

Circling,
Once again,
On this pilgrimage of curiosity.
This story, unfolding, explicating, inscribed,
Still struggles within the nature of its telling.
Strives to transgress
Its flat, fixed life in text.

Enigmatic
Double agent,
Reason is once again in motion,
In a clumsy dance of radical faith, bewilderment
As I swear allegiance to the servant of my intuition.
I offer this poetry,
Laughing as I go around.

Dr. Samson: Thank you Robin. (*Applause*) It is now my distinct honor to introduce you to Dr. Lorri Neilsen, a Professor at Mount Saint Vincent University in Halifax, Nova Scotia. Lorri has taught for over thirty-five years: in public schools, at Mount Royal College in Calgary, at King's College School of Journalism, in a penitentiary, in Northern Canadian communities, and in universities in Australia and New Zealand. The author, editor and co-editor of nine books, she has also been a writing consultant to over fifty organizations in Canada and abroad since 1980. Lorri has been a scholar in residence, writer in residence, and frequent keynote speaker in Canada, the U.S., and Australia. Her poetry and scholarship have won several national and international awards, including two research excellence awards and, in April 2005, a four-year appointment as Halifax Poet Laureate.

Lorri Neilsen: Thanks Dr. Samson and thank you Robin for your important insights about using poetry in your research.

I want to start at the end, with an excerpt from a poem entitled "Phenomenology" from my collection *Combustion* (2007):

> The story comes after comes after, remember? You turn
> the strange into familiar with what is
> at hand. Most of your life is like this:
> memory, mercy, the ballast
> of desire, heavier for the words you've wrapped around them,
> and lighter too.

I was trained as a statistical researcher in the late 1970s, fell in love with ethnography at Harvard in the 1980s, explored many forms of qualitative inquiry including arts-based inquiry throughout the 1990s, and having come out as a poet at the turn of the century, now find myself looking back to the inquiry in which I was a participant—its story and its role in the social sciences—thinking "heavier" and thinking "lighter."

We use language and symbol systems to capture, or fix, at least momentarily, to give our discoveries or creations weight. But ultimately, we know we must let go. Everything, finally, falls away.

Poetry is teaching me this. As a result, I'm questioning the days, months, years of my life I spent advocating for, proselytizing, arguing, defending particular ways of knowing and representing in research, much of which I now wonder if I truly believed. I followed—or was educated into—the herd; at times, I was nimble and led it. But it seemed always to feel like being part of a stampede: adjust direction here; now, adjust direction there. But it was the same old path, with minor adjustments. Did we get anywhere?

Sometimes, my thoughts turn to the radical, and in this case, by radical, I mean the root of things: I'm not sure I have faith in the research enterprise in education and the social sciences at all. I believe in the *need* for research; that's not in question. But I am not entirely sure that we in the academy always do research for the right reasons. We have plenty on this path—myself included—whose CVs, grant-getting, political preoccupations, conference air miles, number of citations, and local or global profiles can distract us, obscuring our view of what really matters.

What really matters? We have to figure ourselves out, know why we're on the planet, know what good we might do, and learn to be present and aware. We need to know our own stories, and be bold about learning what they mean, even if they show us to be callow, small, vain, deluded, greedy for power or control, or compromised. As the novelist Zadie Smith has written about writers, we always know the great ones because they know themselves—they have broken through to who they really are, warts and all. The academic culture of research, as I have found it, is more about control, about hiding ourselves behind belief systems we may not even, in our heart of hearts, understand or embrace; it is more about taking charge of data, following the dictums and assumptions of scientism (which I distinguish from science); it is more about managing material and people outside of ourselves. Sometimes, I fear, it is all about ego—the academic as the child who always excelled in school by mastering the material put before her; she responds to some deep-seated insecurity by choosing a profession that rewards knowledge acquisition with the gold stars of the hierarchy (promotion, grants, keynote invitations, and the like). I can name on one hand the academics I know who demonstrate genuine humility and who do not push an agenda.

These concerns have led me into reading poetry and philosophy and the work of those who concern themselves with fundamentally human questions. As my understanding of poetry has grown these last few years—oh, there is so much more to learn—I've been inspired by the work of philosophers, poets, and theologians. Because I teach inquiry and writing at the graduate level in a small university in Halifax, Nova Scotia, and because I began my career as an ethnographer of literacy practices, I've always understood that our capacity and desire for speaking our stories are fundamental to living.

Of late, I've been exploring and explaining what I call lyric inquiry, using expressive and poetic writing as process and product as a way of understanding myself and the world. To engage in such inquiry, I have been trying to resist the seductive powers of hierarchy, propositional discourse, knowing as trump card, and knowledge as stable, static commodity, useful for standing upon to reach the higher shelves and to stretch the ego, but often of questionable use on the ground. In fact, "on the ground" is a useful term here: in order to understand the lyric impulse, both as a poet and as an ethnographer, I have needed to go to ground. I have needed to duck under the heavy weight of inherited understanding, try to sidestep the lures of academic branding and territorial assumptions, and address basic questions: what is inquiry and why does it matter?

You see the irony. I want to explain to you the value of what I'm calling lyric inquiry, and in so doing, nudge you with intellectual candy: offer you yet another new term, "lyric inquiry." As researchers we want to create terms that tilt our own and others' thinking and that recognize the nuances and complexities of the research process (whether conventional or innovative), and so we create new terms, catchwords, phrases for these nuanced notions. We create even more of that baggage I referred to earlier: visions of citations dance in our heads. Someone may pick up the term; pepper their articles with our names. The term may develop into the kind of cultural currency that creates, and then marks, our academic tribal allegiances. We do love our names and our tribal allegiances.

You can hear my cynicism, but bear with me. Is the research we do, especially in education and the social sciences, as altruistic as we claim it to be? If we really want to make a difference, as one of my graduate students said, we'd quit all this, figure out how to fund, build, and dig a well in Africa or start a school in Northern Saskatchewan or get kids off the streets of Baltimore: we'd just go about doing it. We wouldn't talk about our highfalutin' ideas of arts-based research: we'd take our hefty consulting fees, walk past the phalanx of graduate students outside the door waiting for our blessing and an assistantship, and work directly with people—those young boys in the barrio, for example, who'd thrill at the chance to hold a paintbrush.

But first, we'd figure ourselves out. That's the toughest work of all, and it's not encouraged in the academy, or in public education in general. It's thought of as soft, narcissistic, self-absorbed indulgence. And yet every great writer or researcher I've ever encountered—every inspiring thinker I've known—has spent time figuring themselves out in relation to the larger world in order to know how to contribute. Sometimes the figuring out is done publicly; sometimes not. But the exploration has rarely been characterized by preciousness and self-aggrandizing; it's not about "see me, look at me" but it is about "who am I and what am I doing here?" It's the kind of work done in silence and solitude, work that bears fruit we can take to those around us: fruit such as humility, the willingness to let go of illusions, the lessons of listening, and of reaching out to others.

When I was fifty—over forty years after I'd published a poem in my ninth grade yearbook—I wrote my second poem. Then I wrote another. Now, many years later, I have come to realize that poetry is the closest path to the philosophical, the spiritual, and the pragmatic that I have found. Poetry is a tough master—it demands my full attention to language, to ideas, to others' art, to my own limitations. Poetry asks that I let go, that I accept that my life is not only ephemeral, but that I live it in liminal space: I will never arrive. I must let go—of the hubris of knowing, of believing in books and citations, in the authority of cherished phrases: *research shows, we now know*. For knowledge, add, the poet Charles Wright has said; and for wisdom, take away. Poetry shows me when I am being narrow, selfish, mean-spirited, assumptive, and careless. And poetry shows me my flaws, I believe, because its aesthetic demands are high; it's as though I must aspire as a human being to the standards the art itself has placed in front of me. (Can we reconcile the fact that flawed or evil people enjoy or create beautiful things? I think we can. There will always be exceptions to the great writer/great person equation, but the demands of an art, of beauty, are likely to ask more of people's humanity than less.)

Lyric inquiry (using poetry and prose to tell stories and offer perceptions from our experience) forces me to both understand myself through its practice, and to apprentice myself in aesthetics. My concern with research in general is its lack of attention to the lyric impulse, and, with arts-based research in particular, its lack of attention to aesthetics. When we turned away from the scientistic practices we found constraining, limiting, and arid, we turned to arts in our research practices, with results that were often questionable because they did not address the deeper issues such a shift requires. Poetry as data became simply centered or left-justified phrases on the page, undistilled, clichéd, clumsy and purpled and generic; narrative inquiry often became an excuse to gather anecdotes about bad parenting, toxic teaching, or to sublimate lust for a dissertation supervisor. As a reader, coming away from this undistilled material, I often felt queasy.

In the name of arts-based inquiry, and in a mad and often clumsy scramble worthy of a Bruegel free for all, we took up brushes, pens, grabbed microphones and guitars, ran outside with bubble-making wands, threw ripe tomatoes at one another (oh, the performances we've seen), wrote dewy-eyed or lace-trimmed doggerel, and let ourselves wallow. But was it letting go—really? How much was self-indulgent frolicking in the intellectual equivalent of mudpies and watersplash? How much social progress was there in the research? How much art or attention to aesthetics was in the arts-based inquiry? Worse, was the excess of the confessional the result of a deep exploration of core issues of being human, or just another chance to take the floor in a field where taking the floor is valued. We've taken up exhausted metaphors (quilting, walking, journeys, gardens), to indulge a kind of comfortable limousine liberal scholarship that forces no real assessment, and still, we are rarely left with art. The arts-based research products that have excelled—both as inquiry and as art—are rare, and somehow, these novels, art installations, collections of poetry or photography have served less as exemplars than they ought to have. Others looked at their surface structures, unaware of the deeper shift in approach to being the works required.

The creators of these strong examples understood the lyric impulse—they used lyric inquiry as a means of exploring their understanding in ways that connected their stories or experiences to larger stories—in ways that bound the individual with the universal—and they did so by going beyond expressiveness (a necessary first stage) to attend to the art of the work itself: to contribute to the human condition, and to offer beauty, and their own truth.

I digress, but not really. Let me explain where lyric inquiry comes from. The word *lyric* refers to poetry that expresses a speaker's mood or feeling. In ancient Greece, a lyric was a poem or a song intended by the author to be accompanied by the lyre. *Lyric* and *lyrics* also refer to the words of a song. Any spoken or written language can be described as "lyrical," often taken to mean song-like, personal, heartfelt, and, generally, "poetic." There are times, too, when "lyrical" connotes bathetic, sentimental, excessive, or, as in the term "waxing lyrical," highly enthusiastic.

We all engage in lyric expression. The specific, concrete, sensory, and often intimate language of poetry and narrative makes those genres more likely to be described as lyrical. Because these lyric genres are often more powerful when they are sensory and grounded in the particular, their language is closest to what feminist theorists call embodied; language closer to the body, the senses, the emotions.

Lyric inquiry marries lyric expression with research. It is a methodology that acknowledges the role of the expressive and poetic in inquiry and in the aesthetics of communicating the results of such inquiry, regardless of discipline. Lyric inquiry acknowledges the processes and demands, as well as the tropes, conventions, semiotic and sensory interplay involved in the creation of an aesthetic work. To engage in this inquiry is to engage in all manner of non-rationalist writing—narrative, poetry, fiction and creative non-fiction, journals, prose poetry, dialogue, and monologue (among other forms usually thought of as written artistic expression) to explore for oneself and to communicate to others an issue, dilemma, or phenomenon. It is a phenomenological process and practice that embraces ambiguity, metaphor, recursiveness, silence, sensory immersion, and resonance, creating forms of writing that may become art, or may simply create an aesthetic experience that fundamentally changes the writer's perspective on the world.

Lyric inquiry aims for such an effect on the reader as well. The process and the work are such that their conceptual and aesthetic integrity creates a resonant, or, what reading theorist Louise Rosenblatt has called, an aesthetic effect on the reader/audience. Having undertaken the inquiry process through language (a process that is neither linear or amenable to imposed structure) and having produced a written work of artistic merit, the inquirer brings the artistic work of writing to light not as proof, as with our conventional practices in social science, but as illumination and connection. This process takes time; it takes long apprenticeship; it takes reflection, hard examination.

Lyric inquiry has an uneasy relationship with knowledge as product, commodity, or "trump card." Knowing, instead, is an experience of immersion and expression rather than one of gathering data only to advance an argument. A researcher who creates lyric forms to communicate to readers such engagements emphasizes concrete, specific, located language; concise, artful word choice; and metaphorical, allegorical, or analogical approaches. She emphasizes language that aims to create an aesthetic experience, transporting a reader into a world, a mind, a voice (her own, or others') in the same way as does a fiction writer, a songwriter, or a poet. She apprentices herself to the craft of expression. The effect is not, to use Rosenblatt's term, efferent: a reader does not take away three key points or five examples. A reader comes away with the resonance of another's world, in the way we emerge from the reading of a poem or a novel, from a film screening, or a musical event—physically transported or moved, often unaware of the architecture or structure that created the experience, our senses stimulated, our spirit and emotions affected. Emily Dickinson knew good poetry when the words made her hair stand on end. "Take me there," is a phrase I have often used with students writing in lyric forms: rather than tell me or summarize for me or editorialize or judge—show me. Use vivid, sensory language that I can fall into, that makes the world come alive.

And so finally, what am I saying about research, about inquiry, here?

It's this. Even with the innovative practices in inquiry we've been embracing the last decade or so—arts-based or research creation practices, to be specific— we are still in the clutches of a kind of scientism that wants answers, knowledge as product, generalizations we can apply to new situations, some accountability with regard to authenticity or reliability, and so on. We still want to ask research in the social sciences to do more than perhaps it can.

And when we take up arts-based inquiry to try to address the problem of intransigent scientism, we can fall into other dangerous territory. We take up arts practices without attending to the art and its demands on us. *There is no place that does not see you,* said Rilke, *you must change your life.* Or as Jeanette Winterson has said, *art objects.* Art objects to who we are, forces us to dig further, question it all. In much arts-based work, we considered expressiveness enough. But art asks that we attend not only to aesthetics, but to key principles of living and being: learning how to let go, to be swallowed up by beauty and awareness, to give ourselves over to something larger than ourselves, our small territories of control and domination, our small hedges against the inevitable.

Lyric inquiry continues to teach me that I cannot know anything for very long, that I must relinquish control. When I let go, I open myself to seeing much more than I did as the ethnographer, pen and bias in hand, observing at a comfortable distance. When I write expressively, as a poet or as a prose writer, and I try to make sense of the world through poetry or narrative, the poetry and the narrative ask back in ways that conventional academic discourse does not. It asks back with questions that touch on the emotional, the psychological, the philosophical, the spiritual, and the ethical, as well as the aesthetic.

Emmanuel Levinas challenges us when he asks how we consider the Other. Is it even possible to write or discuss the Other without appropriating, naming, judging, claiming? I can do it only giving the other a face, as he describes it. To honor and acknowledge what I see, not to use it as a CV line, or a boost up some illusory academic ladder.

Let me end this rambling with an example. Years ago my family admitted (imagine the repression and the racism in that word—admitted) that my heritage, two generations back, is partly Cree. Knowing what I have always known about what has been done and continues to be done to the Aboriginal populations in Canada, I suddenly became even more acutely aware of all things Indian. I immersed myself in the story of Anna Mae Pictou Aquash, with the help of a former student and filmmaker, Catherine Martin, and using research skills I have gained as an ethnographer. In order to write a poem about Anna Mae, I needed to learn about myself and my heritage. I can not even begin to fathom the horror she experienced, but by learning what I could, I was open to her story in a way I otherwise could not have been. Using lyric inquiry, I learn I am singular and connected, a drop of blood in a larger pool, that my stories and others' stories are all necessary so that we can help each other learn not who is right or who knows more, but what really matters. How to be wise, how to listen deeply, how to change ourselves so that we can change the world around us.

"Aesthetic spaces"
Margaret Macintyre Latta's story

- A written collage
- Attunement
- Aesthetic play
- Reflexive analysis

Runner: Our next presenter, Dr. Margaret Macintyre Latta, is an Associate Professor and Graduate Chair in the Teaching, Learning, and Teacher Education Program, College of Education & Human Sciences, at the University of Nebraska-Lincoln. She graduated from the University of Calgary, Alberta, Canada in 2000. Her dissertation, based on the art form known as a collage, was titled: "Enfleshing Aesthetic Play: Giving Expression to Teaching and Learning Aesthetically." Margaret, it is great to have you here. As with many of our presenters, I'm sure Margaret will share with you that she did not set out to write an alternative dissertation, but rather, the data demanded it.

Margaret: It is my pleasure to be here to see the future of higher education changing before my very eyes! Yes, my dissertation took the form of a post-modern written collage. There are some image collages included within the text, but the form as a whole was meant to be understood/read as a collage. As an artist, I know any aesthetic experience is both immediate and meditative. It becomes a search in which I am unsure where I am headed. Through playful manipulation of materials and images I arrive at an expressive form. I find expression to involve searching for qualities that show how experience is lived, felt, and understood. I know most existing educational structures do not support or encourage these qualities, and again, this is why I am happy to be here with the pioneers at this conference, whose work does encourage this perspective and will ultimately influence all of education.

In a collage, each fragment can stand on its own but it is intended for them to be viewed and understood as a related whole. I cannot fit living or research-ing aesthetically into fragments. The process involves me in the search to become whole and I understand this whole to be situational, reciprocal, and tentative. Collages are intended to evoke movement, foregrounding specific voices at particular moments, while others move to the middle or back, in an increasingly complex and evolving space. It is really a very "messy" process and tends to stand against the structured realities in most educational settings.

I continue to draw on my dissertation experience, as well as my experiences as a parent, k-12 classroom teacher, and visual artist, in my current role as an associate professor of curriculum studies and teacher education. Educational reforms of the last two decades have focused on objectifying specific learning outcomes resulting in much superficial rather than substantial learning. With emphasis on what may be superficial behaviors, little attention is given to assimilation, internalization, or integration of thought. The contemporary research discussion of the structure of teaching experience that compartment-alizes knowledge, separating pedagogy from content, knowledge from interests, and theory from practice, raises the dilemma I am concerned with. The aesthetic offers a philosophical approach for teaching and learning of all kinds, striving for connections between and amongst disciplines, demanding continuous engagement in reflection and deliberation, and honoring teaching and learning as complex and developmental in nature.

Retracing my dissertation writing experience in thinking about my pre-sentation today elicited a flood of embodied memories that I can best describe as the work of attunement; an attunement gained, lost, and regained, through continual negotiations between self and situation. Attunement seeks out what is called for within the given particulars of situations, demanding attention to process. Through my doctoral research, I became keenly aware of teacher, learner, and learning significances accessed through teaching for greater attunement. My research took place in a public, urban middle school with the mandate to deliberately value the creating process, primary to the arts, within the school curriculum as a whole. Alongside participating volunteers (26 students, their parents, three teachers, and school administra-tors) over a two-year period, I grappled with how attention to the creating processes constituted learning experiences in particular ways. I was constantly reminded in participating classrooms of the fullness and complexities entailed for teachers, learners, and learning. So, the research site and my research task positioned me to continually seek attunement as I considered how to value the creating process in teaching/learning by teachers and students. It was an attunement that I had some prior lived sense of as a visual artist. I knew art-making to be grounded in a close relationship, an ongoing conversation between material(s) and myself as artist. And, I had experienced moments of such attunement in my own practices as a teacher. But, the construction, adaptation, disintegration, and integration encountered as integral to seeking patterns and meanings within these particular classrooms, became a way of living and being that asked me to attend to the process character in the most demanding and encompassing modes ever. Significances persisted, realized again and again through the creating experience of my dissertation. And, these significances continue to form and inform how I work alongside my current doctoral students in my present role as an associate professor in a college of education. I reflect on the power of these qualities, shaping the representative form the dissertation took, and continuing to infuse my work and thinking, acting as bearings and catalysts in all undertakings.

As the inquiry progressed a dominant theme emerged, taking the form of a teaching/learning style I referred to as aesthetic play. It was this style, the nature of aesthetic play that I pursued, through the shapes it took and the spaces it thrived in at the school. Aesthetic play assumed that relational complexities were the essential difficulty that teachers encountered in classrooms. Operatively, it referred to the uncertain and risky process that positioned teachers to continually construct relationships across self, students, and subject matter through dialogic inquiry. A movement of thinking was generated as the personal, social, contextual, historical, cultural, and political relations emerged and intersected. Thus as researcher, I found myself in the midst of many contributing voices—of students, teachers, parents, administration, curriculum, subject matter, context, self, and the research literature. And, I knew I had to dwell within these in-between spaces to explore and converse with the nature of aesthetic play from multiple perspectives.

Conversing with the nature of aesthetic play involved observing classrooms, interviewing participating students weekly, and interviewing participating teachers on an ongoing basis, collecting teacher and student artifacts. The ensuing intersections of multiple voices created a space for me to construct and reconstruct understandings. All were struggling with what attention to process looked like in practice, negotiating the lived consequences for teachers, learners, and learning. It seemed this teaching/learning style I termed aesthetic play was reciprocal in nature. Integrity to its reciprocal nature meant that it was impossible to suggest a model of aesthetic play. There were qualities that permeated the inquiry-guided classrooms engaged in aesthetic play, such as attentiveness, personal involvement, emotional commitment, felt freedom, dialogue and interaction, and projection, instilling greater self-consciousness within the acts of teaching/learning. But, I began to see these qualities as patterns that were continually reconstituted as participants and contexts changed and evolved. My initial analytical written interpretations came up short, over and over again. They reduced the wholeness encountered to concepts to be defined, assumed a false linearity and hierarchy, and diluted the felt beauty experienced through some teaching/learning incidents. I felt this growing representative inadequacy from the beginning. A small, but reassuring voice from within, though, told me to continue to dwell in situation. I valued confidence in process and trusted that a way to proceed would emerge out of attention to process. I knew I was collecting and attending to rich data, so resisted representing the complexity of patterns creating the structures for the dynamic flux of aesthetic play through reductionary treatments of the data. It was clear to me that reductionary measures avoided the necessarily recursive, related, and organic shapes that aesthetic play was taking in participating classrooms.

The data was shared with my doctoral advisor on an ongoing basis and he confirmed that the data was rich and thick, and together we agreed to let the data speak to us. My concerted efforts to vigilantly collect, document, and develop tentative interpretations continued carefully and persistently. I involved participating teachers and students in the ongoing analysis, and the reflexivity that emerged engaged all of us in struggling to shape and give expression to aesthetic play.

As Runner mentioned, I did not set out to deliberately write an alternative dissertation. But, the data insisted otherwise. The form that my dissertation finally took arose out of a lesson I had observed in a participating humanities classroom and a student's response to this lesson: an exercise that asked students to attend to the visual and tactile qualities of fragments of varied material, provided as a means to composing an artistic collage. The teacher purposefully incorporated this exercise to enable students to concretely make connections to composing a story. One student told me in an interview that this exercise was particularly meaningful for her. She told me this almost a year after the experience of the lesson, and was able to describe how she returned to this exercise over and over again, finding insights for her writing efforts. And, it was within the few moments of this interchange that I saw the form the dissertation needed to take. I suddenly realized as the student relayed the significances of the collage-making to her composing process of story writing, that I was longing for an artistic form to reveal the data. I heard in the student's description of the collage-making experience the attention to relatedness within a whole. I realized that what I was struggling to represent was just this, the value and unique contributions of such demands. The collage held possibilities I began to concretely consider.

The collage form embodied the data collected. I knew collage-making to be messy. It was difficult, if not impossible, to regard aspects without acknowledging the influence of other aspects. The form was informed through playing with parts, renegotiating the parts to whole relationships. And, yet, it invited fascination with particular aspects. The messy reality of the collage builder resonated with my in-between position of researcher, attending and documenting the multiplicity of aesthetic play. The collage form gave expression to the flux of understandings generated, revising and redirecting the inquiry itself. The collage form was an artistic medium with traditions that did justice to the data. For example, the historical emergence of collage that broke with Renaissance artists' efforts to confine picture space to reflect one viewpoint and attempted to show more in a single picture than the eye could see from the apparent position of the viewer, was fitting with the thickness of data, the layers and relations encountered throughout the inquiry. A collage always has texture because of the varied materials and layering process, and gluing the textures together are the intersecting planes and surfacing qualities that create patterns, demanding attention to the collage as a whole. The data revealed such relatedness and interdependency, continually asking all participants to see/experience aesthetic play with enlarged understandings. A collage's tactile nature was akin to how in touch with teacher/students, context, and subject matter, aesthetic play demanded. Therefore, collages as experiments in cutting through external frameworks of time and space, purposefully playing with their interdependence, very fittingly confronted what I encountered in writing about the creation of aesthetic teaching/learning spaces.

The construction, adaptation, disintegration, and integration of collage-making described the play I was immersed within as researcher. Through genuine participation as a collage builder, I was reminded that I should not attempt to control aesthetic play, but in fact, be led by it. The collage provided a form that gave life to this movement of thinking. The data collected offered many renderings of aesthetic play. Each rendering was a fragment of aesthetic play, resembling the material fragments of a collage. Each fragment could stand alone, but it was intended to be viewed and understood as a related whole. These diverse renderings of aesthetic play provided a changing context to consider the many facets of its nature and the interplay among parts. The fragments surfaced historical traditions, commonalities, differences, and particularities, which together exuded a texture of meanings. As I deliberately constructed the written collage, forming/informing aesthetic play, I was aware that I needed to involve my audience—the readers. I invited the readers to participate as collage builders too, aesthetically playing along. I hoped that the collage would draw readers into aesthetic play, succumbing to its spirit and authority. The invitation then asked the readers to attend to each fragment as it moved into new directions and details, and also recalled previous fragments and imagined fragments to come. It was at this point that I was able to name this purposeful recursion. The rhythmic repetition of themes and conditions within the data was always present, but ascertaining the purposefulness of such recursion to the nature of aesthetic play became much clearer. It was a dynamic repetition that fostered enlarged understandings, deepening the lived terms and consequences of aesthetic play for teachers, learners, and learning. And, it also informed my researching process, as aesthetic play became my methodology. As the collage builder (researcher) the experience of piecing together the written fragments of aesthetic play was characterized by this style itself, seeking out the parts to a whole relationship in an ongoing search, ever cognizant that there was always more to be perceived and more to be explored.

The construction of this written collage was a slow process. The data collected at the research site and the ongoing reflexive analysis were the collage materials that at some point became a medium for making sense of aesthetic play. These materials, alive in the experiences of students, teachers, subject matter, contexts, and resources needed to be valued for the qualities they held and for the potential they embraced individually and collectively. The collage gave me a form to articulate and express aesthetic play in teaching, learning, and researching that was integral to its very reciprocal, situated, and in-flux nature. I accessed understandings and gained a language that enabled me to confidently defend my dissertation. I was thankful for that confidence, as there were vastly different comfort levels with the final collage form of my dissertation by defense committee members. The confidence in process articulated its own method in the making and I was able to convey this to others. This commitment continued to grow and now in my current role as an associate professor I am ever more confident that there are many significances to be gained from aesthetic play and I work toward realizing these across my teaching, research, and service responsibilities. In particular, how I mentor graduate students always recalls the importance of attending to what is given as the place to begin, responding to what the materials of situation and individuals suggest and reveal. The ensuing aesthetic play is the search for attunement between self and situation. My dissertation writing experience told me it was impossible to separate parts or qualities away from seeking attunement within the act of creating. It was experienced as connected, all parts linked in relation to the vital movement of the whole, belonging to the self and situation within this movement of thinking. In this way, the process of creating positioned participants to be wholly involved. I became very familiar with the vulnerable space negotiating attunement opened into, with risk and uncertainty abounding, but also, pleasure and found purpose. It was sometimes uncomfortable, disturbing, and difficult, but also wondrous. In retrospect, I realized my dissertation advisor had been very wise, someone who trusted in the lostness and foundness of process and gave me the space (and guidance) to negotiate such trust, too. It is a trust I know precipitated powerful qualities, continuing to permeate all facets of my living.

Thanks for letting me share my story with you. (*Applause*)

Runner: Thank you Margaret. OK, everyone. Let's go ahead and get into our groups. By now any doctoral candidate here should be able to construct a title for their dissertation and be able to explain why it will make the world a better place by making a unique contribution to a particular field. Now, with the help of the professors in your group, consider ways Dr. Macintyre Latta's story might inspire creative and meaningful ways to address your topic and present it. We'll resume with our presentations in the morning.

"Inevitable"

Kathleen Vaughan's story

- Bricolage
- Collage
- Interdisciplinary inquiry
- Geographical space
- Ethics of care
- Art theory

Runner: Our next presenter tells also about a multi-modal dissertation using collage. Kathleen Vaughan is a visual artist, writer, scholar, and teacher whose work takes a postmodern, postcolonial slant on thematics such as identity and belonging; memory, storytelling, and the cultural artifact; and spirit of place. Intrigued by the application of fine arts methods to scholarship, she is elaborating collage as a framework for interdisciplinary research/creation/ pedagogy. She teaches in the Faculty of Education at York University (Toronto), at the Ontario College of Art and Design, and through visiting artist programs in Toronto schools. You can find out more on her website, www.akaredhanded.com.

Kathleen's dissertation, "Finding Home: Knowledge, Collage, and the Local Environments," was supported by funding from Canada's Social Sciences and Humanities Research Council (SSHRC) and Government of Ontario in the form of a Doctoral Fellowship and Ontario Graduate Scholarship, respectively. It was nominated for the York University Faculty of Graduate Studies Dissertation Award, the York University Governor General's Gold Medal Award, and, currently, the Phi Delta Kappa International Outstanding Dissertation Award. In addition, Kathleen has just heard that her dissertation has won the 2008 Critical Issues in Curriculum and Cultural Studies Graduate Student Award and the Outstanding Dissertation Award from Arts Based Educational Research (ABER), the special interest group of the American

Educational Research Association (AERA). The Ontario Arts Council has also supported her development and teaching of *Finding Home*-related arts education projects for children and youth in local schools with an Artist in Education grant, so, like many of our dissertations here, this one is continuing to have a positive effect on the world.

Kathleen: Thanks Runner for this introduction. My collage dissertation, "Finding Home: Knowledge, Collage, and the Local Environments," juxtaposes a variety of visual art pieces and a scholarly text in an interdisciplinary inquiry into how a person creates a feeling of being at home in the world. Completed in November 2006 through the Faculty of Education at York University (Toronto, Canada), *Finding Home* was the first multimodal (visual arts plus text) doctoral dissertation in the faculty and indeed—from my department-by-department researches to date—the first such work in the university as a whole. My ground-breaking research was and is still strongly supported by York's faculty and administration, which have nominated *Finding Home* for internal and external awards and funding—often successfully. I am delighted and grateful that while the work of my dissertation was of course challenging and intense, I was always assisted along my way by a supportive supervisor, committee, faculty, and indeed, university.

Looking back now from the "accomplished" side of my PhD, I suppose it was inevitable that I should create a collage dissertation, a work that mixes visual artifacts and illustrated text in a scholarly inquiry. After all, I am a professional artist, with a long-standing active studio practice in various forms of mixed two- and three-dimensional media, and graduate and undergraduate degrees in studio arts. I think 'through' the visual arts, learn about the world and myself in it via visual and literary creation. And I teach others (children and adults) to do the same, through various visiting artist programs in local schools as well as structured post-secondary courses in educational institutions. I am a scholar, too, having completed a first undergraduate degree in the humanities, a bred-in-the-bone love of academia, and a long-standing research orientation to both my visual practice and my work as a consultant in education, broadcasting, and the arts. I undertook doctoral work planning to bring my visual work into my studies and dissertation, and with my university's prior approval to do so. In a way, then, the multimodality of "Finding Home: Knowledge, Collage, and the Local Environments," was already in the works with my application for admission to the program.

Finding Home uses collage to explore two research questions: "what does it mean for a person to find a feeling of being at home in the world?" and "what role can the work of collage play in such a process?" Obviously, my dissertation is an interdisciplinary inquiry, interweaving epistemology and the ethics of care, art theory and practice, cultural and urban theory, history, geography, environmental education, and ecology. Building from my own experience repeatedly walking with my dog, Auggie, through my Toronto neighborhoods,

Finding Home is written as a specific walk though my environs, the text itself a collage of theory, observation-based discussion, autoethnography, and discourse on method. The method that I use is collage, a practice that I began to articulate through my years of doctoral study, one that, I believe, will sustain my interest through the length of my career to come.

In my own thinking, writing, and publishing, I explore collage from an interdisciplinary standpoint, well connected to fine arts and aesthetics. I take into consideration work on collage by education scholars, who tend to see collage as a kind of helpful Rorschach—a tool that allows a new vantage point on text-based research rather than an aesthetic practice with its own traditions, semiotics, and competencies. But for this same oversight, I would find myself linked to the method of *the bricolage* proposed by education theorist Joe Kincheloe. Like collage, *the bricolage* has a sense of the cobbled together. And like my notion of collage, Kincheloe's *the bricolage* is oriented to multidisciplinarity, grounded on an epistemology of complexity, intertextual, based in philosophical inquiry and a discourse of historicity, with a liberatory agenda. But the aesthetic dimension is less developed, and given my own interests and background, that aesthetic dimension is my strong right arm, the basis of my research and my teaching.

Indeed, one of the reasons that I took a collage approach to my subject of "home" was not only to deepen my understanding of my own experience, but also to develop a framework with which to develop arts and environmental education projects with children and adults in local schools and community associations. Toronto is a city of immigrants: more than 49 percent of us were born somewhere outside Canada, as were about one-third of students in Toronto's public school board. Many have come as a result of war or other violence, poverty, displacement. In this demographic reality, work on home and belonging can have important individual and social implications. Of course, work in the visual arts gets around challenges to expression in a new language; and collage itself can be an inexpensive arts option for financially strapped schools, one versatile enough to lead to aesthetic success even for those with little or no fine arts training or capability. In collage, readymade elements culled from external sources can be important representational tools.

In my case, the "ready mades" include archival photographs of my neighborhoods, which I set in chronological series that compared present-day realities (my own images) with those from the past—of that moment 100 years ago, for example, when the terrain that is now a frenetic intersection of buses, streetcars, automobiles and outflanked pedestrians, was once the lush green backdrop to a mounted, hound-assisted fox hunt! *Finding Home* also includes purpose-made elements, large-scale drawings of recognizable neighborhood features, textile maps and sculptures, and paper collages that incorporate images and ideas from each of the text's chapters. These latter were used as an opening image for the chapter in question and were reproduced, enlarged, as "place" markers in the installation of the visual work.

Finding Home was exhibited for four days in November 2006 at Toronto's Gladstone Hotel, an arts-oriented facility not far from the terrain included in my dissertation text and visuals. I chose this ex-university location very deliberately: as a hotel the Gladstone immediately evokes questions of home, residency, migration, and so supported the thematics of my own research/ creation. As well, that this is a "cool" spot, beloved of the city's downtown artists and intellectuals, automatically dusted my work with a certain lustrous cachet.

I was supported in completing *Finding Home* to my own exacting creative and research standards by my arts-friendly supervisory committee, and my supervisor Rishma Dunlop, in particular. Both a poet and a scholar, Rishma wrote a novel as her PhD dissertation in Education from the University of British Columbia, and so was readily able to trust my creative process to produce rigorous results. Indeed, my work has consistently been praised within York's Faculty of Education for setting a very high standard for such scholarship and for breaking new ground in academic/artistic achievement so that others may follow. This is very important to me, and another ambition for my work, which is to make more room within academia for authentic and high caliber visual and collage representations of knowledge. Indeed, in Canada at least, the institutional and funding structures are increasingly being put into place to make such work possible.

My work also benefited from extensive backup from people outside academia, including my invaluable editor, Lori Delorme, who helped with the pacing of my 400-page text, as well as local historians, geographers, naturalists, and community activists and politicians. These individuals' love for their subjects and willingness to share their information contributed great richness and pleasure to my own experience and to the dissertation itself.

These outside supports together with my own personal history of professional practice ensured that I had the resources necessary to create a truly authentic alternative dissertation. Choice by choice along the way, I had the freedom to select the option that served my dissertation as a whole and deepened my own knowledge, understanding, and artistic investigations, without in any way compromising the creative arc of the work. As a result, my dissertation experience was densely rich and extremely rewarding on personal, intellectual, and creative levels. Indeed, through *Finding Home* I have begun to find my academic and artistic home—home for me being an ever-shifting standpoint from which to learn, grow, understand oneself, relate to others, and contribute to communal life.

Part 4

Day four

Documentary film and photographs

A Picture's Meaning Can Express Ten Thousand Words.
(Chinese proverb)

The moral function of art itself is to remove prejudice, do away with the scales that keep the eye from seeing, tear away the veils due to wont and custom, perfect the power to perceive.
(John Dewey, from *Art as Experience*, p. 325)

"Metamorphosis"

Jennifer Mervyn's story

with Beth Ferholt and
Tiffany Honor von Emmel

- Documentary film
- Video ethnography
- Aboriginal children, resilience, and successful transition models
- Critical inquiry

Runner: Our next presenter is Jennifer Mervyn. She describes her dissertation, entitled, "Metamorphosis: An In-depth Look at the Lives of Former Street Kids," as a "video ethnography." Jennifer is a crisis worker who works in hospital emergency rooms and schools doing assessments and counseling for youths under age nineteen in acute mental health crisis. She received her PhD in the Department of Counseling Psychology at the University of British Columbia. She has Metis ancestry and sits on the Greater Vancouver Urban Aboriginal Strategy.

Jennifer: Hello everyone. It is an honor for me to be here and to really continue my own metamorphosis of the doctoral dissertation. As Runner said, my dissertation was a documentary film. It features four British Columbia youth who have successfully left a life on the streets. Half of these young women are aboriginal. Youth in this film tell their stories about life on the streets, and what they had to do to leave that life behind them. Politicians, police, and front-line workers are also interviewed for their input in what helps facilitate exits to homelessness for young people. Concerns raised in the film include lack of available treatment for youth struggling with substance abuse, the need for treatment on demand, the deficits in the "Four Pillars Approach," and the challenges of the Young Offenders Act.

  In this work I take a critical look at the resilience factors in youth leaving the street, and examine the process of transition that successful youth have made. The film generally conjures a lot of questions and discussion about the changes we need to make to help future youth successfully transition off the street.

My dissertation story really started when, after living as a Vancouver street youth, I became determined to help others off the street and to shake up Canada's child and youth protection bureaucracy. My Master's thesis on adults transitioning off the streets was published, but seemed only to garner attention from a small number of academics, and not reach the front lines where the research could make a meaningful impact. So I became the first UBC PhD student to submit a film for my dissertation to help assure people would have a better chance to hear the message. If I was going to put four years into a PhD, I wanted people to engage with my work. Too much research has focused on why youth stay on the streets. I wanted to celebrate the youth who successfully get themselves off the streets.

In the film I focus on four female youth who successfully exited the streets. The students tell their stories about life on the streets and their transition off the streets, including the barriers they faced. I also interviewed politicians, police, and front-line workers. I raised concerns about such things as the lack of available treatment for youth struggling with substance abuse issues, the need for treatment on demand, and the deficits in the current model being used in Canada that is called the "Four Pillars Approach."

I should add that in addition to creating a film, I wrote a 130-page traditional thesis to accompany the film, but it is the film that is beginning to have a far-reaching impact on social perception. Slowly but surely, researchers and clinicians in the mental health fields are starting to take interest in and capitalize upon using film for the dissemination of research findings.

The fact of the matter is that a documentary-style film has the ability to reach mainstream audiences more effectively than would research published in *Counseling Psychology*. Because of its ability to touch those in the mainstream, film can shape the larger discourse on topics. A good example is Michael Moore's *Bowling for Columbine*, which has profoundly shaped the discourse on violence in the United States. Video ethnography is arguably the twenty-first-century version of the case study, the difference being that case studies tell clinical stories on paper while video ethnography lays out the story visually. I chose film for the impact it would have, for its utility in training future clinicians, for its power in raising public awareness of the issues, and for its potential to reach policy decision-makers.

The film ended up as a very costly project. I had no idea about what budget costs would be to make a film. This in itself was a learning experience. Between equipment rentals, camera rentals, camera and editing work, catering costs, transportation costs, and courier services, I estimate that this film has cost approximately $9,000.00. I'm sure that a bigger budget could have allowed for a more professional look to the film, a quicker turn-around time, and better marketing and distribution than I have been able to do with no budget. I did actively seek out funding sources, but because I was a full-time student, because it was my first film, and because I am not a film student, I was not eligible to apply for funding via any of the regular funding routes for film. Moreover, given that film is not the norm in terms of research approaches for counselling or psychology, I was not able to secure funding via those funding sources.

A wonderful outcome of having a film to show and discuss, is the positive media coverage that has been generated. The local newspaper that initially ran my story when I was looking for participants called me to ask for another interview. It is great to have street youth receive positive press for a change, and hopefully this will contribute to a change in how society negatively sees and stigmatizes this population. Shortly after that article came out I received a call from the Georgia Straight requesting an interview about the film. I was also interviewed on CBC Radio the day of the film premiere. *The Province* newspaper featured a large piece on the film. Trinity Western University's Alumni Magazine published an article about the film. The UBC "Ubyssey" just ran a feature story inspired by the film. The media attention and coverage has been phenomenal. I have been invited to speak at many forums where I show the film, and overall it has given aboriginal youth throughout Canada positive role models to encourage them rather than to discourage them with more stories about their problems.

Generally speaking, this film is shouting for more resources for these young people. They point out the startling gaps in service. We need more detox beds, we need more treatment facilities, and we need treatment facilities that are long term and deal with the problems these kids had that first got them onto the streets (which is often some form of early trauma). We need more skilled and qualified workers who are in it for the long run, to be in consistent supportive relationships with these youth. We need outreach mental health services. We need more services that meet these kids' basic needs, such as food, clothing, and shelter.

An interesting point that this study highlights is that the journey off the streets is not a smooth linear path. It is characterized by many exits off and returns to the street before the permanent transition is made. The girls talk about many significant events that led to their exit off the street, not one single event.

It has been interesting how this research has expanded and developed over time. My purpose in the creation of this film was to better understand the process of transition that youth make from street life to mainstream living. I had hoped that the stories of former street kids would educate, encourage, and inspire those kids still on the streets so they will be able to see hope for a better future.

Runner: Wopila tanka, thank you so much. This story is more evidence that arts-based work has at its heart a desire to truly make a difference in the world! I would like to know how many folks out there are planning on a dissertation that involves film? Cool. Beth, would you tell us a little about your project. Everyone, Beth Ferholt is nearing completion of her PhD in Communication at the University of California, San Diego.

Beth: My dissertation will be titled: "Adult and Child Development in Adult–Child Joint Play: Glimpsing the Future through a Playworld." It has two chapters with sections in the form of short films. Some of these films were also a part of my research team's process of data analysis.

In the dissertation I make a distinction between footage and film, claiming that we freed our footage from the category of "data" by pushing it to become "film." I argue, among other things, that filmic representation can be a form of play, and that in our study of adult–child joint play our film-play did not work to show us play that was less "real" than the play we had experienced first hand, but, instead, revealed qualities of the play we had experienced that we could not see without film. Specifically, I argue that in our study the disjointed temporality of film revealed the disjointed temporality of the embodied imagination that is play.

This argument allows for the use of ethnographic film not only as a means of documenting, but also as an object of study. In this way it contributes to a discussion concerning the uses of ethnographic film in the social sciences. The argument that filmic representation can be a form of play also undermines the trend in contemporary play theory to treat play as a means to an end. Play belongs in the classroom not only because it promotes child development of some adult trait or skill, but also because play is of value in and of itself and throughout the lifespan. Furthermore, this argument allows us to acknowledge ways that the methodology of the researcher studying play can be shaped by the play of the children she is studying, and, by extension, ways that the teaching process of the teacher promoting play in his classroom can be shaped by the play of the child he is teaching, and ways that the imagination of adults who play with children can be re-invigorated through the embodied imagination that is the play they are sharing.

The dissertation's methodological argument is tied to an explicitly political goal. I believe that to change the language of representation in the academy is to change who is involved in the process of representation in the academy. To avoid belittling children's play, and also to avoid romanticizing children's play, long enough to learn methods of scholarship from children's play, is to open the academy, if only slightly, to those whom it usually entirely excludes: both to people who are now children, and to our own, past, childhood selves.

The reason my research team used film in our process of analysis is the subject of my methodology chapter, but I use film in the dissertation itself because there are things that I need to say that film, and not writing, allows me to say. For example, in Chapter 3, where I present the playworld activity I will analyze, there are beautiful and emotionally charged moments and relationships that I cannot present in words. I use film to help my readers remember that the play and the methods of analysis that I am describing are both projects defined, in part, by love.

To bring a discussion of such emotion into the academy I found that I was required to turn to art and to life. I ask my reader to remember love in their own lives as they read my dissertation. In return I offer the reader a favorite love story of my own, the object of my analysis, a film. The experience of imagination being represented in my work, and also that quality of the ethnographic film that it will explore, is a fall that becomes a flight, or a flight that becomes a fall. In play, children are lifted above their current potential, achieving that which they could not achieve outside of play, and briefly inhabiting what we could call their future selves. They often appear to both themselves, and to those onlookers who are properly situated, as superheroes, leaping buildings in a single bound. Film allows us to glimpse a future of potential and a future self. Also, in play children push themselves to the limit, placing themselves just next to their greatest fears, and just by those demons that truly threaten their physical and emotional selves. They enter a designated space in which they are at risk because they are challenging themselves, and in which they could not challenge themselves without risk.

Within the frame of film the ability to glimpse a future coexists with the whirling sensation of vertigo, as we fall into a film time that is somehow more our own than the "real" of time unmediated by film. A string of printed adjectives, the usual medium of the scholar, cannot do justice to the experience that I wish to convey and explore in this work. The films that I include, films that attempt to represent adult–child joint play, invite the reader to use their own favorite "love stories" to help make sense of the arguments I make in the dissertation.

In the dissertation I use the metaphor of a golem to describe the need of the researchers in my project to act simultaneously as players and as social scientists, bringing our experience of playing with children back to life in our laboratory through film. In our study we attempted to reanimate our video data using what we had learned from our play with children: we invested our video footage with an emotional life and with agency. The coming in and out of life of a golem is also a metaphor for my experience as a scholar. Sometimes I experience myself, in my attempts to find a room of my own in the academy, as a soulless monstrosity with clay feet. Sometimes I feel that I have been given a soul, but that this soul can be taken away by the powers that be without a moment's notice. Sometimes I see that I do not, at a given moment and in a given place, exist at all within the precincts of the university, that I must, out of necessity, call home—I am merely an emptiness. Simultaneously, it is as an undergraduate and graduate student that I have found my greatest strength. It is within the academy that I have found the people, books, and places that have made me, a few lucky times, air born. This falling flight characterizes my journey towards my alternative approach in my dissertation.

Runner: Tiffany, you also used some film in your dissertation, didn't you? Everyone, allow me to introduce you to Tiffany Honor von Emmel. She is a graduate from Fielding Graduate University and teaches arts-based research methods as a guest presenter in all three of FGU's graduate schools. She works professionally via her non-profit organization named Dreamfish that brings arts-based research and interventions to the world and is grounded in the principles of multiple ways of knowing from a non-eurocentric perspective.

Tiffany: Thanks everyone for your interests and your pioneering work in expanded the boundaries of authentic research. And thanks Runner for the plug. It's great to hear all of these presentations on arts-based and Indigenous research approaches.

I did use a variety of video productions for my 2005 dissertation from Fielding that was entitled, "Somatic Performance: Relational Practices and Knowledge Activism of Bodies Improvising." This study puts the body center stage to show what improvisational bodies can teach practitioners and scholars about knowledge and transformation. It approaches the lived body as both social and ecological—the body as a practice of humanity and as a practice of the earth. Mobilizing the body, it seeks to address an interlocking problem involving industrial patterns of subjectivity, institutional knowledge creation, and ecological and social injustice.

I describe how participants cultivate relational modes of time, perception and desire. I interpret relational practices as transforming of industrial subjectivity.

The research method is performance ethnography. With a DVD-video script and ninety-eight images, I tried to involve the reader in the look and feel of deep participation. The research strategy was to explore the topic of transformative knowledge while immersed in a radical cultural practice—body-based improvisation—which is a participatory art.

I truly believe that if education is to play a positive role in effectively engaging the challenges facing us with regard to social and ecological injustices, the kinds of research approaches you all are presenting at this conference will be necessarily a starting point. After all, the doctoral dissertation is the pinnacle and the starting place for curricular concepts that inform all of formal education. And in these times, certainly film will play a large role in both the research inquiry and its final representation.

"Writing with photographs"
Anniina Souminen Guyas's story

- Artistic knowledge
- Transcultural identity
- Relationality
- Critical visual sociology
- Autoethnography

Runner: Our next presenter is Dr. Anniina Souminen Guyas. She is an Assistant Professor of Art Education at Kent State University. Her PhD is in Art Education, which she received in 2003 from The Ohio State University. Even though Anniina's degree was in art education, she found that her own creative use of photography was still challenged as not fitting the usually accepted formats for art education dissertations.

Aside from FGU, Anniina is one of the few from within the U.S. who responded to our international call for "alternative" dissertations. Of course, Anniina herself and her work are transnational, so perhaps this explains. Anniina, it's all yours!

Anniina: Thank you Runner. My work focuses on issues of (trans)cultural identity, relationality, and artistic knowledge. I live the issues I study in my art, and my theoretical, philosophical, and pedagogical problem solving and concept development center on the issues I find to be important through my relational experiences. I do live in a transnational space in-between two continents and work in philosophically conflicting transcurrents of education, theory, and art. While I continue with my nomadic yet somewhat static and conservative lifestyle that is always defined through temporality, my ultimate goal in life is to learn about humanity and the construction of "reality." I strive to make educated decisions and through my choices in research, teaching, art, and everyday life my goal is to contribute to a livable world that is sensitive to various forms of knowledge. I see my current profession as a very privileged position at multiple levels. Teaching curricular issues and "coaching" future art teachers brings along great amounts of responsibility while also providing access to possibilities of change.

The title of my dissertation is, "Writing with Photographs, Re-constructing Self: An Arts-based Autoethnographic Inquiry." I think the following poem captures its essence:

> My story is about the struggle of learning to speak,
> my story is about learning to write (in any language),
> my story is about becoming an adult,
> my story is about the difficult process of separating my identity
>   from that of my family.

It is about struggling to live in two different time zones, with two languages, two or a thousand ways of viewing the world as a place that belongs to "us" —as a political, authored, understood, theorized physical and social experience.

My dissertation is an arts-based, autoethnographic study, which investigated my adjustment to a foreign culture and social system, my gendered role in a family structure and my growth in academia, as well as explored the use of artistic and self-reflexive methods in the qualitative research process. The primary personal goal for my research was to understand how my cultural identity and self-perception was changed by a life-altering experience. By critically re-evaluating my experiences I investigated the methods for studying identity, artistic knowledge, and approaches to diversity education.

The main theoretical interest in my study was the intersection of artistic/ creative behavior and systematic qualitative research practices. My research participates in further developing the relatively new methodologies of arts-based research and autoethnography, and explores the possible roles and uses of photography and creative writing in qualitative research. The study performs a critical analysis of the involvement of alternative and artistic methods in the process of studying cultural identity. Founded in critical visual sociology and ethnography, feminism, advanced studies of visual methods, knowledge, and culture, as well as contemporary art theory, my study provides a model for using self-reflexive and artistic practices in professional development and diversity education. The methods used were photography, participant observation, photo-writing, memory work, photo therapy, critical essay writing, and public display and discussion of my photographs and creative texts.

My research findings support a critical pedagogy and curriculum that focus on learning about cultural phenomena, artists, visual culture producers, objects and artifacts, and about an individual's culturally situated, and relational identities in their varied and complex discourses. The significance of this study is the exploration of the processes of gaining access to intellectuality and knowledge only available through the emergence of artistic, self-reflexive, and theoretical thinking with the intention of increasing awareness about visual knowledge that has remained largely uninvestigated.

The process became an active re-creation of self: an attempt to understand changes in my self-perception, an artistic effort to create new representations of self, and a systematic practice for developing altered subjectivities that were more sensitive to my increasing awareness of the relationality and contextuality of self. At the beginning I didn't "know" (e.g. internalized knowledge—not an academically learned form of knowledge construction) any other way of being or conducting research. See, I began teaching and working on my PhD in English just a few weeks after I arrived to the U.S. Although I had studied English in school, using it as my primary language of communication was new to me. Besides the difficulties with the language, I was also faced with a major cultural shock including such aspects as my relationship to the strange landscape, how I was treated as a woman in this new cultural and social environment, and my problematic ethnic status (I was mainstreamed and made exotic at the same time). In general, adjusting to the norms, ethics, and standards of the new social environment was occasionally very difficult. I had to find ways to make sense of what was happening to me and find ways to express myself, and I began photographing my surrounding and then writing about these photographs. I call this writing practice "photo-writing" and it involves strong meditational elements and a play with words.

During the research process my relationship with my new surrounding was simultaneously more simple and much more complex through the lens of my camera. "Working" my camera separated me from the rest of the world while also allowing me to pay attention to the little details that I found either aesthetically or emotionally pleasing. I used the camera to translate my surrounding to a "language" understandable to me. Some photos would not "rest" easily but kept demanding attention so I wrote about them. In these photo-writing sessions I found an escape and a relief from the rules of formal English and scholarly writing. Seeing the words begin to form meanings also further developed my understanding of what I found interesting or troubling theoretically or in practice about my actual living contexts.

The pressure, of course, is enormous when teaching and studying in a language other than one's mother tongue. Put it simply, the reason I was able to succeed with my studies was that my mentor and the other supportive people around me understood that I needed to be able to pursue my scholarly interests beginning with my art and from an artistic perspective. During the process photographing and artistic practices occasionally lead the process while mostly working in tandem with the development of my conceptual thinking.

In the end, I am not sure if my research was completed or if I achieved any goals typical and often seen as characteristic for scholarly inquiry. Like my artistic practice, the process never came to a clear end; I set a deadline and publicly "exhibited" what I had. And before the final changes were made I had already moved on; I had changed and so had my writing and practice.

Occasionally, I find myself wondering why I have faced so little resistance from the academic community and I am pleased that I have done reasonably well with publications and presentations. On the other hand, I face resistance weekly, if not daily. I find this a matter of phasing the negative out. I believe that in this area of my life I have learned to behave in a way that does not alter me to others' judgments. Not all my colleagues agree with what I do. Some think that I should not emphasize art creation since I am not an artist according to many institutionalized standards, and since I am not a studio professor, others think that my research is not valid. I was much more vulnerable as a student and I will never forget how I felt when I was humiliated and put down by a board of faculty members who served as judges in an interdisciplinary student symposium. They went as far as to split the available awards so that all the other participants could be awarded. I cried that day but it didn't stop me. I was back at writing the very next day.

I had three themes I wanted to work with: cultural and national identity, gendered identity and generations legacy, and professional identity. After the initial PhD courses in art education I looked for classes to take university-wide and professors to work with whose areas of specialty would enrich my study. Luckily, my advisor never pressured me to limit my interests and to focus on a narrow definition of discipline or inquiry. I finally ended up working with professors from art education, education-sociology, photography, English-folklore-ethnography, and comparative studies. This is reflected in my dissertation. I worked with a different professor on each chapter; however, it was ultimately my personal challenge to piece everything together. Giving presentations at the National Art Education Association's annual conference in 2003 while I hadn't yet finished all my ideas or chapters was scary. This was the first time I exposed my interdisciplinary ideas to the others and I wasn't sure how anyone would react. I was so focused on developing the concepts and ideas, that up until that point I had not really even considered whether my ideas would be accepted by others.

Reflecting back on the process, I am surprised that the committee members never raised any concern about the structure of my dissertation. This freedom of form and construction really helped me to explore the process of learning, writing, and creating. Ideas developed in a more abstract sphere and in a more fluid format that allowed randomness, non-linearity, dis-inter-connections, and relationality to emerge in a way that better reflects my understanding than a "traditional" thesis structure would have. Surprisingly, the final artifact does not include many visuals and the number of stories included is also limited. When I think about my dissertation research I think about the installation I built in the school gallery, and if I need to write about my research I more often return to the video-taped gallery talk rather than to the actual document available through the library. Unfortunately, these are not available to others, which makes me question if the format of my submitted dissertation artifact wasn't a good reflection of the research. Unfortunately, I didn't have many examples to look at and I did what I thought would work.

I hope this brief overview gives you all the flavor of my arts-based dissertation. Thanks for letting me share it with you.

"Photovoice"

Denise A. Ségor's story

- Photovoice
- Ethnography
- Participant stories
- Critical reflection
- Re-interpretation

Dr. Samson: Our next presenter also used photography for her dissertation project, except in this case it was the participants who took the pictures to provide the data for study. It is my pleasure to introduce Dr. Denise A. Ségor. Denise graduated in 2006 from Fielding Graduate University's Human and Organizational Development program. She is a writer and professional who works in the areas of cultural effectiveness, human storytelling, organizational development, and non-profit management. She is currently working on turning her dissertation into a book that will have a broader audience beyond academia.

Denise: Thanks Dr. Samson, Runner, Four Arrows and all the pioneering scholars and presenters who are here this week for allowing me to share my own "alternative" dissertation with you. In this case, as Dr. Samson said, my dissertation integrated women's "photovoices" in that I gave them cameras and asked them to tell us through photos what was important in their lives or what they wanted to tell us or what they wanted for their children.

I have always been drawn to listening to the stories people tell about themselves. In this study I had the privilege of working with elder women in Mizoram and experiencing their stories through their words, their photos, and their willingness to share about their lives with us. The title of my dissertation is "Tracing the Persistent Impulse of a Bedrock Nation to Survive Within the State of India: Mizo Women's Response to War and Forced Migration."

About sixty pages, 14 percent of the dissertation, was a depiction of the women's lives using photovoice and their narrative about the photos and their lives today.

My first time in Mizoram, with a research team from North America and Mizoram, I took pictures in a small village my team visited. I told the people there I would send copies to them. They expressed doubt, because others had taken pictures but never sent the promised copies. What had happened to those photos? How had they been used? At that moment I was keenly aware of my privilege, and of the power I held over these people—the power to go back home and speak for or about them, the power to use their images in any way I chose. When I began putting together my dissertation proposal, exploring how Mizos used their strengths to face the last century of change in their homeland, I wondered what it would be like if I could give women the chance to voice their own stories through photographs that were of their own creation, rather than mine.

One of my committee members, Marie Farrell, told me that as part of a research project in Europe she had given cameras to women so they could document health concerns from their own perspectives. I discovered the photovoice methodology, used in China and Guatemala, which offered women the opportunity to photograph important aspects of their everyday lives, and then evaluate the photos as part of a community health care project. This methodology was the "tool" I had been looking for.

My dissertation was an ethnographic study that explored the intersection between the Mizo independence movement in India during the late 1960s and early 1970s, with Mizo village women's personal experiences of that period of war and forced migration (village groupings). How did the women, their families, and their communities survive such a disturbing time? And what are their lives like today, in light of those experiences? That was the essence of my study. The questions were prompted by Mizos who said no one to this day had conducted such a study with village people, let alone women.

My dissertation included a discussion of Mizos and their history leading up to the disturbance, a discussion of the principles that guided my study (i.e. that communities are resilient, self-generating social systems; and that the living and doing of people in their communities is the core of community knowledge), a deconstruction of prior views (academic and political) about the disturbance (i.e. insurgency), the women's discussion of core Mizo values and a typical day in their lives (using their photovoice and narrative), and interpretations of the women's experiences of the disturbance and forced village groupings both thematically and through each woman's telling of their life-changing experiences. This led to a re-interpretation of the insurgency that was different from "official" views.

After our initial interviews with the women, we gave them disposable cameras and asked them to: "Take pictures of things most important to you, or that you have a story about, or that you would like to remember for a long time, or give to your children." The women could take pictures of anything they wanted. Looking at the photos and sharing about them was the highlight of our follow-up visit when we delivered the photo albums. As a person coming from another country, another culture, another way of living, I learned so much from these women's self-depictions. Their photographing took me deeper into their lives and gave me a better understanding of what they were saying about themselves in the interviews.

My initial idea of organizing the photos thematically would have highlighted important "things," but would have lost the real-ness of their lives. By luck, I decided to try organizing each woman's set of photos into a visual narrative, and boom, her life came into high relief. And all of a sudden, I got it. When a woman said, "I am so busy," I got it. When a woman said, "I am so useless, I can do nothing," I got it. When a woman said, "I am the only wage-earner," I got it. When a woman said, "I love my rice, my pigs, my chickens," I got it. When a woman said, "I am very content," I got it. In presenting the photos, I used not only what a woman said about her photos directly, but also things she told us in the interviews about her everyday life that were directly linked to the photos she took. For instance, Lalchhandami told us how difficult her day-to-day living was because the only wage-earner in their household, her son, was sick and had not worked for over a month. One of her photos was of her sick son. One was of her cooking a meal and drinking water at the same time. One was of her in the middle of all of her grandchildren. The powerful combination of each woman's verbal and photographic narrative showed me what it means to be a Mizo woman, living in a village, surviving day-by-day— the difficulties, the joys, the relationships, the struggles. My hope is that it has the same effect on those who read my dissertation.

"For spiritual reasons"
Christini Ri's story

- Film documentary
- Spirituality
- Ultradian rhythms
- Mixed methods
- Ecological sustainability

Runner: Our last presenter for this series of presentations is a doctoral candidate in the Educational Leadership and Change doctoral program at Fielding Graduate University. Christina left home when she turned sixteen to pursue an education in filmmaking. Christina obtained her Bachelor of Fine Arts and Master of Science degree in Film at New York University and she is planning on representing her doctoral dissertation work as a video documentary. (*Applause*)

Christina: Thank you. I am so happy to be here, both as a filmmaker and a doctoral student, to share my motivation and process for creating a film as a doctoral dissertation.

Before I decided to do a film documentary for my dissertation, the main focus of my work since I started my journey in the doctoral program has been to wrestle with traditional academic research protocol. I found myself continually frustrated by what I read, feeling like I was in a black space with an empty core. Not only did the traditional academic writing style fail to move my heart, but the approach that most authors were using did not reach me. I wanted to create a unique message that would contribute to bringing peace, healthful living, and hopefulness to as many people as possible. I did not think that many of my research papers and writings were helping me. Everything seemed fragmented and unrelated to actual experience, to truth. How would my dissertation be any different?

I was especially confused and concerned about what research method to use. My mind was confused by the differences (and similarities) between them; overwhelmed by the many options; concerned that my approach has elements of several but fully fits none; and frustrated by the need to label my authentic research in the first place beyond a clear description of the logic behind it.

I would have loved to name my approach, "Mindful Inquiry," in honor of the work of Bentz and Shapiro who hail from my own university. They incorporate phenomenology, hermeneutics, critical theory, and the compassionate mindfulness of Buddhism. Although I do rely on some positivist notions about empirical analysis with my use of an MRI case study, which might disqualify me from claiming this approach, my work does look at observable phenomenon and relies heavily on my intuition. I have employed a significant amount of personal interpretation, thus it has hermeneutic qualities. In talking about the effect of mass media on culture, I am definitely using critical theory. As for Buddhism, well, although raised Catholic, most of us South Koreans have Buddhism in our blood it seems, and there is no doubt about my compassion for the subject(s) of my dissertation and my focused intention on whatever emerged during my research. However, Bentz and Shapiro define their method by saying it puts the inquirer in the center and I confess I am intimately connected, but I think it is more accurate to say that I have put human connectedness to nature, or a concern about what we are doing to our natural world, at the center of my project. This may be the same reason I cannot claim my method is heuristic, which seems to require my personal encounter with what I am investigated. My mentor has encouraged me to become personally involved in my research by seeking transformative experiences in nature, but these have not been a significant part of my dissertation per se.

Another item on the long list of research methods is "interpretive inquiry." Interpretive inquiry defines interpretation as related to hermeneutics, which seeks as I understand it to understand the meanings of others with one's own interpretative skills, but is more of an attempt to make clear, to make sense of an object of study that is especially mysterious. This definitely describes how I envision my project, but I do not understand how this does not merely describe all doctoral level research that seeks to make a unique contribution to some field.

Because I did field experiments with human subjects, I thought of calling my research an "experimental design." I do have a hypothesis, but my research plans will not include a control group nor will my subjects be randomized. This, however, is allowed by what is called a quasi-experimental design, which seems to apply to both of my IRB-approved human research portions of my project. However, on closer look, with all the models that seem to be considered quasi-experimental, the "pre-experimental design: one-shot case study" really feels good. This is where I measure the results of an intervention, in this case the watching of my nature film, to see if the results meet my expectations of what would have happened if they had not watched it, even using a pre- and post test to help increase validity. No randomized population, control group, or comparison group is used.

Still, the more I read about pre-experimental designs and the more I reflected on my desire for my hypothesis to remain exploratory and always open to what might emerge, the more I worried that someone might say I am not quite in synch with this type of research. Perhaps my openness to what emerges means I am doing grounded research, another methodology, but no, I have too many expectations and assumptions for this to be how I describe my project.

Just when I thought I could describe my methodology clearly, however, as "combined case studies and confirmatory evidence method" I came across chaos theory as a basis for research and an optional method for describing research that is based on alternative methods of observing reality. After all, having already started my research, I can say that unpredictable and complex factors seems to be leading toward amazing connections I might not have imagined. On the other hand, I am not comfortable with referring to my carefully planned research effort as being chaotic. If I am going to go out on a limb, I would rather refer to my research as "arts-based."

My method could be arts-based for several reasons. First, as I have said, I have used film throughout the process, filming my subjects and in fact seeing the world of my research through the lens of my cameras and analyzing my material with the mind of a filmmaker. Furthermore, the presentation of my dissertation will primarily be in a video documentary format and as many here have said, representation of research is a part of research.

The only problem with my referring to my research as arts-based is that I worry it might not adequately let people know that I've done two significant pieces of more empirical research, one even using an MRI.

This brings me to what I thought would work well—"mixed methods." Since I seem to be using parts of all the methods described above, it seems natural just to say I am using mixed methods, which are generally thought of as a way to collect and analyze data with both quantitative and qualitative approaches. The problem here is that my quantitative data may not be sufficiently rigorous in terms of some of the requirements of those who write about mixed methods. Also, some scholars say that combining the two is not really good research because each stems from a different view of reality.

All of this leads me to really appreciate how some people here have just given their own name to their research method. Or, I could just describe what I plan on doing? I could say that I will start with my working hypothesis that a new kind of nature film may be needed to help motivate humans toward a new appreciation of nature that will, in turn, motivate sustainable practices that might stop the problems of pollution and global warming. (I will analyze the literature to support this hypothesis.) I will then study a sampling of people to see what indications there may be that watching a particular type of nature film might lead toward these motivations. Finally, after analyzing the results, I will interpret them with conclusions that come from both the literature and my interpretative reasoning, intuition, and imagination. And I will do all of this through the creative lens of a filmmaker.

Regardless of all these challenges and how I describe my "method" for research, the idea of capturing people's dialogue, recording sights and sounds, and illustrating the body language and emotional tones of participants is something that, in spite of the cost of a documentary film, I cannot really put a price on. The data will be more honest as a result, and ultimately, a dissertation that will be about truth.

Thank you.

Part 5

Day five

Drama, dialogue, and performance

True drama is only conceivable as proceeding from a common urgency of every art toward the most direct appeal to a common public.

(Richard Wagner in *The Art-Work of the Future*, p. 184)

"Fearless leadership"
R. Michael Fisher's story

with Stephen John Quaye and Blaine Pope

- Performing research
- Fear-based culture of the university
- Emancipatory curriculum
- "Fearism"
- Post-postmodern critical integral theory

Dr. Samson: R. Michael Fisher opens our sessions that relate to dissertations that use plays or other forms of drama to achieve research and representation goals. He is yet another person who received his doctorate from the University of British Columbia. He was the recipient of a $51,000 three-year fellowship for his doctoral work, granted by the Social Science and Humanities Research Council of Canada. Dr. Fisher, it's all yours.

Michael Fisher: Hello everyone. It is truly a pleasure to be with so many people who have demonstrated courage in facing the "fear"-based culture of the academy. I refer to myself as an artist, teacher, researcher, and public intellectual . . . and in some situations . . . a *fearologist*, so this is why I think I'm qualified to make this observation.

The title of my dissertation is "Fearless Leadership In and Out of the 'Fear' Matrix." Maybe, nowadays, post-Al Gore era, a more poignant title would be somethinglike "Global WarMing to Global WarNing: Fearless Leadership . . . ." Anyway, it is a screen-play I wrote as a sequel to the 1999 movie, *The Matrix* . . . and a lot more. Basically, I had to figure out how to actually write/perform my research from the beginning so that it was a contradiction (psychologically, politically, culturally, spiritually) to the "fear"-based culture of university itself. This was, of course, a tricky proposition. In fact, I used arts-based means to work the "trickster" elements of my research and to locate myself in the final product.

In particular, my experiential and intellectual passion has revolved around what happens when fear meets fearlessness. How these are related to the future development of a universal ethic that can help stop the violence in our world, is a question that continues to guide my research. The dissertation used a transdisciplinary approach to addressing this topic, rather than to rely only on traditions, clichés, and one-sided uncritical views about fear that have come from Western scientific psychology and religion. I wanted to use alternative research approaches to see if I could find better ways to undermine, if not eliminate, the unsustainable insanity of human existence—which I see all around me. I wanted to contribute creatively and radically to uncovering the operations ("hidden curriculum") of a ubiquitous *fearism*, which I have come to see as the base of all the insidious "ism" diseases on this planet.

After watching the Wachowski Bros's popular sci-fi action film *The Matrix*, it became evident that this study and dissertation was going to be directed and shaped by the film's characters and meta-mythical narrative. The problem and question that this dissertation explores is "What is the 'Fear' Matrix?" I used the writing of a play to serve as an "arational" modality, that is, as an alternative to rationality, to "get through" or perhaps to expose ("work through") the deep irrational-based patterns of typical research protocols. Thus, I see this dissertation as a type of "fear" vaccination process in which to enact a truthing (rehabilitation) of educational (and academic) culture specifically.

The dissertation is/was a universal curriculum intervention (*cura*), of the sociotherapeutic genre (fearanalysis). It is all theory—it is all practice—all play/performance: fact/fiction. And it is open to critical questioning as to its own aesthetic, epistemological, pedagogical, political, and therapeutic effectiveness.

The dissertation inquiry takes complex, chaotic, and artistic pathways, collaging together multi-layered transdisciplinary processes of an arts-based performative "postmodern" methodology. Although only the text-/image-based dissertation itself is referred to here, there was a substantial amount of research and production of an art installation with seventy-five art pieces and a video performance ritual entitled "Platinum 'Fear' *plat du jour*," which was exhibited in 2002–2003 in various forms and locations, including a public art gallery and a curriculum and pedagogy conference—which is foundational to this entire doctoral work. As well, I read/performed the screen-play (6–8 hours) in seven locations—in various groups—across western Canada during 2003, before I defended and wrote the final draft of the dissertation. From the beginning of getting my research office in 2000, I transformed my space in the academy into an art studio. The dissertation defense presentation was an artistic performance, costume and all.

The play opens with Part One (102 pp.) and an introduction to a polyvocal chorus that includes nine pages of back-to-back quotes all copiously endnoted and from scholarly references. Revolutionary fictional dialogue with Ken

Wilber (critical integral theory) and Daniel Cohn-Bendit (historical figure) serves to introduce the intellectual problematics of understanding the "Fear" Matrix. Part Two (230 pp.) is the performance of a sequel and critique of *The Matrix*, written through a general cyborg feminist lens. Part Three (27 pp.) summarizes the methodological problems of the dissertation.

At one point, in an earlier draft of the dissertation, I wrote that I was utilizing a "voluntary performative schizoidal praxis" as methodology. In a nutshell, that means that I had to "go crazy" (deconstruct–reconstruct over and over) during this process and processing of the subject/object relations involved in this research inquiry. The presentation of the research also has schizoidal qualities, because I wanted to ensure an "authenticity" to what I produced, went through, and what I think most of the post-9/11 (and postmodern) world is going through, in some way. The dissertation presentation had to "mirror" some "reality" of what I was picking up and learning and going through (and suspected that most everyone else was too—albeit, they are usually less conscious of it than I). All very disconcerting, exciting, terrifying, uncertain, dangerous. I couldn't write "straight." I couldn't be "straight-faced" about any of this work. I couldn't explain the "Fear" Matrix. I had to perform it (with all the nebulousness that goes with it)—and I had to show that there is "little clarity" about anything when it comes to what this dissertation (emancipatory curriculum) was all about. The reality was/is: I was/am overwhelmed by it all—but I chose to be and I work at figuring out how to do that well (healthily), and educatively. Sure, its "transformative" (whatever that actually means, when going in an out of the "Fear" Matrix). Bless their hearts, my research committee had confidence in me pulling this off. They all appreciated arts-based approaches, more or less. The enormous scope of studying fear and education, from a transdisciplinary (all encompassing, integral/holistic) perspective "forced" all of us to reconcile that there is no clean and simple way to answer the research question: "What is the 'Fear' Matrix?" So, we played with it. Reality is, as I saw it from the beginning, that my research committee (and the doctoral defense assessment people) would *resist* any notion of fearless leadership and an epistemological fearless standpoint (which I implied throughout, but never articulated directly). Why? Because I knew they were all "Agents" of the "Fear" Matrix itself—of fearism (of a university institution and academic culture that works on fearism)—and thus, would become 'enemies' to everything I was writing, doing, saying, performing —(at least, I suspected that, based on my life experiences prior to and during my graduate Master's degree in the same faculty). There was a "battle" between "me and them"—oh, yes, this was (still is) a consciously chosen dichotomous (dualistic) relationship. My task was to perform this relationship dynamic fearlessly (in the deepest and most rigorous way I could). I was ethically committed to not approaching them in "fear." I tried to convince them to do likewise with me and this project—(that's a long story)—but they never quite figured that out—or, never wanted to figure it out—or they never let me really know up-front that they figured that out. I am not sure which. Mostly, they had "puzzled" but smiling looks on their faces every time we crossed paths. I did find out they thought my work was "extremely important." But as to how to approach it in a scholarly manner—well, I think they were probably, most of the time, as confused as the researcher. I wanted the research committee members right *in/with* the script, the play, the dramatics. I suppose I'm a bit of a "trickster" that way. So, maybe that will help "introduce" myself to this group dialoguing on the "authentic dissertation." I look forward to hanging out with you all.

Dr. Samson: With all due respect to Dr. Fisher, to Runner, to all our presenters, professors, and students in the audience, I must say that I am at this point myself "confused!" What I've heard just now makes it difficult for me to see how new knowledge that is validated by the academic community has or can emerge from such a wild approach to inquiry! I mean did your dissertation produce a new theory about fear?

Michael: Yes and no. It is a transdisciplinary postmodern critical integral theory of "fear"—which boils down to making "fear" a whole lot more complex than previous theories about fear. I don't articulate the fine details of a "clean" new theory—a lot of it is implicit, and a lot of it is performed theory—arational—art as theory. Mostly, the new information produced could be summed up as involving the methodological problematics of "knowing fear" (in a "culture of fear" or "Fear" Matrix)—that's the thrust of the dissertation.

Dr. Samson: Hmmm. Your opening question/problem was about creating a new universal ethic that relates to "fearless leadership." Did you come upon or define or support such an ethic?

Michael: No real "clean" universal ethic was created nor did one emerge as "the" ethic. It was more an opening to how an embodied, performative, arational, and arts-based pursuit for such an ethic must be, at least, grounded before such an ethic can be "lived." These questions, with all due respect, Dr. Samson, I mean, the very idea even of a nice clean rational description and empirical support for an ethic to counter fear-based thinking and actions, reveals, I think, why typical academic assumptions stifle any true realizations that can change our situation for the better!

Runner: I see a couple of hands rising out there. Stephen, what's on your mind? Before you tell us, please introduce yourself.

Stephen John Quaye: I'm a new Assistant Professor at the University of Maryland. In 2007, I received my doctorate in Higher Education at Pennsylvania State University. My current research concentrates on the influence of race relations on college and university campuses and my own dissertation used a critical race theoretical framework. This is why I want to endorse what Michael did and what he is saying. I know what he did can be confusing to many people, but it is the confusion that I think makes it appealing. Dissertation writing does not have to be neat and clean; life is messy and uncertain most of the time. I sometimes wonder whether going into academe is the right path, as there are so many standards and norms in writing that they make me cringe. However, I've decided that avoiding it is not the solution, but instead to try and promote change by entering that system. Although, I feel that this system continually stifles my creativity.

As a Ghanaian/American student, I continually struggle with merging my Ghanaian culture with my American culture. I grew up in a family where story telling and sharing were valued and seen as important ways to convey one's emotions and thoughts. Family was everything and success was not seen through an individual. If I achieved, my family achieved, and my success was not due to solely my skill or aptitude. Rather, I did well because my family enabled me to do so. Yet, I quickly learned this was not the case in my American culture. Learning was defined as individual effort. A person achieved because she or he studied hard, and those that failed needed to pull themselves up by their bootstraps. Therefore, according to my American cultural values, there was pressure to compete and leave others by the wayside in doing so.

As a doctoral student I was ready—ready to write in ways that aligned with my Ghanaian heritage. Yet, when I wanted to tell stories in my classes, faculty members silenced me. They told me I was not fulfilling the conventions of "academic" writing; meaning, I was not detached from the text writing in a passive way. The dissertation should be an experience in which the doctoral student writes in a voice most meaningful to her or him. Multiple forms should be accepted and encouraged—poems, dramas, personal narratives. The dissertation is the final chance for the student to show what she or he learned about the research process. Communicating those lessons learned in ways that are passionate, different, and subversive to academia's norms promote opportunities for change and personal growth. How maddening this can be to students whose cultures and values do not align with dominant ways of thinking, being, and acting. The dissertation writing process should not be one in which students' voices are stifled, but rather, a chance for students to be creative, experience joy, and challenge themselves and dominant standards. As a new professor, I will also work with students who desire the same—to push their boundaries and the walls of academe so that their cultures and voices are respected and heard. The research process should be one in which students self-reflect on who they are. As Michael showed us, it is nearly impossible to not be changed when working with humans; we see their struggles, experience their vulnerabilities, and better understand ourselves through listening to their narratives. Therefore, it is so important for emerging scholars to explore their identities as they conduct research. Our research works when we invite the messiness that personal subjectivities entail. This "messiness" is important and why Michael cannot answer Dr. Samson's questions like Dr. Samson wants.

Runner: Thanks Stephen. Blaine, you'll have to be our last comment before we move on. Everyone, Blaine Pope is a Columbia University Professor of Environmental Science and Policy and is currently working on his PhD in Human Organizational Development at Fielding Graduate University.

Blaine Pope: Dr. Samson, if I may. I understand your confusion and concerns. Yet don't you see that what is happening in our world—what *we* are doing to our world—is much more a product of the so-called "logic" of Western reason and academic research? If fear is the root of propaganda and compliance, then a study of an antidote to fear would naturally do the dance that Michael's dissertation did. It would have the "messiness" that Stephen is talking about. It is this kind of multi-leveled awareness that might bring us out of the insanity Michael referred to when he talked about what we are doing to the planet.

For my own dissertation I developed a concept I refer to as "Terracentrism." Broadly speaking, Terracentrism is a holistic, cross-disciplinary way of viewing, framing, and discussing seemingly large and/or complex issues. I offer it and discuss it in terms of it being a tool that will help people get started on a new path, a path that is open enough to allow for wide latitude in terms of approaches. We need situated and diverse alternatives to the inadequacies that I had been finding in the literature on international political economy, global studies, world systems analysis, philosophy/spirituality, and ecology. In fact, what I sought to do was to unify each of these themes under a broader tent. But the academy keep wanting us to dissect everything so it fits into the kind of box I feel Dr. Samson is wanting Michael's work to go into.

The fundamental issue is to be able to apply elements from one's own cultural background—whatever that may be. I am grateful to the members of my dissertation committee at Fielding Graduate University who, with minimal persuasion, were willing to go along with me in this somewhat innovative approach. I think I was able to convince them to go along with me because, I believe, the individual components of this approach made sense to them; furthermore, the unifying elements of Terracentrism seemed to satisfy the committee members' own desires for a kind of holism in the analysis of complex global problems. I hope more and more doctoral committees can share this desire!

"Out of the cage"

Karen Lee

with Peter Gouzouasis

- Storied dissertation
- Personal experience as data
- Creative non-fiction
- Autobiography/autoethnography
- Importance of mentor support
- Stressful repercussions

Runner: Our next presenter is Dr. Karen Lee. She received her doctorate in Curriculum Studies from the University of British Columbia in 2004. She is a Faculty Advisor and co-founder of the Teaching Initiative for Music Educators cohort (TIME), at the Faculty of Education, UBC, Vancouver, BC. Her research interests include performance ethnography, women's life histories, autoethnography, writing practices, and arts-based approaches to qualitative research. She is a writer, musician, music educator, and researcher. I understand that Karen's doctoral supervisor, Dr. Peter Gouzouasis, is here also and will say a few words to us about Karen's dissertation journey as well. Peter is the Chair of Music Education at UBC and 2003 recipient of the Sam Black Award for Excellence in Education and Development in the Visual and Performing Arts. Karen, it is all yours!

Karen: Thank you Runner, and my greetings to everyone. My dissertation, "Riffs of Change: Musicians Becoming Music Educators" is a storied dissertation that researches the inherent shifts and extensions in musicians' identities as they transform into schoolteachers. My research explored literary studies, arts-based research, and feminist-based literature. I investigated musicians' lives in practicum, university, and school-based contexts. I discussed the nature of institutional education and the musicians' conflicts with love, loss, pain, wisdom, and change.

I represented my research in the form of eight short stories and an auto-biographical account of my experience. The stories are considered creative non-fiction as I tell stories about what happened with an artful presentation of real people and real events. My stories were told with a clear eye and alert imagination. In them I examined musicians' beliefs, education, and experiences, focusing on their identity issues as they transformed into music teachers. The stories confront and challenge and steer readers into critical places of thought and unexpected spaces of change.

My research led to several important ideas. It revealed that some musicians benefited in their transitions to teachers if they collaborated in the story-writing process, and if they were mentored by a school advisor who was also a professional musician. It proved the value of autobiography in resolving my own conflicts relating to the musician/teacher dynamic. I also learned that exploring issues from multiple viewpoints and writing styles enables people to gain new insights that help make change possible.

Because I was asked to tell my story about the process of my adventure into an arts-informed dissertation and because time is short, I want to share with you the thoughts that went through my mind the day I waited for my doctoral committee to determine the outcome of my doctoral defense.

It's been forty-five minutes and the anxiety causes me to reflect on the arduous and challenging journey of writing a storied dissertation.

Don't panic. It's only my doctoral defense. It demonstrates intellectual depth, breadth, dexterity of knowledge. The last and most challenging exam I need to pass: *viva voce*. I stand and wait, try to figure out what happened. Nothing comes. My hands shake, my heart beats. I rub my stomach, feel it coming. I close my eyes and let my mind lapse. I wear my black suit, something for formal occasions. An actress in costume, I just performed. After forty-five minutes, I retreat outside while the jury deliberates. An unusually long time to wait. *Will I graduate?*

I remembered my decision to choose an "arts-based research" project as the conceptual, theoretical, methodological underpinnings for my research. To write a non-traditional storied dissertation. To open up new epistemological and political ways of seeing and saying.

I reflect on my journey as middle-aged daughter, lover, mother, scholar. My voyage has been wildly unpredictable, dark with secrets, evocation, and celebration. I recall the hurdles in a flood of memories. A lump in my throat, clay in my hands. No choice but to wait. Going back inside for after-defense small talk would crumble this moment into dust. Instead, I unpack years of murmurs about writing a non-traditional dissertation. A fine rain starts to fall. Pushing back my hair, I tell myself I will graduate. A damp mist takes hold. Years earlier, when my dissertation was born, I searched to express the emotion of the magnum opus. A steady sound of writing behind closed doors; I divided time between my daughter and my dissertation. She wanted to attend convocation. Habitually, she drew with stubby crayons beside me.

Calling from fog
My daughter
When will you graduate?

It's March. I remember, we are arguing. My supervisor is a skeptic. It's a cold winter morning. My hands shake, my heart palpitates. I walk to a large, blue building in the opposite corner of the quadrangle. I could probably convince him to go for coffee, could probably afford the cost. My doctoral supervisor likes to eat and drink when we talk. And I need to change his mind. Provide a convincing argument for writing a storied dissertation. He must understand that my dissertation needs music, poetry, autobiography. That subjective knowing contributes to academia. That an alternative form of representation would contribute new knowledge. But arts-based research is novel and problematic for him. Originally, I had decided to write a traditional dissertation by interviewing musicians with structured and semi-structured questions. But after in-depth interviews, coding, ordering, categorizing could not explain their experiences. Instead, writing stories about their experiences would express their emotions and dilemmas with change.

I vividly remember arguing. And how the appointment was sabotaged. I had brought him a cup of tea that he knocked over. "You put the cup in a bad place," he mumbled. With paper towels, I cleaned the mess. Closing my eyes, I recall music between us. Harmony, the interplay of notes. We walked at the beach. A rainy, blustery day. Bit by bit, he unleashed his stern words. My waking nightmare unfolded:

"This arts-based stuff seems somewhat," he paused, "subversive. Know what I mean? Research needs to be systematic."

"What do you mean?" I asked.

"That there must be some sense of coherence. A clearly defined purpose and problem. A certain sense of structure. Structural corroboration, not multiplicative corroboration—even Eisner says that. I mean, considering the state of research in our profession, how can you hand in a dissertation that's merely a series of stories?"

Indeed, there are arguments against personal experience as data. Questions about assumptions, collection, analysis, validity, presentation, and subjectivities that influence data. Questions about the artistic process shaping research that acknowledges the aesthetic, physical, emotional, and intellectual.

It's June. We are still bantering. Images surge like a stormy wave. Finally, I decide that any more grief, resistance, and I'll leave him. Yes, find another supervisor. Get on with life: write, defend, graduate. As is, I'm dead from hardcore cigarettes. Dead from swollen meetings, redolent of half-lit winter mornings. My hands shake, my heart beats fast. I hold articles in one hand: Ellis, Barone, Eisner, Rambo, Richardson. I curse at myself, be more persuasive. I curse writing, curse research. Curse him, curse his skepticism. But I wait. Wait for the bilious feeling to pass. Visualize myself being brilliant, persuasive.

Suddenly, he smiles and waves in the doorway. As he opens the door, I step inside. I remind myself that the *raison d'être* for visiting is to make a decision. Yes or no. I take a deep breath while he begins to speak.

"How are you?"
"Not good."
"Why?"
"I need to talk."
"About what?"
"I need to write a storied dissertation."
"What? I thought we talked about this. A thesis like that will never get you a job in our profession."
"I'm not worried about a job, Peter. I'm more interested in the best way to tell my student's stories."
"What about putting food on the table?"
"Seriously, Peter, I need to share some articles with you."
"About what?"
"About stories being research."

I explain I started a course with a poet, writer, researcher in language education who discusses how artists use art, dance, story, poetry, multimedia in narrative research. I list narrative researchers: Bruner, Cixous, Greene, Kundera, Lather, Goldberg, Wooldridge, Bateson. I tell him about the rewards of writing. About autobiographical writing as a method of discovery. I write to find out about love, death, good, evil, personal, family. Indeed, it is research to be a laborer of words. Like many, words and images fill me. I write poems and poems write me. I even share how my poems and two stories have been accepted for publication.

There is silence. Then, he takes a deep breath. We've had small arguments but always resolved them. The way scholars go about polemics like pantomime puppets, one walks in front, the other behind. As the silence deafens, I stand to leave. "Wait," he halts me, "I need to read those articles."

Later, I don't remember how long but it seemed like eternity, he scheduled an appointment with me.

"How are you?"
"Okay."
"I read the articles."
"Great."
"Let's eat and talk."

It's August. We go for sushi on Tenth Avenue. I smile and he smiles. I wear shorts and a t-shirt. I'm an actress in costume, celebrating. Long shadows of the sun make patterns on the table as we drink water. Immediately, I turn toward him. Thank you, thank you for reading the articles. I stare deeply into his eyes, thank you. My voice cracks, I hold back tears. I taste my California roll. Lunch is easy, comfortable. There are silver flashes, blue lights. As we eat, I remember to tell my daughter, "I will graduate."

Now it's January. The day of my doctoral defense. I recall the last two-and-a-half hours. I sing and read poetry, sing and read stories, sing and read autobiographically. I sing the song my stepfather taught my daughter.

> Tell me a story.
> Tell me a story
> And then I'll go to bed.
> You promised me you said you would.
> You better give in so I'll be good.
> Tell me a story
> And then I'll go to bed.

There was a drum roll, a downbeat to defend how stories teach. How everyone is from a story-telling tribe. How great stories bring metaphors to life. How adults and children use stories to gain insight about the world. As artist-as-researcher, researcher-as-artist, I play musical excerpts from the musicians in my research. But the oral exam was loaded with super, colossal, intellectual questions, the dialectic. A tribute to Socrates. On the edge of inquiry, I staggered as academic questions gain dimension, often wake me in the middle of the night.

Finally, the grueling questions end. A motionless winter morning imbued by the hurdles: my supervisor, emotional hurdles, oral defense, and the deliberation. Inhaling, I focus on my publications on autoethnography, performance ethnography, women's life histories, writing practices, and arts-based approaches to qualitative research.

Soon, a celebratory Chinese lunch at a restaurant with my friends and parents. Then, dinner with my parents and daughter. I want to tell her *I will graduate*. Fidgeting, I watch the misty waters dance on the pavement. My heart speeds up, my teeth chatter. There is itchiness from nylons. I want to wear jeans, socks, and boots. It's cold. Nothing I can do to make the wait go faster. It's the deepest part of the day, just before the final verdict.

That night, after sharing the news with my family, my daughter draws a picture of me in cap and gown. It has the caption: "Congratulations Dr. Mom!"

Runner: Thank you so much for sharing this. I think the way you presented in itself proves the power of stories to move and inform us. Dr. Gouzouasis, were you the supervisor in Karen's story?

Peter: Karen's defense was rough. She had the lingo and knew the literature, but didn't answer some questions in a satisfactory manner. Some examiners felt she didn't elaborate on the basic ideas that enabled her to use stories as data. When the questioning came back to me I tried to ask questions that would lead her to address the concerns raised in the external examiner's letter. The argument that followed when Karen left the room was not pleasant. I was left alone to conduct a forty-five-minute defense of the defense. Unfortunately, the missing committee member, the poet who inspired Karen to pursue arts-based research, was 3,000 miles away on sabbatical.

My major concerns with an arts-based dissertation remain. Very few music educators are involved in this approach to research. Three years after her defense and with numerous journal publication credits to her name, Karen would have an even more difficult time finding a position in a music education department in the U.S.A. And it is not an approach I recommend to everyone, because it requires a commitment to both personal artistic growth and the development of multiple research skills.

Karen's narrative, like many others of those at this conference who have dared to move out of the standard academic box, is an emotional story. I learn so much from working with all of my graduate students. I always read the material they choose for their literature reviews, and in most cases go beyond the scope of their project. In Karen's case, I initially thought her intentions were a passing fancy, a fad. Then I started reading books and articles on my own—Eisner, Connelly, Clandinin, Riesman, Richardson, Barone, Sparkes. I had begun to form my own ideas and I wanted to see where she was connecting with arts-based educational research. She was more ready to compose a creative non-fiction dissertation when I was intellectually prepared to go on the journey with her. We grew together. A supportive, knowledgeable advisor is crucial.

Karen: Remember Peter, when I reminded you of the cage that day in your office when I was crying and you tried to console me?

Peter: Yes, twelve years ago when I met Karen in a class, we were in a room that had a huge wire fence dividing it. We were trapped in there with computers. We called it "the cage." We used to say that they put us in there because of all the crazy music we were composing. Anyway, Karen reminded me of it during her stress about the dissertation, saying that she felt like she was still in it.

I just wanted to add to Karen's story that it is vital that students who are choosing to move in the direction of alternative dissertation find supportive networks among faculty and students. They also need to factor in the role of change in relationships that they might experience. People go through so much "skata," to use a Greek term, to make things work. And I mean real scatalogical experiences, in the name of academia. Believe me, I've been there and dealt with a lot of heavy stuff.

Some people are stuck in modernism, others in postmodernism. They're hung up on dualisms and manufactured binaries. They're stuck on their own stance and afraid to change, but we have to rethink the way we see the world. When people stop growing they can't connect ideas any more. Change brings about the need to reconstruct and reconnect, to rethink the ways that we see the world, to adopt a new set of lenses. Sometimes, that doesn't happen. People stop growing, they can't connect anymore, probably because they can't get away from relativistic stances to see how the relational, the relative-relative, supercedes the mere relative.

As musicians, Karen and I live and breathe music, and our understandings of all aspects of music—performing, composing, improvising, listening, studying—are ongoing and expressed through a variety of media, in a variety of forms. For us, synthetic, split binaries of teacher-artist, teacher-researcher, researcher-artist dissolve into a relational, inclusive perspective of an understanding of the artist/researcher/teacher. Our personal experiences in music teaching, learning and performing inform our research and our research informs our teaching, learning, and performing. That music (i.e. art) informs our research and research informs our music may be further elaborated as each aspect of artist/researcher/teacher simultaneously nurtures the other—creating and being created—in an ongoing process of living inquiry.

Runner: And not everyone can be a musician or a painter, right, Peter?

Peter: The artist is in all of us, especially the story teller. However, it takes a lifelong commitment to an art form to live up to the title of artist. And the strongest, most coherent, vibrant examples of arts-based educational research demonstrate Eisner's principle that the art informs the research and the research informs the art. The researcher's integrity and lifelong commitment to the arts is crucial in the creation of meaningful arts-based inquiry.

"Hybridity"
Annie Smith's story

- Performative inquiry
- Participatory performance
- Autoethnography
- Accoustmatic text
- Elasticity

Runner: Our next presenter is Dr. Annie Smith. Annie is a faculty member at Grande Prairie Regional College in Canada and received her doctorate in Curriculum and Instruction at UBC in 2006. Her research interests encompass community rituals, participatory performance, and her "fledgling" theory of elasticity. She is creating a new field called "participatory performance and pedagogy." Her dissertation is titled, "Elasticity, Community, and Hope: Understandings from Participatory Theatre Performance." Annie's teaching and research is informed by the Indigenous understanding of the relationship of all beings to each other. She worked on the reserve at Itattsoo and was trained by the Nuu-chah-nulth Tribal Council in child protection and community development. "Even though I am non-native, I have taken the teachings I was given as a foundation for how I try to live in the world and how I work as an educator. I hope that I can be understood to be an ally and not an appropriator." She is an aspiring author and she presents often. Annie, welcome!

Annie: Thank you Runner. It is an honor and a pleasure to be here. I've titled my brief talk, "Hybridity, the interdisciplinary dilemma," so I'll start with the question: "What does it mean to be a hybrid creature?" If you are an artist and an academic, a practitioner and a theorist, a student and a professional, in what ground can you thrive? Are you branded a mule or a hybrid seed—

infertile, intransigent, inconsequential? What tensions can hold you in the in-between spaces of hybridity? My doctoral experience was a probing into the tensions of the academy and the tensions within myself.

I call the approach to my dissertation, "Performative Inquiry." It began with a research project I conducted in the summer of 2004, a six-week "participatory theatre laboratory" with eight undergraduate students in the Theatre Program of the Department of Theatre, Film and Creative Writing, at the University of British Columbia. Integral to the laboratory were six participatory theatre performances with day camps in the Greater Vancouver area. Seven youth leader participants from three of these performances and two student actors were interviewed six to eight weeks later to discover what they remembered of their experience with Participatory Action Theatre. Their responses cover a wide range of interests, focusing predominantly on the value of involvement.

My conceptual explorations encompass the late twentieth-century movement towards audience involvement in theatre performance, theatre for education and social change, performance studies, and the relation of the artist, as mystic, to the community. "Community" is a contested term: I borrow from the Amerindian understanding of community to ground my own interpretation. I perform this inquiry as an ongoing journey of discovery, using stories from the Tricksters' Theatre tours, my initial work in participatory performance, to propel the journey between stopping places of reflection.

Elasticity, community, and hope, are three concepts that have risen through my exploration of the experience of participatory theatre. Elasticity bespeaks the dynamic of interrelationships between people when they perform together. I identify what participants have reported as a "feeling of community" when performing together. My dissertation explores how participatory theatre performance can generate feelings of belonging that go beyond the performances themselves, and theorizes an elastic connection between performing together and feeling a sense of community. The value of feeling community is that it may reveal an emergent culture of hope in situations where people perform together.

I never had any intention of doing a non-traditional dissertation. At my first conversation with my supervisor I expressed my desire to write something that was straightforward—nothing fancy or radical. I suppose she knew better than I did, that doing arts-based research would lead me into more convoluted paths than I could envision that early in my process. I was fortunate to be accepted into a program that allowed for innovative, interdisciplinary, non-traditional scholarship. I was unfortunate in that, during my first year as a doctoral student, the program came under academic fire for "lack of rigor" and was almost terminated. After two years of turmoil and distress, the program was resuscitated under a new name. Nevertheless, my experience as a doctoral student began on shaky ground and left me feeling sour and angry with the implication that non-traditional research was less than rigorous. The sentiment that was voiced, jokingly, among those of us now tarred as "radical," was that we were at least "vigorous" which was preferable to being afflicted with "rigor mortis."

Although my intention was to write a traditional dissertation, my research was non-traditional in that I was working across two disciplines: my program was housed in the Faculty of Education and my research was facilitated through the Department of Theatre, Film and Creative Writing in the Faculty of Arts. I was always getting caught in between these two different cultures, particularly with my vocabulary. My education committee members were horrified with my use of words such as "truth," "reality," and "didactic," which were perfectly acceptable in theatre culture, having quite different connotations.

My research was non-traditional for theatre because I did an empirical study. It was confusing for education because I was also exploring theoretical understandings from performance studies and creation spirituality of the dynamics revealed in the empirical study. To add further to the confusion, I realized that the theatre experience that had propelled me into the research needed to be brought into the work, thus introducing an autoethnographic element.

As I said, the "methodology" that I chose to employ for my research is "performative inquiry," as developed by Lynn Fels in her doctoral work at UBC from 1996 to 1999. Although I was able to gain insights into performative inquiry from a course taught by Lynn Fels, there was no institutional support given to this methodology. I was also using the methodology to explore the dynamics of performance itself, rather than using performance to explore a research question that was independent of the performance. My first question was: *What happens between people when they perform together?* This question required people to participate in a performance, thus requiring a performance to be created and enacted. But the content of the performance was secondary to the experience of performing together.

A further complication was that the form of theatre that I wanted to explore was "participatory performance." What had intrigued me in my theatre practice previous to entering into my doctoral research, was the engagement of the audience when they became full participants in acting a play. In this form, the "actors" facilitate the audience members to become the actors. There is no separate audience watching the play. Everyone has an integral character role to play in the drama.

My first hurdle was to get approval from the Ethics Board for my research project. I did not know how it would be feasible to stage a public participatory theatre event and have each audience member sign a consent form. How would one advertise such an event? "This is your chance to act in a play, but first you will have to read three pages of academic language and sign a consent form." And if I wanted to video-tape the performance the "risks" were higher. Who would see the video? Could people be identified? And of course there would be children there, which made it even more complicated as parental consent was needed for them to participate. And what were the physical, psychological, and emotional risks to people being involved in a theatre event? How could they be protected? From what? The medical research model just didn't fit what I was trying to accomplish.

I had to modify my research to fit the BREB (ethics review) criteria, which meant that I was unable to research what I most wanted to. I settled for more controlled performance situations with child audience participation at summer day camps, interviewing the youth leaders after the performance events. Although this research is important and valuable, I despair of ever being able to empirically research the many variables of a public audience's participation in theatre performance and the potential relational dynamics of those participations.

While it may seem that I am complaining about the strictures of ethics reviews, I am not in any way saying that we shouldn't have to follow ethical guidelines. What I am saying is that the current model that is being used in social sciences research does not serve art-based research projects where the language, the parameters, and the goals of the projects are in different domains.

Once the ethics hurdle was vaulted (with less difficulty than I had supposed), I was able to accomplish my research project with few difficulties. The next hurdle was finding the form for my dissertation. I have mentioned that I wanted to bring my previous theatre experience into my dissertation. I had been writing short stories about my experiences directing and touring with an Aboriginal theatre company in rural British Columbia. As I was writing the stories I realized that I was charting not only the geographic journeys of the theatre company, but also my internal journey of epiphanies and realizations that had led directly to my doctoral research. I was challenged to incorporate these stories into my dissertation even though my committee was at first resistant to these bits of creative writing that did not seem to have direct connection to the research project.

My desire to write performatively was supported by Jacques Daignault's understanding of "accoustmatic text" as explained by Lynn Fels. Daignault says that a text can never repeat reality; it doubles it. This idea echoes Antonin Artaud's understanding of theatre as doubling reality. This idea is important to me because I wanted to use my text performatively, not to attempt to replicate the participatory performances but to double them. My chosen way to do this was to invite my story-telling self into the dissertation.

Once my storytelling self moved into the text, it was irrepressible. It seemed that every time I needed to explain a concept I was telling a story. In my efforts to explain to my committee why I needed the stories from the theatre tours and why they would be interspersed throughout the dissertation, I found myself telling about a canoeing trip through the Broken Group Islands on the west coast of Vancouver Island. It was through telling this story that I began to understand how the stories worked within the dissertation: they were the paddles between islands. The islands were the chapters of text that addressed the traditional foci of dissertation chapters—methodology, research project description and data, literature review, theoretical analyses. The stories invited the reader into an imaginative space that had a throughline of its own that influenced the reading of the theoretical chapters. I invited the readers to make their own sense of the work and asserted that their interaction with the text would add new meanings to its continuously created performance. They were participants in a textual performance that doubled the theatre performances.

There was some resistance to my introducing story telling into the dissertation. Here, I was able to fall back on Native theorists such as Jace Weaver, Kimberley Blaeser, and Joanne Archibald to assert the importance of story to cultural understanding and learning and community. My second research question was: *What do people mean when they say they experience "a feeling of community" when they perform together?* The Aboriginal understanding of the relationship between story and community undergirded my understandings from the research project and supported the format of my dissertation.

The last hurdle that I was faced with was the warning that arts-based research methodologies were being scrutinized within the academy. I was warned that my defense could be really tough in terms of having to defend my choice of methodology. This entailed a rigorous rewriting of my methodology chapter where I had to provide an ironclad case for my choice of methodology, a thorough explanation of the methodology, and what felt like an "apology" to justify my interpretation of the methodology. At this point, the extra re-writing, which was not about my research, but about appeasing academic policing, was emotionally draining. It also meant that I would need to pay for another term's fees without any support through graduate student employment, my four-year time limit having been reached.

What have been the benefits to choosing to write a non-traditional dissertation? The biggest benefit has been that I really love what I have written. I am proud of it. It is authentic because I am in it; my voice is heard. I think that because I was committed to my work it generated interest from other graduate students and also from the other communities of which I am a part. There were over thirty people at my defense, which incorporated story telling and some audience participation. We sat in a circle; each person there was seen and also witnessed each other. This was a radical act. I do not know yet what the other benefits will be. I think they depend on who reads my work and their response to it. At this point, I am glad just to have maintained my integrity in writing and finding ways to support my choices. I hope that my example may support others who find themselves struggling to be true to their hopes and desires in bringing their research into the public domain.

Now that I have finished my doctorate and have a position teaching, I still wonder about those of us who are in "in-between spaces," having done interdisciplinary work. The academy, even as represented by UBC and its willing-ness to allow arts-based research, remains quite rigidly aligned with more traditional approaches and subjects. I hope this conference will play a significant role in seeing that innovative, "cutting edge" research is authentic-ally encouraged and rewarded in the real world of employment at universities. Thank you.

"A grim fairy tale"

Kevin Kirkland's story

with Katrina S. Rogers

- Fictional narrative/playwriting
- Performative exploration/inquiry
- Mythopoetics
- Anti-oppressive pedagogy
- "Taboo" topics

Runner: Now it is my privilege to introduce our next dissertation author, Dr. Kevin Kirkland. Kevin is another one of our presenters who earned a PhD from the University of British Columbia using an arts-based model. In fact, as I'm sure he will tell you, in this case his dissertation supervisor made the recommendation that he consider writing a form of fiction to achieve his dissertation goals. I think this shows how far ahead the Canadian universities are in contrast to most in the U.S. Kevin currently works as a music therapist for the Extended Care Unit at the UBC Hospital in Vancouver, Canada. Kevin, the stage is yours. Thanks for being here.

Kevin: Thank you Runner, and thanks to all of you who are here to truly move higher education toward ever increasing opportunities for creative, sustainable, and anti-oppressive research. I am a gay man researching taboo topics in education and am performatively re-working and "re-righting" my history of mother–son incest as part of that work. Drawing on sourcebooks on wounded story tellers, mythopoetics, performative inquiry, and anti-oppressive pedagogy, my dissertation demonstrates how people can reclaim their voices through narrative approaches, including the fairy tale, even a "grim" one.

I began my doctorate, choosing to research mother–son incest through anti-oppressive pedagogy (in a theme of topics that are silenced such as mental illness, difficult subjects, homosexuality, within the text). I chose my topic based on my own childhood experience that had emerged at age thirty-seven to be dealt with in therapy and in life (one of three children in my family who had been severely sexually abused by our mother). I had a very supportive dissertation committee but we encountered great difficulties when it came to ethics approval because I proposed using autoethnography. It was just too taboo for them, it seems, and despite all the counterarguments and rationale I provided they suggested I change topics altogether. As Runner mentioned, my supervisor suggested fiction. "Why not write it as fiction?" he suggested. I began the writing all over again. It was more satisfying and, I believe, more richly written, than what would ordinarily have basically been a review of the literature and a dry stance on trauma at the center of educational pedagogy.

This topic, never covered in any other dissertation I could find, came to life and to accessibility for the reader (of an otherwise potentially heavy read). I titled the dissertation, "A Grim Fairy Tale: A Mythopoetic Discourse on Trauma, Taboo, and Anti-oppresive Pedagogy." The dissertation is a critical, performative exploration and analysis of mother–son incest as a site for educational inquiry. Particular attention is given to the sexual abuse of gay males and the effects of abuse across the lifespan. The text challenges and re-enacts personal and social perceptions of taboos as spaces of silence, trauma, and transformation, drawing on discourses of anti-oppressive pedagogy and narratives of healing. The arts are performatively incorporated in the healing process through the use of music (a CD of original and pre-composed music accompanies the text), personal photographs, sketches, and poetry. What stories are privileged while others are silenced? What narratives are (not) told, written, and lived in life/education? Anti-oppressive pedagogy writers believe that performatively reworking oppression is a necessary approach in working against oppression and for shifting inaction to action.

My mother taught me most things I know about incest; the rest I learned during the dissertation process. Discourse, dysfunction, drama, and disruption come together in the once upon a time land of mythopoetics and narratives that (en)counter oppression *embedded* within the fabric of societies. The chasms in life's education result from the gap between knowledge and acknowledgment.

I was thirty-seven when a psychologist drew the forbidden knowledge out of me. Research is influenced by what we *don't* ask. Until that time, no one had asked me the question that opened the dam: "Was there anything about incest?" I had never equated a woman with sexual abuse. I thought I was the only person in the world whose mother had used her child for planned and regular sexual assaults. The literature would prove otherwise, as would my family. The youngest of seven, I wasn't the only one. I knew an older brother had been abused, but we had long maintained a tacit understanding to remain mute because of our mother's enormous power in the family dynamic. I later discovered that one of my sisters—aged sixty-two at the time—had also spent many nights in our mother's bed, victim to the blanket of incest that shrouded our family. Our alcoholic father slept upstairs and also worked nights on the railroad, giving her free and chronic access to us. The damage done from our mother's actions has had lifelong repercussions for the three of us.

A year later my entry into doctoral studies drew me to change topics. I wondered, "What if I placed the trauma of sexual abuse at the center of pedagogy?" Schools didn't teach about sexual abuse when I was a kid. I was all too familiar with a curriculum of silence, having grown up gay in a predominantly Catholic small town in northern Alberta. But now here I was, pursuing a PhD at the University of British Columbia with a supervisory committee willingly engaging with the (socially constructed) ultimate taboo. It was time to put culture on the couch.

I found inspiration in the coursework, such as Kogila Adams-Moodley's course called "The Politics of Memory," Susan Edgerton's summer course, "Trauma and Education," and Lyn Fels' "Performative Inquiry," among others. To my amazement and healing, I had found an academic setting willingly supporting the transgression of educational boundaries. Because I planned to use autoethnography, it was deemed best to go through the Behavioral Research Ethics Board (BREB). What are the ethics of writing about taboo subjects? What narratives are (not) told, written, and lived in the academy? Can my memories constitute a methodology? The man at the desk who issued ethics application forms asked, "Is this a behavioral study?" "Yes, I think so," I said hesitantly. "Well, are you interviewing people or dissecting animals?" "Um, no, neither. I'm using autoethnography." He frowned, puzzled. He figured there were sections that wouldn't apply to my approach, but to fill it in as best as possible. I wondered to myself: Where is the *I* in the academy, which seems to be consumed with valid knowledge of the Self only *through* the Other?

My text would also focus on sexually abused gay males, a seemingly correlative "double-edged sword" in my existence. What emerged from initial literature reviews demonstrated my experience was far from unique. Had anyone written an autobiographical dissertation on the subject? I couldn't find one. I envisioned a conceptual work that would be anti-oppressive, incest literature and gay male sexual abuse-based, exploring educational institutions as sites of conspiracies of silence or the crumbling of boundaries, using writing as healing. I submitted twenty copies of the ethics application to the BREB. "No," came the reply via Carl. They had serious concerns: was I stable enough to undertake the work? Shouldn't a psychologist be on my committee? Wouldn't my committee become enmeshed with me because of the presumed highly emotional content of the topic? What about libel? And above all else, they questioned: Does this constitute research? I crafted a six-page reply, rebuttal, and clarification. The Ethics Chair said the Board wouldn't be considering it again: he gave it an unequivocal no. "Why not change topics?"

The Ethics Chair wouldn't speak to me about it, nor correspond with me. As principal investigator it was technically Carl's research, Carl's incest.

Although he recognized that this could have been experienced as retraum-atizing, through Carl's spiritual warrior guidance I saw that the main focus was to complete the dissertation. Advocacy could be carried on afterwards; one must choose the walls you want to sound your trumpets at. We circum-navigated the boulder in the stream of dysconsciousness. I would use f(r)iction as an anti-oppressive device to tell my story, thus bypassing the need for ethical review. I must clarify one point: it would be easy to self-righteously villainize BREB, but they do serve a vital role. I recently applied for a research grant that once again connected me with UBC and BREB. In one section of the ethics application it asks what other methods are being utilized, including auto-biography and action research. I would like to think this is the beginning of a more inclusive concept of what constitutes research.

My committee was looking for a creative text, and I realized I needed permission to engage in the creative process of writing. "A character," Carl suggested, "mulling over the issues." I began the dissertation again. I started with a character brewing over some thoughts. I wrote one page and quickly reached a dead end: he needed dialogue. Freire had said a quality of anti-oppressive pedagogy was the dialogical. Isn't this the very nature of pedagogy? Isn't the education about sexual abuse and its prevention for all? One girl in four, one boy in six. A cast of characters stewing over how things are and how they came to be emerged. It demanded performativity. Paul, a retired professor and now a school librarian, is about to read a fairy tale with the literature appreciation group one evening, telling them: "I only know three things about it. One is that it's a fairy tale. The second is that it's autobiographical. And third, every word is true." In order to transgress the boundaries of silence I also had to transcend my own edges, including talking openly about my research topic and engaging in the unfamiliar territory of arts-based writing by doing sketches, poetry, and playwriting. I also added old photographs of me and recorded a CD of original and pre-composed songs. Soon a cast of characters, each with their own assorted histories, beliefs, attitudes, secrets, and silences, gathered together one evening for a reading of a contemporary fairy tale. The dissertation title became clear: the result for the cast of characters was a mythoclasm: the collapse of previously held myths and legends on personal, familial, and social levels.

Mythopoetics (*mythos*, meaning plot; *poesis*, story making) involves writing and creating meaning for life stories. We tell stories for the sake of other listeners, for the purpose of sharing knowledge. Drawing upon sources about mythopoetics, arts-based research, performative inquiry, and anti-oppressive pedagogy writers such as Kumashiro and Freire, I demonstrated how people can reclaim their voices through narrative, arts-infused approaches. Anti-oppressive pedagogy calls us to performatively rework oppression and to shift inaction to action. Such writing is bound to be seen as contentious and disruptive, even "inappropriate," because it challenges our resistance to envisioning education as a place for speaking and teaching about difficult subjects, social change, and emotionally charged topics.

Act I. Gathering of characters each with their own perspective or history of oppression. Stage is set for the reading of a modern day fairy tale by an unknown author. *Bluebeard* is used as an example of how tales promote ways of knowing and being in the world, how they promote oppression and social attitudes, and especially how myth justifies victimization. I had read that *Bluebeard* was based upon the real life Gille De Rais. I discovered subsequent to the dissertation the truth behind the fairy tale—that De Rais was a raging pedophile who raped and murdered between 40 and 100 boys. The fairy tale metamorphosed his legend into that of a devilish rogue who killed seven wives. The disparaging theme of the naïve, curious woman desperate to marry a man with money was reinforced in favor of silencing the secondary underlying atrocity while perpetuating violence against women as an everyday occurrence. The most important thing I learned through the dissertation process is that *myth justifies victimization.*

Act II. Reading of the fairy tale with its revelation of mother–son incest, the fall out, conflicts, education, and discovery that the author is a member of their group. A fairy tale opens up the world of make believe. By combining *currere,* to run, with *narrare,* to tell, the text challenges the traditional silences where we run *from* telling to where, as Carl said, we run *with* telling.

Act III. The author presents his manifesto, including a summary of the literature of mothers/females as perpetrators of sexual abuse along with the secondary theme of indicators of abuse in gay males.

Act IV. An interview on the Larry King show with the fairy tale's author, models the process of awakening to knowledge from individual to group to larger society. The aftermath of the small group is discussed, including the suicide of one member by drowning because of her own history of abuse, emphasizing how often it's "too little, too late." Further data, research, reasoning, and conclusions are carried through questions, arguments, and support from a guest panel. *Fairy tales can come true, it can happen to you . . .*

My research seeks to open up much needed conversations about experiences that have been largely rendered silent and prohibited; it promotes ways of living with a commitment to seeking wellness in the world.

Why does it work? It uses narrative encounters to elucidate meaning. It demonstrates the need for narrative practices that develop useful repertoires of both an imaginative and practical nature. The text also emphasizes the value of personal transformation and openly questions whose histories we are teaching and promoting. It seeks to trouble the separation of academia and life. Moreover, the play problematizes oppression in education and demonstrates performative ways of dealing with traumatic histories and events. Engaging with mythic and symbolic writing and characters had a rapture and rupture all its own. The writing at times became so powerful, the text so alive, that I would find myself excited in anticipation of what was unfolding or in front of the toilet bowl heaving yet again. These were necessary avenues for moving beyond the text.

The moral of the story is that it is unconscionable and unethical that sexual abuse continues to dwell in exile on the periphery of educational discourse in many school and academic settings. It is tragic that university classrooms and ethics committees continue to silence the individual voice of witness, victim, survivor, student, teacher. We must include subjects that arouse emotion, that trouble and disturb, that provoke and evoke, because these subjects are within the lived experiences of many people. We are called to empower those who have endured abuse to write their stories and to be their own researchers, archaeologists, and architects so they can rebuild personal and educational foundations. (*Audience applause*)

Runner: Thank you Kevin. I think your story is a powerful illustration of the connections that can exist between other ways of knowing and teaching, and critical issues of our times being given attention in higher education.

To add to Kevin's presentation, I've asked one of our guest scholars to say a few words. Katrina S. Rogers is an Associate Dean of Research and Practice at Fielding Graduate University and is Director of FGU's Institute for Social Innovation. She is currently involved with an important project relating to sustainability and globalization in Canada, as well. Katrina.

Katrina Rogers: What intrigues about Kevin's and others' work being described in this conference is the overall sense of adventure, and perhaps the kinds of courage that often accompany adventure. We say, let us step off the cliff of our disciplinary selves and seek the narrow and sunny ledges below. We say, let us experiment with language and let us seek to know things by different means. Let us not assume we understand what the elephant looks like by examining only the trunk. Let us embrace the mystery that is embedded in our own understanding. This takes courage, the kind of scholarly courage Kevin needed to do his important work.

In my own work, it all started with a dream, a dream with a nightmarish quality. The creature swirled out of the mist in front of where I was sitting, crouched with several others in a circle. "How do we come to know things about the world?" said the creature to my mind as it, too, huddled with us in the fading light. Some say that it has to do with categorization; we know things when we can name them, classify them, and sort them on to the different shelves where knowledge is kept. Others say that we know things through experience; in the doing of the thing, it becomes clear. Still others say we know nothing at all. At best, we glimpses shadows of reality, as our minds and bodies experience the world and interpret both its abstract and concrete qualities.

"It seems to me," the creature reflected, "that it all comes down to inter-pretation." Hardly an original thought, I groused to myself, but then stared at the light and wondered. The hot, dry, high desert wind blew over us, slowly beginning to quiet, to let us know that the day would soon be ending and night would fall. And it was in this wondering that I woke up, feeling hot and lightheaded, as if the wind, and the creature, were still present in my bedroom.

I began to think about whether it would be possible to use the ancient art of interpretation as a way of understanding some "thing" in the contemporary academic world. I had been studying history, politics, international relations, and environmental problems. All of these subjects were taught to me, and I learned them through the lens of liberalism, *realpolitik*, and the other hege-monic forces of the disciplines at the time, caught by their attractive neatness and false clarity. Globalization is good because it allows a Western style of life to pervade the planet, which is better than Indigenous culture. Ruining the planet? No problem. We will simply solve our environmental problems with technological fixes. Rather than question our assumptions, we shall simply pretend that evidence to the contrary does not exist.

I wrote my doctorate about international relations in the waning days of the Cold War, which in itself was an assumed construct that neglected the reality of many other parts of the world outside the Soviet–U.S. political construction. I took on the assumptions made by political scientists and argued that interpreting their actions as texts in a hermeneutic sense gave us far more insight to past, present, and future events and trends than the tired old theories that were based on political ideologies. Furthermore, current theory ignored both the understanding and experiences of the people in most of the rest of the world.

Authentic curiosity (and the adventuresome spirit to act on it) is a char-acteristic important to understanding. One way to think about using such curiosity would be to aspire to the kind of embodied scholarship represented by Kevin's work. Embodied scholarship means embracing the full nature of both our heads and our hearts to bring to bear on epistemological questions. It offers a comprehensive way of knowing, which doesn't privilege certain methods or others, or certain cultural norms over others. It is both *personal*, grounded in the sum of the individual's emotions and thoughts, and *intellectual*, rooted in a tradition of holism. I have greatly appreciated what I have heard thus far in this conference and look forward to hearing more!

"Masks in metaxis"

Warren Linds's story

- Circular hermeneutics
- *Theater of the Oppressed* and *Forum Theater*
- Transformative drama
- Body–mind work
- Hermeneutics/phenomenology
- Performative writing

Runner: Our last presenter in this session on drama work in dissertations is Dr. Warren Linds. He was an instructor in the Faculty of Education, University of Regina and in the Saskatchewan Urban Native Teacher Education Program. He is currently an Assistant Professor in Applied Human Sciences at Concordia University. His doctorate is another one from the University of British Columbia, which seems to be, along with Fielding Graduate University, the source of many of our most creative dissertations being represented here. His interests are in the facilitation and development of transformative drama processes through a performative writing and research methodology. He is also interested in the exploration of drama as an anti-racist pedagogy and how embodied and reflective experiences of improvisation in teaching are developed. Among other publications, he is a co-editor of the 2001 text, *Unfolding Bodymind: Exploring Possibility Through Education*. Warren.

Warren Linds: Hello everyone. I'm honored to be here at this conference. I have been a drama workshop facilitator for fifteen years before, and during, the writing of my dissertation. This involves engaging with groups through theater games and trust exercises. This process explores verbal and non-verbal communication and comes to an understanding of social issues directly from experience. Often, these workshops end in a *Forum Theater* presentation. *Forum Theater* is a theatrical approach where a problem is shown in an unsolved form, to which the audience (spect-actors) is invited to suggest and enact solutions. Many alternative solutions are enacted in the course of a single forum—the result is a pooling of knowledge, tactics, and experience.

I wrote a poem that came to me at a moment when I felt I was stuck writing my dissertation in Language and Literacy Education at the University of British Columbia about my work facilitating these processes. I wrote:

> Explorer, Mentor, Interrogator,
> an Animateur, Provocateur, Difficultator.
> An Instructor, Friend, Expert, Guide, Presenter, Planner,
> Coaching from the side . . .
> Or just along for the Ride?

I think it sums up how I felt about a year before I eventually defended. I had submitted to my committee what I thought was a completed dissertation. The text consisted of several chapters about my work as a facilitator. Using a variety of writing styles to share my experiences and doing a critical analysis of my stories, the dissertation's structure reflected the framework of a drama workshop—entering the workshop space, having a talking circle, introducing the facilitator, group building and trust exercises, developing scenes, performing a play, and discussing the implications for action (i.e. for facilitation). One of my advisors said to me then, "You have written some wonderful texts, but I am not sure I know what *you* think about what you have written."

The comment was a challenge to me both in terms of my writing, and in terms of what I was writing *about.* I felt the underlying question was "*What is this body of the facilitator and how can we begin to understand it in all its various forms of relationships within the workshop?*" The approach I was using in theater workshops was based on adaptations of Augusto Boal's *Theater of the Oppressed* where participants engage in a collective creation process to develop short interactive plays about social justice issues as they experience them in their lives. In this creative process, actors develop a short improvised play out of their own experiences. In inter-acting with audience members who are spect-actors (in that they intervene, on stage, taking the place of particular characters at certain moments in the play), they are constantly shifting between the character they are playing and their own experiences.

I thought, you don't write *about* this kind of thing; you write *through* it. I wrote the major sections of my dissertation in several parts about experiences that had happened to me as drama workshop facilitator, both recently and up to thirty years ago. Thus these layers upon layers of experiencing were writings I had some distance from. I re-visited, re-collected, and re-newed my acquaintance with these experiences with/in these texts. I was also the origin of these texts, yet these texts announced me as facilitator. So, the temporal distance from the physical experience helped me to re-illuminate them, but it was still a challenge to get to know the text of my living experiencing as "object" while also continuing to be engaged with it. This seemed to be a vicious circle but it wasn't. I applied Hans-Georg Gadamer's approach to hermeneutic text as articulated in *Truth and Method*. In the circular hermeneutic process of making what was familiar to me strange and in re-acquainting myself with the unfamiliar, I re-discovered facilitation. At the same time I engaged in an interpretation of my experiences, which, I hoped, opened up spaces for others to engage with.

My particular focus in the dissertation titled "A Journey in Metaxis: Been, Being, Becoming, Imag(in)ing Drama Facilitation" was the role of the body and mind (bodymind) of facilitator and participants in workshops as we journeyed into a co-emerging awareness of senses, personal and social histories, the landscapes we work in, and the relationships that intertwine through the constant ebb and flow of dramatic interplay. I played with forms of texts, languages and styles in order to enter into the text(ure) of the worlds of facilitation. Bringing together body mind world and spirit, I hoped we would come face to face with experiences remembered and reconsidered. Through writing, I re-awakened the memory of my senses and re-connected with them in the moments of "performing" my teaching. Writing from and through such a sensing body means that my reflection on practice was not only just a reporting of experiences, but also a celebration and expression of the multi-vocal, multi-layered experiences that is the development of drama facilitation skills. Through such poetic and expressive writing I explored ways that enabled an evocation of the world of drama in my text.

Wanting to "walk my practice" (of interactive workshops) through the dissertation, I hoped to enable the reader/audience to participate in the text by opening their senses and emotions to, and enabling interactions with, our experiences of the text as a living medium. In addition to my commentary, I hoped that themes and content would (e)merge with/from readers' interests as they read.

Perhaps through this interactive process I was also trying to open up the possibilities of the transformative drama process, where style, expression, and its significance in particular social processes leads to new processes of communication, understanding, and action. Such poetic and expressive writing enables an evocation of the world of drama, allowing the reader/audience to participate in the text. Opening up my senses to the momentary present, the text enables a mutual triggering between and amongst I as practitioner/writer and the reader/audience, with the text as living medium.

Writing thus becomes a form of performance that brings forth experiences that become present; first in the writing, then the reading. This idea of performance is clarified by looking at it as a translation from the French word *représentation*. Moving from the English sense of the word (descriptive fidelity, to "stand-in" for something) to one French sense (performance) moves us beyond approximating or substituting for experience (and experience not as something separate from me, but part of my life). Performative writing is not a description of a past event; rather, it abolishes time, making the past immediate and present. In bringing the reader past and forward to the future, some solid ground is created. But this solid ground in the moment of the present is swept away if we pay attention to our interactions with the text. The past and future become traces, as the text and the reader pass through the transitory present of reading. Such texts are plays with no final curtain, with all the ambiguities that implies, where, through particular forms and styles of writing there is space for the writer and the reader to engage *through* the text. Being "writerly" means the authors don't attempt to control the actions or feelings of the reader but, instead, create a structure where individuals can bring themselves into the text. When there is such room, there will be discomfort, ambiguity, and uncertainty about what we will discover about ourselves through the story that is being explored.

In response to my advisor's question, I was drawn to the idea of "masks" as characters of the facilitator speaking through the dissertation. Drawing from Brecht's clowns and Boal's Joker, and extending the idea of embodied reflection in a workshop, I developed masks as commentators that are involved in the facilitation of the workshop. This exteriorization and distancing through writing of my inner dialogues about facilitation brings in the in-between-ness between the workshop stage and the world.

These dialogues speak through four points of view as I wrote them "into being." Their perspective helped me understand, as well as unfolded from, my sense of the work. I saw them as points of departure that helped me in a hermeneutic process that deepened my understanding from, and through, the patterns of my facilitation. This process of interpretation and interrogation through the theatrical mask developed the skeleton connecting it to a body (inter)acting in the landscape of the workshop. Taking a journey into each "mask" meant looking at what I saw through it, (inter)acted with it, and felt/thought inside it. The masks chosen, per se, were not examined in depth, but my musings/trying outs/exploring of what this perspective *might* mean kept options for action open and projected possibility around every corner. This enabled me to distance myself from my practice as well as explore its familiarity. In other words, these "masks" became hermeneutic interpreters within me, and each one commented in a form of "workshop notes" at different times within the workshop/play process. In this interaction of writing masks into being and reading the main sections of the dissertation, there is an interplay between content, methodology, and re-presentation, with each section intertwining with the characteristics of the particular mask that will comment on it.

The masks I chose were based on, and integrated into, the structure of the dissertation—that is, the workshop plan. *Shaman* (embodying energy), *Diver/*

Diviner (intuiting acting), *Wri(gh)ter* (sensing creating), and *Joker* (transforming bridging). Each commented on one appropriate section of the workshop/ dissertation. I concluded the dissertation by gathering all four masks around a sharing circle and discussing what had come before (staging departures).

I brought one of the masks with me for you all to see. This one is div(*in*)er. It looks like an unusual mask. One that takes risky jumps but, at the same time, also develops a sense of intuition. It might seem to you now that this is a split personality, but it is two personalities working together, acting and sensing together as they find themes through the theater activities and then propose them as subjects for thematic exploration through improvisation and scene-building. When this mask is called div(*in*) er, it intertwines the acts of divining—probing from above, and diving—jumping in, to get below the surface.

When I put on this mask, a new kind of knowing emerges from this process of interstanding between I the diviner, I the diver and the not-I, the other. *Diving* and *divining* connect so we begin to see everything in new ways. Thinking of learning drama facilitation as a quest means that diving cannot result in pre-determined outcomes. I find myself underwater, where things appear differently from how they looked from above the water. Pretty stones I bring up to the surface look plain in the air. How light refracts underwater means that even if I see something from above, I find it difficult to grasp. The knowing I gain in any process changes in its application. Through drama new versions of our story, in new languages, emerge to be explored at a distance away from our day-to-day experience. I hope this brief presentation gives you a sense of my journey. (*Applause*)

Dr. Samson: Very nice Warren, but why would not a dissertation committee see all of this as merely a self-indulgent exercise. Can you comment on the effect of this on your work after completing the dissertation?

Warren: Yes. We often just think of our dissertation as a text that will sit on a shelf somewhere. We don't think of the effect of writing it on our own teaching and research practice. But much as my workshop facilitation attempts to link the world of the workshop to the world outside the workshop (that participants bring in), I have found my dissertation is also connected to my practice as an Assistant Professor of Applied Human Sciences at Concordia University and in continuing my work as a theater workshop facilitator. For example, there is one effect on my own teaching that I hadn't anticipated. I now ask my students to pay attention to their experiences in class and to write about them. I ask them to engage in reflective writing, but to start with description about what happened, then to engage in critical analysis. To me, writing this way is an important aspect of academic and practical work that hasn't been paid attention to very much in works on action, or participatory, research. There is a difference between merely noting that an experience occurred or that you had a particular response to something, and thinking about how you responded to an experience, why you had a particular response, and what you learned from the experience and your response to it. So the work I did in my dissertation writing has carried through with helping both undergraduate and graduate students look at their own learning, particularly in becoming effective facilitators and community development workers.

"Passion and sparks"
George H. Elder's story

with Sandra K. Winn

- Dialogue
- Social communication
- Neuroscience
- Accessibility

Dr. Samson: George H. Elder is our next presenter. He received his PhD in Speech Communication/Rhetoric from Penn State in 1990 with a minor in Psychology. His dissertation, "The Scientific Foundation of Social Communication: From Neurons to Rhetoric," was subsequently published as a book with the same title. George has given me a note here to read as part of his introduction, so please know that this was his idea, not mine. I don't want to get in trouble with anyone, especially him.

(*Reading*) George is a former coach, bouncer, weightlifter, drug addict, dreamer, and petty miscreant who was led by fate into becoming a scholar. He is ill-equipped by disposition to deal with academic pretenses and politics, but he was felt to have promise by those he studied under. As a scholar, he sought to find a scientific basis for how communication literally changes our minds. He dove deep into the neurosciences during this quest, and when he broke surface he realized that the only way to describe the processes involved to a humanistic audience was via a story. And so he led each chapter of his dissertation with an ongoing dialogue that described general principles in a user-friendly fashion. He then turned to an academic narrative, appendices, and footnotes for the remainder of each chapter to please the scholars. The effort was long and intense, and was eventually published as a book. After George got his degree . . . he walked away from the academy altogether. He simply did not fit that community, and now wanders the world unfulfilled—a good teacher, forever seeking students that he will never find.

George: When I first presented the ideas I had for my dissertation, no one on my dissertation committee felt anyone could satisfactorily describe how communication induces actual morphological changes in the brain because the subject was both broad and deep. Moreover, it was felt the scientific material would be so far outside the humanistic realm as to be beyond interpretation by most members in our "rhetorical" community.

Nonetheless, I demonstrated how the story could be told in a user-friendly way via dialogue, and my committee members condescended—rather reluctantly—to allowing a dialogue to introduce each chapter. A subsequent narrative section would express the contents of the dialogue in a "scholarly" fashion, along with notes and appendices. And so I spent over three years writing the story.

It was a monster project, involving 1,800 sources and many drafts. The dissertation ended up being 1,500 pages long, but condensed into a 450-page textbook. In fact, my dissertation was published as a book by NOVA Sciences, and was the first dissertation to be so published in a very long time by someone from my department.

I am sure that "The Scientific Foundation of Social Communication: from Neurons to Rhetoric" didn't sell more than a few hundred copies, but it was worth the effort. And the dialogue is easy to read—and thus accessible to a lay audience. Indeed, the dialogue discussed stories and schema theory à la Bartlett and some of his early work on the subject. Yes, an old Eskimo tale is discussed in the text, along with how the narrative form interacts with our creation of meaning.

Before I decided on using dialogue, I had taken several playwriting classes. I used this technique because the subject matter I addressed was very complex —as in neuroanatomy and related processes that form the basis of what we call thought. A dialogue allows one to relate complex information in a casual fashion—one that is not encumbered with footnotes, endnotes, and other inclusion that ruin the flow of ideas. Moreover, ideas can be wrapped up in emotions via the use of dialogue, and that has a power in itself that we seldom see in most academic texts. In fact, academic writing has to be the most tedious ever devised, and it stifles creativity in many ways.

The purpose of the dissertation and book was to review and apply modern findings that provide theoretical, critical, and practical insights into rhetoric's classical canons of invention, arrangement, style, memory, and delivery. Collectively, the still-vibrant canons address persuading, informing, and pleasing audiences, although they also embody many other pedagogical and communication-oriented purposes. However, the text is not bound by the canons, because findings are also related to a wide range of contemporary communication doctrines and scholarly perspectives. Hence a postmodernist may benefit from examining how schema theory is useful in explaining the formation of epistemes while a classical scholar can find valuable new insights into how the ancients' mnemonic systems operate.

My dialogue is between a taciturn professor emeritus of neuropsychology and a graduate student in rhetoric. The dialogue is accessible to all readers, regardless of their expertise in communication, psychology, or the neurosciences. There are narrative, notes, and appendices sections that follow each dialogue, and these allow readers to address the subjects that the dialogues cover in a conventional and very detailed fashion. In addition, chapter schematics and other referencing tools provide readers with easy access to information. This format allows anyone from a novice to upper-level researcher to glean valuable insights into how the mind operates and changes, and it makes the work an extremely useful teaching and reference tool.

I can also explain the chosen format by way of dialogue:

DR. GREGG: I have to tell you, Alexander, I'm not at all sure that a dialogue is a good way to write a dissertation.

ALEXANDER: You've told me that before. But I'm addressing an audience that knows next to nothing about the processes occurring within our brain as we process information. This changes our brain in physical ways, and that's the essence of what rhetoric does.

DR. GREGG: You don't have to convince me. I've written a lot about it.

DR. CORNWELL: I think Richard's concern is that your dissertation committee and many others aren't accustomed to reading dialogues.

ALEXANDER: I think they've all read Plato—and seen lots of movies and plays.

DR. GREGG: Yes, but Plato wrote about definitions, and general themes—such as what defined "good." You're going to discuss extremely technical matters, such as how neurons are interlinked to form memories.

DR. CORNWELL: And how communication plays a role in that process.

ALEXANDER: Then what better tool can there be to tell the story other than a dialogue? Our earliest learning experiences involve stories. Gosh, I can still hear my mother's tales about selling vegetables on the streets of West Lebanon, New Hampshire. The memories are fresh and clear—like how she used to secretly buy candy with some of the daily take. And then there was Ted and Jane, Dr. Seuss, and on and on. And after all, Dr. Gregg, isn't a good lecture a story?

DR. GREGG: In a sense. But it's a story that's predicated upon students being on the same page with regard to knowing the underlying material. And I'm telling you, understanding how the sensory organs process verbal and nonverbal inputs isn't like comprehending a typical Grimm's Fairy Tale! And that's just the first step in examining how communication can modulate memory.

DR. CORNWELL: And thus behavior. I believe a dialogue can describe these processes, yet it's a difficult thing to do. I'm a neuropsychologist, but I fully understand how important it is for messages to be tailored to audiences. And I would think your audience is very accustomed to reading what you call linear narratives. So why should any academic indulge your fancies when it comes to reading a dialogue?

DR. GREGG: Paul has an important point. Dialogues don't do a thing for me. Maybe that's because we favor what we've become accustomed to—but that doesn't make my point any less valid.

ALEXANDER: Are you going to tell me that humans aren't accustomed to telling and hearing stories? We were children long before we became academics. We could dream and wonder. We loved listening to stories and telling them to friends. And I've heard both of you tell wonderful stories, so please don't say you've lost the ability! It's the damn academic style that blinded us to accepting the way we once were. We wear the academic style like a robe and badge of achievement. Eventually, we arrive at the stage wherein we cannot tell one piece of literature from another because they all sound the same.

DR. GREGG: I'm not sure I accept what you say. I think a style has evolved that allows us to examine points and counterpoints in a rational way. Notes and footnotes permit us to see the support for what is being said, and to reflect about its veracity.

ALEXANDER: But what is there to really reflect upon? There is no real disagreement within the text! A fair academic may present a few straw-men dissenting opinions that he then knocks down. And he can do that because the text is dead. The opposition simply isn't there to provide a good counterpoint because we're all taught to think and write in an essentially monological fashion. You may bring some counterpoints to the stage, but many do not. We become passive and uninvolved, as likely to fall asleep as we are to learn. God, I hate writing like that. Footnotes, appendices, and sources are substituted for passion and sparks.

DR. CORNWELL: But you have to consider what Richard is saying. I like the idea of a dialogue, but how will you answer Richard's concerns?

ALEXANDER: I'll do what I dread. At the end of each dialogue, I'll include a heavily annotated text that reviews what the dialogue presents.

DR. GREGG: Then you've doubled your workload—and for what gain?

ALEXANDER: The dialogue will allow readers to grasp the essential points in an easily understood fashion—while the narrative permits academics to garner greater insights into various details.

DR. GREGG: Can you prove what you say is true?

ALEXANDER: I can cite study after study that shows the story form is more readily assimilated and remembered than is academic writing.

DR. CORNWELL: Yes, there is lots of literature on that. But I think Richard needs more of a reason for considering this format than a dialogue allowing the essence of various points to be more easily grasped.

ALEXANDER: It's not just the dialogue format! We know that the emotions evoked by dialogues and stories can help people memorize general themes and many details.

DR. GREGG: Well, we know emotions can help memory formation in some cases. But do you think this can work in a dialogue about memory formation?

ALEXANDER: I know it can! Because if the people reading this dialogue knew the whole story, they'd realize I'm talking to two dead teachers who helped the dissertation we're discussing become a reality. And you ripped my heart out when you died, Dr. Cornwell. It was so damn unexpected.

DR. CORNWELL: It's kind of ironic. I was reading one of you're dialogues at the time. I think it was for Chapter 3 or 4. It all seems like a dream now.

ALEXANDER: It was a nightmare for me! They found your notes in the hospital. They were beside your bed. I didn't even know you were f'n sick! And there you were, reading the text right before the heart surgery that killed you. And when I found out, I cried. Good Lord, how I cried. Tears are welling up even as I type this. You were the brightest man I ever knew—and you understood . . .

DR. CORNWELL: I tried to understand. And please don't shed tears for me.

ALEXANDER: And your last note on my text was, "This can work." That's what drove me to complete the project.

DR. GREGG: Your passing was a shock, Paul. I remember how hard we tried to find another outside member. But I was still skeptical about the project working. And let me tell you, using both the dialogue and essay approach produced a 1,500 page monster—with 1,800 sources.

DR. CORNWELL: I had a feeling that would happen. Perhaps an annotated dialogue would have been better.

ALEXANDER: Yes, that's what I'd do if I had to write it again.

DR. GREGG: But I think the narrative helped sell the work as a book. And quite frankly, I was a bit surprised when it got published.

ALEXANDER: I hope I did right by you, Dr. Gregg. Your death bothered me a lot.

DR. GREGG: Well, I lived long enough to see your work published, and that made me feel good. I wish you had followed up on it though—although someone like you cannot survive in the academy. You're overly temperamental. And don't feel bad for me! I've no regrets about dying. In the end, it was quick, and I wasn't looking forward to more chemo.

ALEXANDER: I still think of you. I always liked your table analogy. We are all friends gathered at the feast of life. Every so often one leaves the table, and another takes an empty seat. But the dialogue goes on and on.

DR. CORNWELL: And do you think this dialogue has accomplished anything?

ALEXANDER: I wasn't given many pages. But the subject was introduced, and we showed that a dialogue project can work in an academic setting. And perhaps we also showed the power of emotion in helping us to form memories. I sure hope we did. I miss you two.

DR. GREGG: I think the ancient Egyptians believed that as long as your name is spoken, you're never dead.

ALEXANDER: And that is yet another story. I am heading your way, my friends, but there is still some way to go.

(Enter Verity)

VERITY: Ah, you still seek certainty in a Universe of constant change! It is impossible.

ALEXANDER: I seek a bit more certainty than can usually be achieved by using the written word—and especially when using a dialogue. After all, the readers can only guess and assume what we meant about this or that.

VERITY: There is nothing the matter with that! The poet speaks to our heart and moves us. The direction each one goes may not be the same, but the movement is made. Is this a bad thing?

ALEXANDER: It might be if the poet wanted to share a very specific emotion or thought.

VERITY: Only mathematicians seek such certainty! But the numbers they use paint ideas in much different ways than words.

ALEXANDER: Yes, even Plato turned toward numbers in the end. He felt numbers were less prone to misinterpretation than are words.

VERITY: What a silly man! The mathematic has the syntax and tools to guide the exact understanding of relationships between this and that—how you describe them—variables? So yes, this more exact meaning can be communicated, but math does not move us to commune in the same way as words. Can one describe hate, love, greed, or lust with math? Can one write this page as a set of formulae?

ALEXANDER: Well . . .

VERITY: And now you will say truth is One, and lies are 3? These numbers are—they are now merely being used as adjectives, adverbs, nouns, and such things. The way they are used comes from the social convention, and they have no meaning outside that. To say to the Moslem woman that she is a 10 will only meet with confusion. So do not tell Verity that these numbers make the meaning easier to understand. You, my friend, are dead wrong.

ALEXANDER: You understand more of the philosophical underpinnings of Western society than you intimate! But I'm far more interested in the reader finding the meaning I wish to convey! If I cannot communicate what I intend, then any form of writing is both futile and dangerous.

VERITY: How selfish you are! And how little you understand the observer's need to create meaning. This is the thing called freedom! It is part of what we are and how we think.

ALEXANDER: You're advocating chaos under the guise of freedom! Some may make conclusions that are completely opposite to what I or any one else intended. Can't you see the harm this could do?

VERITY: I do not believe free thought can be such a bad thing.

ALEXANDER: So a student assumes that any meaning he or she creates is correct, and goes through life this way. There is thus no right or wrong answer. Indeed, there is no right or wrong. A certain law means what I interpret it to mean, and thus I do as I wish. This results in a society wherein the perceptions of the individual can assume ascendance over the common good.

VERITY: So our little dialogue can bring an end to civilization? Is this what you think?

ALEXANDER: Here I seek to find meaning and truth, and you go off on tangents.

VERITY: And what of Verity's desires? Do I not have the right to speak as I will? Do I not seek to describe the reality we share in my own terms? How the sun and wind feels on my skin. How the sand on the beach feels underneath Verity's feet. But you go on and on about the words and control. Was it not you who just said words were useless because they mean different things to different people? Now you tell Verity you can make the words mean what you intend or what the reader interprets?

ALEXANDER: I cannot achieve perfect . . .

VERITY: You writers, you have the greedy little minds. But if you truly understood the words, then you would let them be free.

ALEXANDER: But I believe in freedom! I never said words didn't mean—W-w-where are you going?

VERITY: For the long walk.

(*Applause*)

Dr. Samson: Thanks George. You seem to have touched a chord with folks if I am reading the audience body language correctly. Sandra, I see you would like to respond. Folks, Sandra is from Albany, New York and went to school at the State University of New York in Albany. She is currently an Assistant Professor at the Albany College of Pharmacy and teaches communication in the Writing Center. Sandra.

Sandra K. Winn: Well, I resonate with much of what George has said, not only about communication, but also about his frustration with the academic resistance to his doctoral research. Creating and maintaining a dissertation panel was one of the most stressful experiences of my doctoral program. I changed panel members several times. Some of them just left my committee without telling me. Sometimes, it was due to the professor changing jobs, or it was due to philosophical differences pertaining to my dissertation topic. Or someone did not like the methodology used for data collection and disagreed with my ideas about emergent education practices. It was really a nightmare.

Let me begin with some background information before sharing why my panel "experience" was so difficult. After getting my Master's degree, I was encouraged to get my PhD in the education field. I researched what was required to complete this degree and decided that I would prefer to pursue a degree that allowed me to create a curriculum for myself. Thus, I switched to a Doctoral Arts program in Humanistic Studies. The focus of this program is to merge two fields together and study these through a humanistic lens. This appealed to me since my interests lay both in the fields of education and communication. I felt that how students and teachers interpersonally communicate was under-studied, thus, my choice was made. I found that, because of my interest in progressive education, the education department was not quick to embrace my work. Instead, I found my home in the communication department and actively pursued studying and understanding progressive educational practices through a communication vantage point. I loved it.

This brings me to my panel. Like my classes, my dissertation did not follow the typical format. Upon completion, the paper very much looked like other qualitative research. However, its content never followed the popular strain in the education field. I sometimes wonder if this is why one of my first education department faculty members took another job and never told me that he was leaving. After having collected books to read for my comprehensive exams and meeting with him regularly, this person just left without a word or explanation why. It was very disconcerting as I began the search for a professor who was willing to work with a student who was determined to look outside the box and do something different.

I thought that I found this person. He agreed to be on my panel as well. He changed the entire comprehensive exam list and sent me off to study all new educational titles. The list is comprised of twelve journal articles or books; books comprised most of my list. I studied for four months. I sat for a six-hour written exam on communication, education, and humanities concepts. This was followed by an oral exam with the entire panel present. In the exam, I was questioned by all present about the answers I gave on my written exams. At one point, I was challenged about an answer I gave in the education component. I had answered the question the way that I believed the panel member would have wanted me to answer it. However, my panel chair knew that I believed differently from what I wrote on the exam. Hence, the debate began. I did give my argument against what I had written, which was a surprise to everyone except my chair. I passed the exam. However, after this, the person from the education department asked to be removed from my panel without explanation.

At this point, I had to find another person to serve on my panel as my education representative. I went to ask another faculty member who is well versed in and committed to qualitative research methodologies. When I described what I had planned for my dissertation, she quickly declined to join my panel. Her reasoning was that she was not comfortable with doing emergent research, which required that my questions came out of my data. The hunt began again.

This time, I bypassed having anyone represent education on my panel for my dissertation defense. I had requested that I no longer have to look for someone from education to work with me. Instead, I had two people each from communication and humanities sit on the panel.

At my proposal defense, I approached my research very differently. I had collected all of my data first and designed questions based upon what I was seeing while in the field. I wrote my proposal from this. When my defense date came, yet again a large academic debate ensued. This time, I was not the recipient of the questioning only an observer. The panel became divided as to how my final dissertation document should be written. The humanities professors felt that the dissertation did not need any research component at all, while my chair (who was housed in the communication department) felt that research was essential for relaying my subjects' experiences, albeit the research methods and presentation were not traditional.

After my proposal defense, I felt that I wanted to have an education professor as part of my panel process. I looked to a person who was not on campus. She was a professor elsewhere. I wrote my first 100 pages and sent this out to the entire panel to review. I received comments from this professor that referred to the need for triangulation and validity in my methods. My approach to my dissertation was not traditional. I was not going to use any quantitative means to prove my thesis. I wanted to relay the experiences seen by the students and teachers to explain a different way of learning. Triangulation and validity didn't fit into this model and neither did this education professor. With this, I abandoned the idea of having any education professor sit on my panel.

When it came to the final defense of my dissertation, the initial two humanities professors changed due to philosophical differences and I had four education professors leave. At my defense, I had one new humanities professor, no education professor, and my two initial communication professors. They questioned me as a colleague on my work, which they were all intimate with by this point. They encouraged me to publish this work and were visibly proud of my accomplishments. I am grateful that my chair stayed with me through the whole process; he was supportive, encouraging, helpful, and open to approaching materials in a very innovative and different manner.

Thanks for letting me share this story with you, as I know many of you have faced or will face similar challenges. I just wanted to encourage you to stay true to your vision in spite of the resistance you might receive.

Dr. Samson: Thanks Sandra. Well, we've run out of time, so we'll see you all tomorrow!

Day six

Autobiography/autoethnography

All art is autobiographical. The pearl is the oyster's autobiography.

(Federico Fellini)

"The educator's voice or 'the club?' "

Sigmund A. Boloz's story

- Autoethnography
- Critical autoethnography
- Poetry
- Field notes

Runner: Our sessions today are about biographical stories, whether autobiographical or the stories of those researched. As with all of our presentations, these defy classification. Forms of representation include poetry and the world's first electronic dissertation.

Our first presenter has not yet completed his doctoral dissertation, but he is a distinguished educator and an acclaimed poet in his own right. His story, however, reminds us of what can be lost when we dismiss autobiography from academic legitimacy. Valuable "new knowledge" from Sig's remarkable twenty-two-year history as a public school principle on the Navajo Indian reservation might have been lost to school reform literature had he chosen to join "the club," rather than stay true to his goal. Sig is currently a Lecturer at Northern Arizona University.

Sig.: Thank you Runner. It is a pleasure to be here and my decision to write a critical autoethnography has been confirmed by listening to the previous speakers. The title of my proposed dissertation is "A Critical Autoethnography of the Role of the School Principle in School Reform: A Twenty-two-year Journey within a School-wide Literacy Development Effort." It describes and brings meaning to twenty-two years of school reform efforts within one school site located entirely within the boundaries of the Navajo Nation, as documented through the daybook (journal) entries of one school principal. These school reform efforts are defined as those specifically related to the development of the school's integrated language literacy program. With it, I seek to uncover the personal meanings and implications of school reform of one individual as a participant within multiple cultures: the culture of the school, the culture of the community, and the culture of the wider educational system. Using the lens of a critical theory perspective, the focus is on the principal's documented recollections of agency and resistance which were recorded as the events unfolded or shortly thereafter. This study contributes to the literature addressing school reform by examining those efforts from within the process and identifying the lens through which progress can be made in improving school reform efforts.

From 1980 until my retirement from public school education in 2002, I was the principal of a small, rural school district located entirely within the Navajo Nation in northeast Arizona. The school was located in one of the four poorest counties in America. Nonetheless, we received numerous national and state recognitions including superior designations from the International Reading Association and the National Council of Teachers of English, and the U.S. Department of Education's ultimate performance stamp as a National Blue Ribbon School. As important, this school, which serves a mostly Native population and which employs an almost entirely Native teaching staff, has been awarded the extremely limited and highly sought-after Arizona A+ School title three times in an eighteen-year span, and more important, during one of those years was named The Number One School in Arizona.

Each year from 1984 to 2002, I crowded the pages of three to four daybooks with diagrams, observations, vignettes, memoirs, and reflections about staff, students, and the personal (family) and educational communities that affected our work. The writing and reflection was important to me; however, I had never had the time to look back at the process and to try to understand our journey.

With a wagon-filled experience but without a degree, I eagerly considered the possibility of beginning a process to examine the contents of my daybooks as a part of the formal doctoral dissertation. Yet, exploring the sixty-eight daybooks, which spanned my years as principal, as a data source for a dissertation immediately met resistance. The "gatekeepers" informed me that a dissertation had to emerge around "new material," not work that had already been completed. Although my daybook entries represented years-upon-years of reflection and were neither written nor collected for the purpose of being used in a dissertation, the potential data source did not meet with approval.

I was, of course, disappointed. I felt that my daybooks are an innovative data source and important to the field for at least three reasons. First, few research efforts concerning school reform are longitudinal in nature. My study might provide the only twenty-two-year perspective of one school's struggle to search for quality. Second, most school reform research is conducted by those outside the process, and my research focuses on the inner workings of a group of practitioners. Finally, my dissertation reflects the efforts of a rural and under-served population. Too often, mainstream social scientists focus on educators as the Other—and, however well-meaning, end up defining us as a problem to be solved. Rather than looking again at the failures of underrepresented groups, my reflections on these years of journals would afford a chance to study success.

As the semesters clicked away, although I received support for my ideas from a number of people, the pressures to abide by a more traditional definition of "acceptable research" grew. Regardless of my more than thirty years of experience in the trenches of actual schooling, I was informed that if I wanted to be admitted as a member of "the club," I would "have to forget what I knew about writing and relearn to write as a scholar." Also, I was asked by some, how would I prove that my entries are "valid" and not simply the rantings of a self-serving educator? True, I was the person responsible for the journal entries and these were my interpretations of the experiences described. I admit that others may have seen these experienced differently. But, as important, what did I understand and might those perspectives be valuable to some others?

If all of this was not discouraging enough, because I had been admitted to the doctoral program within the department of teaching and learning, another apprehension expressed to me was that I was seeking a doctoral degree from the wrong department. Regardless of the research that placed the importance of leadership at the center of effective change, somehow the principal was being viewed as outside of the educational process. By now I realized my plans would not work and I gave up on them, putting my daybooks back into storage. I felt betrayed. The same people who told me "this was my dissertation" were also telling me at the same time, "as long as it fits the unwritten rubric of 'the club.'"

Nevertheless, others knew of my journey and of my daybooks and were supportive of my unconventional view. Their expressions of interest rekindled and emboldened the possibilities. Surrounding myself with professionals who I respected and who were receptive to learning along with me, my methodology was narrowed to ethnography, to autoethnography, and finally to critical autoethnography.

At first, ethnography was seductive because it uses as its primary data-collection technique the writing of field notes, either in situ or as immediately following the event observed as ethically and logistically possible. Many researchers affirm that the spontaneous, intimate diary is one of the best sources of personal documents.

Although ethnographic research has been established over the last century, it also relies on the old anthropological adage that the researcher must make the strange familiar. The question that is seldom asked, however, is strange and familiar to whom? In the standard roles of ethnographic researchers we are forced to ignore the personal connections and experiences and to view other people as objects of scrutiny, as the Other.

Whereas some question autoethnography as a "myopic view of scholarship" and as "narcissistic" and "in danger of gross self-indulgence," I was drawn to the methodology. In autoethnography the researcher uses personal experiences and highly personalized accounts in a culture to reflexively look more deeply at self–other interactions, turning the ethnographic gaze inward on the self (auto), while maintaining the outward gaze of ethnography—looking at the larger context wherein self experiences occur.

As I continued to investigate autoethnography, I was intrigued by the questions: Who speaks?; and On behalf of whom? Critical theory is inherently a critique of the reproduction of social order that is sociocultural theory's central theme. I was drawn to critical ethnography because it primarily studied power and its effects on societal relationships. My daybooks were ripe with reflections concerning disenfranchisement and my struggles to understand those who attempted to use legislation to control us, and how our lives as educators and as vibrant human beings were and are still affected by such control. My daybooks also reflected resistance and the critical interrogation of the power relations in this society that produce many of the inequalities on display in classroom, schools, and across districts. In short, the critical ethnographer acts as an agent for change using the power of critical skepticism to comprehend organized power and knowledge.

Critical autoethnographic inquiry seeks to uncover the personal meanings and implications of school reform of one individual as a participant within the multiple cultures affecting that school. My dissertation contributes to the literature addressing school reform by examining those efforts from within the process and by deconstructing one way in which progress can be made in improving leadership as well as teaching.

As my daybook entries suggested so many years ago, educators still struggle to understand the critical importance of school reform efforts as a vehicle for social betterment. While a consensus about the actual problems and the promises of possible solutions may vary, the voices of educators must be heard and added to the discussions. The real issues about school reform may always be those about power, politics, and control, but adding the voices of educators into the discussion may even result in a system that also values learning, and school reform may one day become something we do with educators, rather than to them.

I'm sure that my challenges are still before me, but as a result of scholars such as those here this week who have paved and are paving the way for storied dissertations, I am inspired to stay true to my vision! Thank you.

"Calling on spirit"

Sarah MacDougall's story

- Capacity building
- PeerSpirit circle
- Group process
- Spirituality
- Transformation
- Focus groups
- Interpretive ethnographic inquiry
- Autoethnography

Runner: Our next presenter is Dr. Sarah MacDougall, yet another graduate from Fielding Graduate University. She received her degree in Educational Leadership and Change in 2005. Sarah retired from high school science teaching after thirty-three years and is now an independent consultant, coach, and Shamanic practitioner who directs her own company, Maribec, and works with individuals and groups using the process of PeerSpirit circle, the topic of her dissertation, which was entitled, "Calling on Spirit: an Interpretive Ethnography of PeerSpirit Circles as Transformative Process."

Sarah: Thanks Runner. It's great to be here with scholars from around the world who understand that we are not likely to stop the social and ecological injustices surrounding us if higher education does not embrace the kinds of research being represented at this conference.

PeerSpirit circle practice challenges dominant ideologies based on the concepts of hierarchy and individualism through providing a means to equalize power. It allows all voices to be heard and honored and leads to action based on the collective wisdom of the group. I think of it as a methodology that can be used to create professional learning circles in which teachers engage in action research in the classroom and as a platform for professional meetings in all areas of education.

Twelve years ago I was introduced to PeerSpirit circle, a specific circle methodology conceptualized and articulated by Christina Baldwin in her book *Calling the Circle: the First and Future Culture*, published by Bantam in 1998. Sitting in a PeerSpirit circle, I experienced connection. My voice was heard and honored. I felt at home with a group of peers. I also felt deeply connected to Spirit, to something beyond my own fragile, human ego, something I could not define intellectually, but that I felt at the core of my being. The experience of circle is what brought me to my quest for understanding circle in its symbolic form and in its physical manifestation as a way of creating community with other human beings.

In addition to doing traditional ethnographic research, I wrote two autoethnographic chapters describing my personal life experience with the symbol of the circle and my personal journey through the dissertation process. My dissertation committee required that I write a strong, research-based rationale for including my personal story in the dissertation and why it would help answer my dissertation question, "What happens in a PeerSpirit circle that can foster personal and collective transformation, and ultimately lead to social action intended to create a more just and equitable world?"

Those of us who work with this format are familiar with what happens in circle that creates an atmosphere or field that is different from that in other group settings. Sometimes this happening is referred to as *magic*, which implies that it is beyond the cognitive realm, something intuitive that is difficult to articulate in words. I found a definition of magic that seemed to express what it was we were trying to say. In the Introduction of a book entitled, *Dreaming the Dark*, author Starhawk, defines magic as, "The art of evoking power-from-within and using it to transform ourselves, our community, our culture, using it to resist the destruction that those who wield power-over are bringing upon the world." With Starhawk's definition in mind, I crystallized the research question into "Does magic, as defined by Starhawk, happen in PeerSpirit circles?"

The focus-group work that I did with my PeerSpirit colleagues gave me continual feedback with regard to my narrative writing. At one point, they told me that my writing seemed disjointed and hard to follow. They said the way in which I wrote about the focus-group findings left them with the impression that I was not in charge of how I was presenting the material. What ensued was an emotional time for me, as I came face-to-face with the issue of speaking out, with taking my own authority around how to translate the research findings into an academic discourse while at the same time trying to challenge the hegemony of long-standing academic tradition. My colleagues reminded me that I had authority in the realm of PeerSpirit circle. I had done the personal, transformative work, had integrated circle into my life, had relied on Spirit for direction in the research process. They said to me, "What you are doing is not a head trip, but a soul journey." And so, I went through a rite of passage witnessed by my PeerSpirit peers, and entered the writing of this dissertation standing on my own authority, while holding the sharing of all co-participants in sacred space, paying close attention to presenting their words with integrity, doing my utmost to allow myself to be a hollow bone, a vessel through which their wisdom could emerge.

Our ancestors met in circle, sitting around the fire for warmth and security, to make decisions about survival in their daily lives. I believe we have much to learn from the peoples who have gone before us. Meeting in this format was a necessity, as the problems our ancestors faced required their collective wisdom to find and implement solutions. Today our world has changed drastically in many ways, but I believe our problems still require the gathering of our collective wisdom in order to solve our many complex and critical problems. We need to build our capacity to relate to and honor one another in the face of increasing distance introduced by sophisticated technology, social structures that isolate individuals, and the competitive and hierarchical nature of our organizations. My dissertation ultimately is about how we can regain the kind of structures and attitudes that can bring a new collective wisdom to bear on our world's problems today.

In my dissertation, circle history is organized around the concept of the Medicine Wheel, a sacred circle divided into four equal quadrants by lines extending from east to west and from south to north. Aboriginal peoples used the Medicine Wheel as a way of teaching about the need for balance, connection, and unity. I chose to use the Medicine Wheel as an organizing principle because it incorporates circular rather than linear thinking. The Medicine Wheel concept not only lends itself to viewing any topic as a system with all aspects interconnected, but also changes the mind-set that conditions have a beginning and an ending. For me, the mental image created by envisioning the turning of the Medicine Wheel generates the hope that circular thinking leads to transformation, which, I believe, is the goal of attaining knowledge.

Beyond the Medicine Wheel metaphor and my bringing into the research process my personal voice, I also integrated stories that evoked emotion with the intention of engaging the reader in a transformative experience. Laurel Richardson, a postmodern ethnographer, inspired me to translate some interview material into poetic form. The writing of these poems was an extraordinary experience. In reading the interview transcripts with an eye to capturing the essence of each of my participant's stories, I related to the material in a very different way than I had when originally analyzing it. The end result surprised me. I felt I knew each woman in the group more intimately. Poetizing their stories also grounded them in historical and social context.

I also ended my dissertation with an allegorical story, told through the medium of the sacred Medicine Wheel, to invoke the circle and the idea that human progress is continually changing rather than moving toward a final destination. This story came to me through my imagination. To engage you in the story, I ask you to envision in your mind's eye the sacred circle with its center and four directions as the foundational layer and then, with each turn of the Medicine Wheel, another circle superimposed over the previous one. The story begins with the foundational layer, Aboriginal history, then spirals into human intellectual developmentas layer two, and on into PeerSpirit circle practice as the third turn of the Wheel. Hopefully you will hold this vision to imagine where the turning Wheel might take all of us here beyond the third cycle.

"I've got to be me"
Carol Parker Terhune's story

- Naturalistic inquiry
- Black feminist epistemology
- Black feminism as a standard of validity
- Lived experience
- Matrix of domination
- Dialogue

Runner: As we have said often throughout the conference, trying to pigeon-hole our presenters' dissertations with methodological labels has been a little crazy and we have done so only to help readers of the transcript have an idea what general direction the dissertations took for the sake of easier referencing. Our next presenter's dissertation is an example of how difficult it is to do this labeling. Although her dissertation was not ethnographic or biographical per se, we felt that in essence it was very much a product of her lived experience. Carol used her dissertation journey to realize her desire and need to be heard. Not just to be heard, however, but to be heard in a voice, language, dialogue, and experience that was authentic to her.

Carol Parker Terhune received her PhD in Human and Organizational Systems with Fielding Graduate University. The title of her dissertation was "The Experiences of Black Middle Class Women who Relocate to a Predominately White Environment: A Critical Hermeneutic Inquiry." Carol has used her dissertation to inform others, particularly those in the dominant culture, of the experiences of women similarly situated. Through interviews, presentations, and consultations she has worked to shed light on the plight or difficulties of being one of a few or the only one in countless environments. Carol will again use her work in her role as the Interim Director of Oregon Master of Public Health Program to build community, increase dialog, and expand paradigms on authentic conversations and the importance of acknowledging the value of the lived experience.

Carol: My interest in the experiences of Black women that relocate to predominately White environments is a personal one. I moved to the predominately White Pacific Northwest six years ago. Although I was raised in a mixed community, my school and my friends were predominately White. I was never cognizant of being Black until I was about ten years old and a new student in my elementary school called me a "nigger." The word, however, held no significance for me. A few years after this experience I moved to the Midwest where my world became predominately Black. The adjustment was traumatic for me. I went from buying into White hegemony to being confused to being pro-Black to being an activist against racism. I became somewhat obsessed with trying to understand what it means to be a member of my race, to finally gaining an understanding of what it means to be a part of the human race. From that time, I spent most of my adult years, more by circumstance than choice, in predominately Black communities gaining wisdom and understanding of self within a racist society and why I had been previously called the "n" word.

Having spent the majority of my life situated in extremely diverse metropolitan cities, my experience at finding myself to be the "only one" in not only my workplace (which had become commonplace after achieving a certain level of education) but also in my daily walks of life were quite unsettling. Relocating forced me to examine and solidify who I was as a Black woman. I found that it had to be defined by me, instead of how others were attempting to label and (re)define me. Who was I and who was I becoming in this predominately White environment that I had previously known so well? I felt somehow trapped in the "Land of Oz" where all the characters had been cast and I was being forced to choose which one I would become. What I have come to anecdotally understand is that my experience is not unique and that other Black women who have relocated have also faced similar challenges. There exists for me a pull for homogeneity and conformity—a push to dissect that part of me, the Black part of me as I had come to define it, and to replace it with something that is socially constructed and defined by the dominant group; more specifically to reconstruct me in the image of a White American. However, rather than assume one objective truth exists about this experience, I decided to explore the stories of other Black women who relocated. My dissertation was designed to explore and make meaning not only of my experience, but also the experiences of the women in this study. I think my dissertation, though I agree with Runner about labels, is best described as a "naturalistic inquiry" although it certainly is based on an autoethnographic or situated story of my life.

Naturalistic inquiry suggests a holistic and intuitive approach to research. Embracing this framework it was important to me as a Black female researcher that I study Black women using a Black feminist epistemology that embraces and honors their experiences as valid. It demonstrates the limitations of traditional epistemologies and allows knowledge to be constructed by those who have lived along the margins. In addition, to gain an understanding of their experiences the social and historical context in which Black women find themselves had to be taken into consideration and a critical paradigm supported this standpoint. Therefore, I used a Black feminist viewpoint along with the interpretive framework to develop a critical hermeneutical approach to conduct my research.

Was this process readily accepted? Well, let's put it this way, I had to change my entire committee and start over. The thought was that my work would be a weak introduction of me into the academy. Discussing "black" and racialized issues from a qualitative perspective for the sake of giving voice and informing the world about the continual plight of not just African Americans but more specifically African American women was not "real research." A better approach was suggested to me, which was to compare and contrast the experiences of Asian, Hispanic, and Black women, using a quantitative scale, to see what was different. Although this may have resulted in a dissertation of interest, what of the uniqueness of Black women? What of the uniqueness of their experiences? Historically, Black women have been instructed on the insignificance of their experiences, particularly in relation to the larger issue of race and/or gender. That we must pick sides and discontinue subverting the "cause" by talking about race in the company of White women or gender in the company of Black. To compare and contrast the experiences of racial groups would only allow for the issue of gender to play a prominent role in my dissertation, moving intricacy of the duality of race and gender to the back burner.

I must note that this resistance was done so with the greatest of intention and with the desire to assist me in conducting outstanding and critically acclaimed work. However, the question that nagged me for months was, "Why was my proposed research interest not outstanding, and why would it not yield critically acclaimed work?" Although I attended an academic institution that prided itself on social justice, diversity, and authenticity, the underlying message was that it is ok to play in this world while doing your course work, but assimilation and conformity were the requirement when producing publishable work. This felt to me like more than a rejection of my work, but a rejection of me.

Reassembling my committee, although stressful, was not difficult and I found individuals who felt my work was necessary, needed, and had to be done. The next hurdle for me was using a Black feminist epistemology as the core theoretical and methodological framework in my dissertation. As a Black woman, positioned at both a critical and interpretive paradigm, I hold to an ontological perspective of social relativism and historical realism. My multiple realities are shaped and constructed within the context in which I am and have been situated. Black feminist epistemology is both subjective and transactional;

therefore, any research method used to obtain the experiences of Black women must be appropriately grounded in a process that will not disturb the natural context of the phenomena (their experiences) of interest.

Incorporating Black feminism within this research paradigm allowed for the placement of Black women to be at the center of the inquiry and assured that their experiences would neither be discounted nor diluted. Black feminist thought demonstrates Black women's emerging power as agents of knowledge and provides intellectual space for the validation of their lived experiences. We are in a unique position to study the lives and experiences of other Black women. Therefore, having experienced relocating to a predominately White environment, I become uniquely qualified to examine these experiences in other Black women.

I found it necessary to "teach" my committee about Black feminism and why using this was critical in my research. My new committee members were willing learners and equally convinced that my use of this framework was necessary and important. The tricky part, however, came when establishing standards of validity. In qualitative research, Lincoln and Guba's validity standards are considered foundational. However, I felt, with the guidance of a Middle Eastern colleague and mentor, in keeping with the truth of my work I had to again use the standards of Black feminism as my standards for validity. This was new territory as there was nothing in the literature that supported this proposition.

Validity, trustworthiness, and credibility in qualitative research are essential, of course. Researchers are responsible for presenting the framework used to ensure the validity of their findings. As I said, the validity of my research was grounded in "Black feminist epistemology." Patricia Hill Collins in her book *Black Feminist Thought* describes this as being four dimensional. These include: (1) the lived experience as a criterion of meaning; (2) use of dialogue in assessing knowledge claims; (3) an ethic of caring; and (4) an ethic of personal responsibility.

The *lived experience as the criterion of meaning* was met by the very nature and focus of this study. Through the experience of relocating to a predominately White environment, the women developed new knowledge and wisdom, thereby giving them an "expertise" in this area. The use of dialogue in assessing knowledge claims came through the dialectic and conversational nature of the interview process. Through the telling of their stories and experience both myself and the participants were able to assess knowledge claims while co-creating new knowledge. Validity or member checks were employed through the use of dialogue, discussing the interviews and the researcher's initial interpretations of the data to ensure the experiences of participants were accurately captured. Empathy, emotion, and personal uniqueness were met through the researcher's ability to share her own experiences and accompanying emotion on relocating to a predominately White environment. The *ethics of care* was achieved through the laughter and tears of the shared experiences.

Finally, the *ethics of accountability,* through my interpretation of Collins' work, was achieved in three ways: *walking the talk*; *the matrix of domination*; and *reflexivity. Walking the talk* means living the principles of Black feminist epistemology, which not only serve as a way to record and disseminate knowledge gained through the experiences of Black women, but also work toward the betterment of those experiences. The research served this purpose. It not only raised awareness of the experiences of Black woman, but also provided practical implications for improving the conditions of Black woman who relate to a predominately White environment. In addition, the *matrix of domination* required Black women to remain cognizant of their multiple positioning as both oppressor and oppressed, as it relates to race, gender, and class. Analyzing the participant's stories through this matrix also added to the validation of the research and clarity of the knowledge created. Accountability also required that I work to safeguard Black women from further stereotyping and pathologizing. My research included safeguarding the participants as well as the Black community in Oregon. Collins has frequently noted that knowledge is a critical component of domination and resistance rhetoric. Knowledge claims cannot be solely one of victimization or heroism if Black women are to embrace and understand themselves holistically, taking ownership and accountability of their lived experiences. Black feminism suggests there is always choice and power to act no matter how bleak the position. It is through the dialectic nature of knowledge creation that Black woman become aware of their social positioning, through stereotypes and pathology, so they can work to deconstruct then reconstruct their stories. The information shared by the participants in this research about themselves and the Black community of Oregon is situated knowledge (and could be argued subjugated knowledge) representing a partial perspective or building block of knowledge to which additional knowledge must be added to attain a full and clear picture.

Was it worth it?

In the end I believe it was all worth the effort. In the back of my head as I was doing my work I wondered, "Am I doing the right thing?" However, every moment I spent interviewing the women, reviewing and analyzing data, and pouring my heart and soul into this work let me know that it was indeed the right thing to do. In addition, my research was featured in the local business journal in my town and noted as important work. The reporter won an award for her article. She also did a follow-up piece on my work. My dissertation has been published in two journals and I have had the privilege of presenting my work around the world, including Australia and Hawaii. Most importantly, however, the women in the study and other women who have read about my study have called me and thanked me for giving voice to their experiences. They thanked me for sharing what was commonplace to them but an apparent constant source of mystery to those people around them. They thanked me for caring enough to ask about their experience and acknowledging that it is indeed different, unique, and complicated from other racial groups as well as other genders. Although these women thanked me, I had to reciprocate because the experience gave meaning, value, and voice to my personal struggles, dilemmas, and experiences as a Black woman. Voice, both the obtaining and proclaiming of it, was critical for me as a Black woman, especially living in an environment where I feel multiple attempts to silence or limit my voice. Providing a forum for the voices of Black women to be clearly heard was a deeply embedded motivator of this research. I am thankful for the journey and the commitment to be me.

"Appreciative inquiry"
Jeanie Cockell's story

- Appreciative inquiry
- Autoethnography
- Transformative education

Runner: Next it is my pleasure to introduce to you Dr. Jeanie Cockell who has come all the way from Nova Scotia. She is an Educational and Organizational Consultant and a dynamic facilitator whose background includes many years as an adult educator, including college teaching and leadership roles. She is a leader in appreciative inquiry as an organizational development process, a research methodology, and a foundation for fostering collaboration in groups. Jeanie "makes magic" with teams for more appreciative learning, leading, and working together. We have asked her to talk a bit about her "appreciative inquiry" dissertation because it is also based on her own consulting practice and, as such, is in many ways her story.

Jeanie: Thanks Runner. It is great to be here and I am very excited to be here with so many other amazing and inspiring people.

Let me begin by explaining what I mean by "making magic" with teams. "Magic" is the team transformation to more authentic inter-connections where appreciation is combined with critical reflection to enhance goal achievement and relationships.

My doctoral study of the meaning and value of "making magic" had a profound impact on my consulting practice, deepening my understanding of facilitating groups and of who I am as I facilitate, doing what I have been called to do.

The title of my dissertation was "Making Magic: Facilitating Collaborative Processes." I received my degree from the University of British Columbia (UBC). The purpose of my research was to examine the meaning and value of "making magic," facilitating collaborative processes. Further to what I said earlier, in this study the term "making magic" was a metaphor for the peak experiences that happen when facilitating collaborative processes with groups (two or more people) in workplace, community, and/or classroom settings. Four other educational/organizational consultants joined me in this inquiry, which was itself a collaborative process that I facilitated in three stages: interviews; collaborative conversation; and data analysis.

Two key areas of literature, appreciative inquiry and transformative education, inform and are informed by this study. I used appreciative inquiry as a research methodology and the models, theories, and applications of appreciative inquiry inform our practices of "making magic." The transformative education literature added a critical lens that is lacking in appreciative inquiry, the notions of the impact of social structural differences on people's ability to appreciate and be appreciated.

The primary findings of this inquiry are the notions of critical appreciative processes, and "making magic" through being present, vulnerable, and courageous. Critical appreciative processes combine the appreciative and the critical. These processes could enhance the possibility of magic, the transformation that happens when groups of people collaborate effectively by being interconnected and authentic, present, with each other. The group transforms to be more than the individuals put together and/or the group process aggrandizes the learning. Critical appreciative processes could create sacred spaces, holistic spaces that take into consideration the spirit and emotions as well as the intellect and body. Facilitators intentionally create these spaces for the possibility of "magic" through a variety of strategies and by being present, vulnerable, and courageous themselves, being who they are, as they facilitate.

My doctoral dissertation was alternative methodologically, in representation, in the use of the metaphor of "magic," in the findings, and in the literature examined.

Methodologically, there were several ways that my research was alternative. I used appreciative inquiry as a main approach. It is also a main part of my facilitating work, the work that I was studying. Appreciative inquiry, at the time, was new to my department at UBC. Appreciative inquiry is a type of action research that focuses on what is working well, in my case, the "magic." Appreciative inquiry makes use of narrative inquiry and collaborative inquiry. I used narrative inquiry to collect, analyze, and represent my data. I used collaborative inquiry because I was doing what I was studying—facilitating a collaborative process with other facilitators. Another significant alternative approach was that the main part of the collaborative conversation took place online by e-mail. I also took on multiple roles. As well as being the researcher, I was the facilitator of our collaborative process and a participant in it. I told my stories as well as represented the others' stories told to me and shared in the collaborative conversations. The autoethnographic element was strong and linked it all together.

My representation is also alternative. My dissertation opens with a picture of my magic facilitator wand and with a snippet, my term for a small story taken from interviews or the collaborative conversations, or written to illustrate "magic" in some way. I began my dissertation with the snippet, "The Birth of the Magic Wand," which is one of my stories that represents the inter-connection between my personal and professional life. Revealing my vulnera-bility through such an autobiographical story felt very alternative, and being vulnerable in order to be present was an important finding of my study. I use the metaphor of a magical quilt for the whole dissertation. It is a quilt of snippets sewn together with notions and threads from the literature and themes from the study.

The use of the metaphor of "magic" is also alternative. As one of my parti-cipants said, when asked why she wanted to participate, "I'm interested in participating in this study because I like the idea of contributing to an aca-demic study that has magic in its title! Given the highly rational and quantitative nature of some academic studies, this feels like a mildly subversive activity, and it appeals to me. I expect it to be an opportunity to reflect, learn, clarify, grow—to hear the stories of those who engage in magical work." She was right. We all felt that this had been a very profound opportunity to reflect on our work, together with others who do similar work. It is unusual for independent, self-employed consultants to have such an opportunity. As another participant said at the group's final face-to-face collaborative conversa-tion, "I think it's a gift to be able to reflect on one's practice. For me it's a vertical and a horizontal gift. The horizontal gift is the circle both online and here, hearing and experiencing and the vertical is digging down inside myself and being able to talk on a very, very deep level."

The findings contribute to the alternative nature of knowledge in that they support a holistic view of learning and group transformation to more authentic interconnections through spiritual and emotional as well as intellectual ways of engagement. "Magic" happens when facilitators and participants are present with each other and to do this requires courage and vulnerability. The findings are not a "how-to" list of "making magic," although the stories do include techniques. More importantly, the stories represent the spirit of human interactions.

Last, my juxtaposition of literature from business and education was alternative. The appreciative inquiry literature is found mainly in business literature. Transformative education literature added an important critical and spiritual dimension to appreciative inquiry. As a result, my research contributed the notion of critical appreciative processes through which facilitators create sacred spaces where participants are appreciated and respected for their differences (appreciative inquiry), and where social structural impacts are acknowledged and challenged (transformative education).

At UBC, I was encouraged by my professors to use the learning experience to deepen my own practice. My topic developed with the support of my professors and the other students in my doctoral cohort. The cohort was a "magical" team with much wisdom among us. We were all in our mid-careers with lots of life and work experiences that gave us this wisdom. Recognizing my wisdom and strengths did not occur at the beginning of the program. I had to grow in my own sense of strength and ability to contribute to the university as well as to learn from those around me, both the professors and students. It is easy to lose one's sense of strength and knowledge in traditional university settings. My advice to others is to recognize what you bring as well as what you need to learn and, most importantly, get a supportive open-minded advisor who wants to learn from you too, and who knows how to handle the university's systems!

I was fifty-one years old when I began my doctorate in Educational Leadership and Policy and fifty-five when I completed it. When I began I was in a career transition having started my own educational and organizational consulting business two years before. At the same time I had held onto some security by teaching mathematics half time at the college where I had worked for many years. The doctoral program helped me to give up this security and concentrate fully on developing my consulting practice as well as immersing myself in doctoral courses, research, and thesis writing. This happened because the topic I chose was based on my consulting practice and by doing this research I enriched my practice. The program helped me to see my passions and to follow these in my consulting practice. The following story from the end of my dissertation is an example of the kind of work that I am passionate about and my inner voice is calling me to do.

Does that always happen?

After handing in the first draft of my thesis, I facilitated an appreciative inquiry and community development workshop for federal government employees to introduce them to some basic appreciative inquiry concepts and models to use in their work with First Nations' communities. It was a lot to do in four hours. None of the participants were First Nations. Four participants were "trainees," expected to be there as part of their job training. The rest of the group included their supervisor, the trainer who had hired me, and two others who worked in the team in other capacities and who were interested in the topic. I could sense as the "trainees" came into the room that some of them were not keen to be there. "Oh, dear," I thought, "this will be a challenge," feeling a little nervous about how they might receive me. I introduced myself (and my magic facilitator wand) and proceeded to build an appreciative climate. I presented some theory then they did appreciative interviews and group development of provocative propositions and images around the topic of working with First Nations' groups. I talked about the impact of power and privilege on people's ability to be appreciative. Throughout the session, I told stories and they told stories, stories of our experiences working with First Nations' groups. The transformation to a more engaged and connected group began in the climate setting and increased through the interviews gaining further momentum in the group work, and was fully apparent in the whole group debrief and closure. In the closing circle, passing my magic facilitator wand around, each person spoke in a very emotional way about the power of the experience and their appreciation of each other. So I wasn't surprised when Mary, who had hired me, called me later and asked incredulously, "Does that always happen?" She was amazed by how much had happened, all the original outcomes and, more powerfully, the unexpected outcomes, the depth of emotions that people shared and the transformation of the group to an interconnected whole. "How wonderful," I thought to myself, "she saw the magic."

"Being in harmony"
Adair Linn Nagata's story

with Valerie Bentz

- Mindful Inquiry (critical social science, phenomenology, hermeneutics, and Buddhism)
- Bodymindfulness
- Autobiography
- Phenomenology
- Embodied emotional resonance
- Relational attunement
- Appreciative inquiry

Runner: Our next presenter is Adair Linn Nagata. She is a Professor of Intercultural Communication at the Rikkyo University Graduate School of Intercultural Communication in Tokyo, Japan and also teaches at the Graduate School of Asia-Pacific Studies at Waseda University. After careers in international education and corporate training, communication, and organizational development in a global financial services company, she earned her doctorate in Human Development from the Fielding Graduate University. Her publications focus on the cultivation of consciousness and communicative competence in intercultural relationships and for intercultural researchers using *bodymindfulness* and Mindful Inquiry. Both her scholarly activity and her teaching emphasize pedagogy that encourages integrative transformative learning in intercultural education and peacemaking that begins within and can radiate out from a person with coherent energy in ever-widening circles.

Adair: Thank you Runner. It is an honor to be here among such remarkable people whose doctoral journeys have reflected their hearts as much as their minds.

My own dissertation story really begins back in 1970 when I was first living in Japan. There I discovered a new talent of which I had previously been unaware. I seem to have had an innate ability to disturb the famous Japanese sense of *wa*, the harmony existing in a group situation before I appeared on the scene. My presence, especially my arrival in the group, would often result in a change in the atmosphere and what was happening; a shift in the conversation; and in the worst case, a dispersal of the people who had been assembled there. After a while, I began to realize that these things did not just happen; something I was doing was causing them.

Eventually, when I had the opportunity to do doctoral study in human development, I found myself researching a question related to these communicative and relational difficulties that I was seeking to understand. Gradually, I realized that the problem was a combination of my way of doing and, more fundamentally, my way of being; but I wondered how I could change such basic things about myself. It seemed that if my international marriage to a Japanese man were to survive, if I were to be able to raise my children honoring both their Japanese as well as their U.S. American heritage, and if I were to be able to work well with mainly Japanese people, I needed to learn new ways of communicating.

As I tried to understand what I was experiencing and what might be necessary to shift it to a more satisfying and effective way of communicating with Japanese people, the research question that eventually emerged took the following form: What is the embodied experience of being in empathic resonance with another person in an intercultural interaction? I used "Mindful Inquiry" for my dissertation. Here I am referring to the concept described in the book by the same title by Bentz and Shapiro. I am so honored to know that Valerie Bentz is going to talk after me. My Mindful Inquiry into this mysterious phenomenon resulted in a change in my way of being that was also expressed in new ways of doing things. Since beginning to teach at the university level in 2002, I have aspired to promote this holistic kind of transformative learning experience for my students, who are mainly Japanese but also include men and women with diverse cultural backgrounds and nationalities. Ultimately, I use the word "bodymindfulness" to describe my approach.

Bodymindfulness is an approach to becoming aware of and adjusting our inner state. The term *bodymind* emphasizes the systemic, integral nature of lived experience, and mindfulness is a Buddhist concept and practice of cultivating awareness. Bodymindfulness is the process of attending to all aspects of the bodymind—body, emotion/feeling, mind, and spirit—in order to grasp the holistic personal meaning of an internal event and to use the resultant understanding to communicate skillfully. Because bodymindfulness can help us to access and to understand the prerational structures of our meaning perspectives and how we express them, it promotes self-reflexivity in the moment and ongoing integrative transformative learning.

My dissertation, while situated in my own autobiography or autoethnography in which I integrated twenty years of dream journaling and years of field notes, is a Mindful Inquiry into the realms of relational and transpersonal psychology, which was pursued using the four knowledge traditions of critical social science, phenomenology, hermeneutics, and Buddhism. I used multiple texts including my own phenomenological writing and the transcripts of interviews with twelve interculturalists to write an eidetic phenomenological description of embodied emotional resonance: the bodily experience of relational attunement. I explored its functioning on two levels in face-to-face interactions—intrapersonal and interpersonal—as the basis for a somatic epistemology. Descriptions of intercultural applications of bodymindfulness demonstrate the practicality of this research. I consider that my work on intersubjectivity extends that of Alfred Schutz into proprioceptive, somatic-emotional realms. My lived experience of Gadamer's three levels of hermeneutics suggests that my work moved into a fourth level with active implementation of my understandings in intercultural interactions. I believe applying understanding of emotional resonance and bodymindfulness has generic value in human relations as a form of everyday peacemaking.

I feel fortunate that I did my doctoral work at Fielding and was mentored by Jeremy Shapiro and Valerie Bentz. Matt Hamabata and David Rehorick who also served on my committee were encouraging and wonderfully supportive. My gratitude to these four people and Barnett Pearce is unending. They allowed me to attempt the seemingly impossible task of making sense of my life of fifty-eight years (the data I was integrating included twenty years of dream journals, five years of field journalling and all my KAs, three years of phenomenological protocols on my topic, fifteen protocols of trance sessions with my psychospiritual counselor, and the transcripts of twelve interviews with other interculturalists), developing a new way of being, and gaining the confidence to work in more challenging and effective ways. I am happier now than I have ever been in my life. My relationships are more satisfying, and my work is more fulfilling.

That said, I only recall one discouraging comment, which surprisingly came from a particularly beloved professor who was a renowned social psychologist and a truly gentle soul. She cautioned me not to pursue my fascination with subtle energy and emotional resonance because it was too close to the edge of what was academically serious or acceptable. I remember this comment, but it did not dissuade me. I was already conscious of being on a path that was leading me over the edges of my own limitations, and there was no way I could have stopped myself from pursuing my Mindful Inquiry to its tentative conclusion that found its fullest expression of all that I *knew* about it at the time I submitted my dissertation.

I was also conscious that I was becoming a PhD for my own development and not because I had a particular career goal. I had already "retired" to write my dissertation and never expected to become a graduate school professor, an ongoing process of integrative transformative learning. My dissertation process helped me to become more authentically and consciously my, now bicultural, self, and I am delighted to be passing on this opportunity to my students. Thank you. (*Applause*)

Runner: As Adair said, her mentor and co-author of the remarkable book, *Mindful Inquiry in Social Research*, and many other publications, is here to say a few words. It is my pleasure to introduce you to Dr. Valerie Malhotra Bentz, PhD, Professor, School of Human and Organization Development, Fielding Graduate University.

Valerie: Four Arrows, my colleague at Fielding, asked me to join you at this conference and enter the dialogue on alternative creative dissertations because I wrote (with Jeremy Shapiro) *Mindful Inquiry in Social Research*. This book is a guide to a dissertation process which is centered in the consciousness of the researcher, and which asks the researcher to fully examine his/her role as researcher through the rigorous processes of phenomenology, hermeneutics, critical theory, and Buddhist principles. It asks writers of dissertations and other researchers to be mindful of the effects of their dissertation on the participants. Researchers are urged to be clear about ways in which their research and its products may ameliorate oppression, suffering, and injustice, not only of humans but of all beings.

Dissertations are not written, however, with a main goal of entertaining either the writer or the reader, although I do think that boring oneself and a reader is not desirable or even ethical. But boredom is in the mind of the reader. Many of us have struggled to read through Marx' *Das Kapital*, however, it was a great and most important work in human intellectual and social history.

Dissertations, whatever form they take, necessarily make knowledge claims and claims to truth regardless of their epistemological style. In this age where the news media have merged with the entertainment industry, if universities are the sole remaining bastions for standards of truth, if they lose the credibility and the relevance of their research, they lose the point of their existence.

In my search for truth and expression as a scholar and professor over the past thirty-five years, I have moved through the range of epistemologies and methodologies. I have written theoretical works, quantitative empirical works, through qualitative. I have become a phenomenologist because I believe that the basic tenet of phenomenology, that is that we can only know with and through the screen of our consciousness, is irrefutable. Yet phenomenological methods give us rigor to get to an understandable level of "truth" or "truths" that are also directly related to practice and to life experiences. Similarly, since all we know is a matter of interpretation, hermeneutics is necessarily a part of all research. Researchers must therefore, make their hermeneutic strategies and stances explicit rather than hidden in the interest of what in current jargon is called "transparency."

Critical theory's assertion that power distorts communication must be addressed, along with the economic and political basis of our knowing lest our work unwittingly serve oppressive powers. I was pleased to see Adair Nagata was invited here to talk about her dissertation. Other FGU students, including Dudley Tower, Bernie Novokosky, Pam Young, Mary Beth Haines, Sandra Simpson, Lucille Dinwiddie, Linda Wing, Gloria Cordova, Valerie Grossman, Rita Lustgarten, David Haddad, Sandra Coyle, Helen Turnbull, Judith Hochberg, have also written dissertations that were creative, important, and rigorous and inspired or guided by phenomenological work and by *Mindful Inquiry*. Their topics included empowered consulting, to walking the mystical path, high performance teams and feminine wisdom leadership. My book, *Transformative Phenomenology*, co-edited with colleague David Rehorick will highlight the work of a dozen scholars, most of them doctoral dissertations, in which the research process also transformed the researcher.

My own epistemological style has moved over the past thirty-five years from traditional methods to phenomenology. My style has also increasingly involved writing in the first person and presenting personal experiences as relevant to the topic. My most recent work is a work of fiction, in which some of the major theorists and philosophers I have written about over the years are fictionalized as characters. In this way I was able to express the emotional depth of my long-term relationships with philosophers George Herbert Mead and Martin Heidegger. My protagonist is married to one and involved with the other. My novel, *The Time Travels to Nazi Germany of Dr. Victoria Von Dietz*, illustrates ways in which a woman's research and scholarship is not separated from practice and results in overcoming oppression. I am seeking a publisher or agent. Let me know if you have any ideas. (*Laughter*)

Well, my commendations to all of you for being here and for the important work you are doing with your learning and teaching at this level.

Runner: Thanks so much Valerie for a "from the horse's mouth" overview on mindful inquiry.

Part 7

Day seven

Participants' voices

Memoir is a window into a life.

(William Zinsser, from *Inventing the Truth: The Art and Craft of Memoir*, 1995, p. 11)

"Knowingness, negotiation, and beauty"

Recognizing and sharing Indigenous knowledge and voice

Doreen E. Martinez's story

- Ethnography
- Cultural knowledge
- Authentic biographies
- Academic gatekeepers

Runner: Well, we have made it to our final day of the conference. Today will be a full day, however. Our first presenter is an Assistant Professor in the Women's and Gender Studies Program at Northern Arizona University. Like most of our presenters, her dissertation story does not fit a clear "category," but her honoring of the Indigenous perspective is clear.

Doreen: Thank you. It is good to be here. My paternal grandmother is Mescalero, Apache and my paternal grandfather is Mexican of Indigenous lineage. My maternal grandparents are "Pennsylvania Dutch." I am a "first generation college student," and I have acquired a few of those precious pieces of parchment (I think our degrees are still printed on such.) I have a Bachelor's in Psychology with an emphasis in Group Dynamics, a Master's of Science degree in Sport and Exercise Science, a graduate certificate in Women's Studies and that beloved doctorate. My purpose and ambitions continue to focus on developing long-term relationships between institutional entities and knowledge systems with various Native Nations and Indigenous communities/efforts. I especially want to address epistemological issues of oppression and discrimination while nurturing, recognizing, and providing beauty the space to flourish.

In 2003, I completed my dissertation at Syracuse University in Sociology. I had completed a qualitative/ethnographic research project centering on Indigenous women from seven Nations: Apache, Lakota, Omaha, Onondaga, Oneida, Pueblo, and Winnebago. It had been a journey that spanned over ten years and included an array of experiences and events. We had been to movies, to restaurants; we had celebrated birthdays, weddings, and grieved together; we had participated in ceremonies, gone to PowWows and box lacrosse games; we shared, and developed very strong relationships. For my actual research, I asked "What is medicine?"

Along the way, I had had to negotiate the ever-present lack of knowledge or sense of how to be a community member, how to build respect and be humble—as a researcher. They, the research scholars, had pressured me to "get the interviews done," "just go down there [to nation territory] and knock on doors," "you need to do this on our schedule," and it was even *suggested*, "why don't you go with the healer when she goes and sees someone." I was struck with the push and lack of appreciation regarding such an intimate relationship. I wondered if they would tell other students to just invite themselves along on doctor's or physicians visits. It was a constant struggle, for when I said, "It's not time," or "I can't just invite myself," they only saw it as resistance. I was a student who simply avoided doing the work, or a student whose work failed to be significant enough to warrant more consideration or understanding.

The college "gatekeepers" and I had debated and I had to frequently fight their linear expectations, the demands to be an expert that would allow me to tell my "informants" about their lives. Somehow, I was to be the expert of *their lives*. I was told, "They don't know gender. It's your job to identify it." We had fought over the meaning of race—that it is much more than a theoretical social construction. It is a lived experience, a sense of culture, ancestry, and variations in humanity that are too often oppressed through prejudice and colonization. I know the history of the development of race as a tool of oppression. My argument was that Indigenous Peoples have cultural knowledge, a sense of self rooted in their ancestry, a knowingness of being and breathing; an understanding of nation, of interdependence, of place and space. My perspective only provided more questions and uncertainty regarding my legitimacy and the subsequent value of my research. Who is this student who sees race as a concept outside of practices of discrimination, attempts at colonization and genocide efforts? Who is this student who embraces a knowingness of breathing as an artifact of culture knowledge? Should this student be a student? Our student? The gatekeepers failed to verbalize it; yet, I could feel their critical harboring eyes that were guised in intellectual tradition—their response to "knowingness" (another concept I developed and incorporated), was that it was unknown or unfamiliar or if I was *lucky*, someone thought it was one of those new age or ancient ideas (again ripping it from the hearts of knowers, who did know that this—this knowingness—is about a complete quintessence of experience: a knowingness of the mind, heart, body and soul that is embodied in all our relations). It is an Indigenous ancient cultural—and yes, racial—knowing.

And then, there was the push to develop and own this idea of "intimacy plus" that I had developed. I had merely being trying to emphasize the role of intimacy within medicine ways, which is intimacy that extends and is much more than the default psychological notions of intimate relations and/or intimacy via another (typically a very individualistic experience.) It is intimacy plus because it is borne out of an Indigenous consciousness, an ancient cultural consciousness, which is and must be experienced in relation to others. This intimacy is lived today within our past, present, and on-going histories (carrying our culture within the very sinew of our bones, of our existence.) The phrase—intimacy plus—although it may have worked for some readers, seemed cheap and incomplete to me. So, I accidentally on purpose focused my efforts elsewhere.

And then, there was the issue of informant biographies. First, to honor and respect the women, I had pushed for them to be referred to as participants or women (naming them in some way that was about being people; more than research tools). I also had to do so to honor my own needed humbleness—my place—and respect; to make active my belief of their knowingness, *their expertise*. My research proficiency—my role/status—lay in my knowingness of time being circular, a communal expression and intent in language, active respect, and honor of our consciousness that knew, explicitly, of the connection to our ancestors, the interdependence to all our relations, and the needs of the seventh generations.

Yet, I was informed (and knew via my own "schooling") that qualitative and ethnographic research often includes biographies of the "informants." My reply to this request/perceived need was, "The women know and describe themselves in other ways and I'm uncomfortable truncating and Westernizing it." The women's focus and understanding of themselves reflects a much larger placement and connection to community rather than individual biographies (the expected qualitative/ethnographic typification). We went round, and round, and round about this legitimate authoritative expectation. Although, reflectively, I was focusing on the round/circle dialogue while they seemed to push the straight and narrow path. Finally, I was talking to a mentor (a friendly gatekeeper—one who kept the gate open and/or let me know where the keys were). They asked me who I viewed was the audience of my work. I had come to know that I wanted to offer this material to Indigenous Peoples as a way of celebrating and honoring our lives. Yet, I had come to strongly understand that the audience I wanted to receive it was primarily non-Native readers. My desire was to increase the understanding, comprehension, and consideration of those non-Native "others" to/with our lives. So, I had to ask myself, what do they need to make this transition of understanding, comprehension, and consideration; to at least read it? Well, okay, biographies it is then.

The next question, though, was what the content of the biographies would be. The "typical" biographies contain individual demographics of job title, years in profession, marital status, number of children, etc. Yet, again, I questioned this framing. The women know themselves as communal members. This demographic data would skew the representation of their lives. However, this is that non-Native reader expectation/need/desire. I decided to merge the women's knowingness and the target audience expectations. I cited a little regarding the expected demographics such as number of children, grandchildren, or jobs they have had (in plural as they had noted.) Yet, I made sure I also gave a flavor and picture that depicted their lives as much more—as their understanding. I also believed it was important to reflect our relationship in these biographies, situating my location/position with the women. Therefore, the biographies included information such as where we met, how long we knew each other and in what context; they included favorite types of cars, the fact that one participant still owed me a pair of moccasins, one had a job as a mermaid once, or that another took me on the "nickel" tour of her homeland. These more complete—whole—biographies I could share. The women all reviewed their biographies and made any changes before they were included in the shared research.

Then, again, I had to negotiate where the biographies would be placed in the body of the dissertation. "Typically," they are placed at the end of the text. This felt rather unacceptable to me. The women are much more substantive. How could I place them at the end as part of the references or citations? Then it was suggested that I place them as an appendix to the methods sections. To me they would end up as an add-on in that location, also unacceptable. It was unacceptable for me to place them as an appendix. I struggled for some time to find a resolution, the right thing to do; to be just. There are no other models I could find or anyone suggested. Finally, after spending time in reflection, I had the idea that they would be their own chapter. Yes, their own chapter. And, it made most sense that they followed the methods chapter, prior to the substantive chapters, which were rich with their words.

I "defended" my dissertation after seven years of doctoral studies and work. I was ready, anxious, nervous, and excited. One other element to my work was that I kept the women's words as closely verbatim as they had shared and spoken to me. "Typically" data is "cleaned-up" (utterances, repeats and so forth removed). In my cultural knowingness, I knew that these utterances, repeats, and such are necessary to read, to see, to even struggle through while reading their narratives, their stories. To omit these cultural idioms would omit the essence, depth, and necessary emotive "guts" of their lives.

During my dissertation defense, a member of the committee stated, "You know I have read a lot of dissertations and I have never said this, but at times when I was reading yours I had to say to myself that this work is beautiful." After he said such, I recall breathing a deep soulful breath. It worked, that is them—these Indigenous women—their beauty made it through the negotiation of knowingness.

"Caught by culture and conflict"

Dixiane Hallaj's story

- "Fictional" vignettes
- Epigrams
- Language issues
- Anti-oppressive research

Dr. Samson: Our next presenter is Dr. Dixiane Hallaj who earned her PhD from George Mason University in 2006. Entitled, "Caught by Culture and Conflict: Palestinian Refugee Women's Perceptions of Illiteracy and Education," it won the 2007 Illinois Distinguished Qualitative Dissertation Award, which Dixiane received at the 3rd International Congress of Qualitative Inquiry.

Dixiane: I'm very honored to be here and to have my dissertation selected as one of the "authentic" ones for this conference. I began my doctoral work when my youngest son was completing medical school with the goal of accumulating the credentials I need to start family literacy centers in Palestine rather than to launch an academic career. Those facts probably have a lot to do with my dissertation not fitting the accepted template. Oh, and along the way I also founded OPAL (Organization to Promote Adult Literacy) to facilitate my work.

So how did my presentation differ from the traditional five-chapter dissertation? For starters it was nine chapters long. It included fictionalized stories that incorporated elements of several interviews but adhered to none. It did not focus on a research problem, but rather on a social problem. Therefore the discussion focused on suggestions for further social action rather than suggestions for further research. Last but not least to some in the reviewing hierarchy, I deviated substantially from APA by setting off my vignettes in single-spaced blocks; I included epigrams in some chapter headings that were not only single spaced, but in a smaller type font. The direct quotes from the interviews had non-standard margins, non-standard line length, non-standard type style and, incidentally, a lot of non-standard content. Luckily, although these "flaws" were brought to my attention page by page, with enough sticky notes to reconstruct a small tree, I was allowed to keep my deviant formatting.

No, I was not just trying to be different. My concentration on adult learning and my focus on the women in Palestinian refugee camps as a dissertation topic in a school of education that was very K-12 oriented was difference enough. I was brought to these differences in an effort to communicate both my topic and the words and context surrounding my participants as effectively as possible to an audience that came from a very different world. I am sure our Indigenous presenters at the beginning of the conference have faced many of the same difficulties. Speaking a different language is more than having different names for the same object. A language embodies a culture—it reflects a way of thinking and a worldview particular to that culture. Translation is not simply substituting an English word for a non-English word.

Not only were the women I wanted to portray separated from my audience by language and culture but also by experiences of life-long suffering and oppression. And yet, as women, they do the same things women do the world over. They bear children and try to make the lives of their children better than their own. They serve their families in the best way they can. They rejoice in their triumphs, no matter how small. They share the pain and give support and encouragement when there is failure and disappointment.

Again, I address my Indigenous colleagues when I speak of the suffering of a people whose land was taken from them, a people who were enclosed in refugee camps living under conditions of poverty and squalor—a sometimes unbearable fate for a people who had farmed their own land and breathed the air of freedom. Many are lost along the way. Some are lost to the violence of resistance but many more are lost through despair.

How can we convey these things to the colleague sitting by your side who has not had such experience? His knowledge of violence, poverty, and oppression are limited to the newscasts that are almost indistinguishable from the feature films and entertainment that come from the same screens into his living room. His children feel oppressed wearing last year's fashions to school. The children of the women I write about worry about being shot while walking to school. They are occasionally shot as they sit in unheated classrooms trying to concentrate on curriculum that often seems totally irrelevant to their world. Yes, the schools are free but sometimes the students find the price they must pay to take advantage of that schooling is too high and they stop going to school—and illiteracy continues.

My quest for a way to tell not only the story of illiteracy, but to set it in a context that was wide enough for it to make sense to the comfortable mainstream American reader led to the non-traditional presentation of my dissertation.

My professor of qualitative research methods, who later became my chairman, had exposed me to many widely (and sometimes wildly) different studies that used qualitative research methods. He encouraged his students to experiment with their own work. He taught that the traditional second chapter should be viewed as a conceptual framework that included more than a review of literature in the field. The researcher's worldview and life experience contribute as much or more than the literature to the conceptual framework.

As my chairman, his style was that of a minimalist. I told him I could not see a logical way to put the literature of trauma into a literature review on women's literacy without discussing the results of the research. His answer was, "Then don't put it there." I told him I wanted to build more context around the individual women. His answer was, "Then do it."

The work began in earnest as I listened to the interviews over and over again. I had to make sure that I translated correctly and then I listened again to make marginal notes. I revisited the questionnaires and, freed of the constraints of the software I had used originally, I paid particular attention to the actual words of the open-ended responses and the marginal notes of the field workers. I began to dream in Arabic again and many of the dreams were set around a plain wooden table talking to the women. They never lost their identities for me and I wanted to portray them as they were—real people with real hopes, real dreams, and, unfortunately, real pain. I could not do this solely on the basis of the words of the interviews—too much had remained unsaid. My tongue had revealed to the women more than just my foreign birth. The Arabic I speak is not the language of the academic but the language that the women themselves speak. Unlike comparable situations in English, this difference is one of vocabulary rather than grammar or use of slang—it is not a "lesser" language, but rather the language of home and hearth. While the academic switches from one register to the other at will, the women and I shared the fact that this was the only Arabic we spoke.

I wanted a way to present the words of the women in a way that would convey the cadence and feeling of the original. Arabic is a very colorful and poetic language. I decided to format the direct quotations from the interviews into short lines that corresponded to the natural pauses in their speech patterns with extra lines separating either long pauses or changes in topic. I then further set it off from my own writing with italics. The end result was that the quotes had the look of poetry and at the same time encouraged the reader to read with the cadence of the actual voices of the women. In my eyes it added value to the women's words and adhered as faithfully to the original as possible through translation.

Having done what I could to give the proper feel to the language, I needed to have a way to show the two-way relationship between illiteracy and the hardship of the women's lives. I needed to show, for example, how poverty does not exist in isolation. How could I ever convey the horror I felt when the first woman came into the room and ordered her son to open his mouth to show the "doctor" his black stubs of teeth? Who had said I was a doctor? How did the child not get dental care sooner? She complained that the camp dentist was going to pull the teeth. What was the use of that when they were going to come out anyway when he got older? Did that have a place in my study? I felt that it did. That event was a living example of the research that connected low education levels with increased hospital use and increased health costs. It was also a living example of how lack of education narrows ones horizons. The woman had no prior knowledge that allowed her to think of a doctor in any but medical contexts. She also had such little experience in that realm that the concept of specialization was not known to her. A doctor was a doctor and should be able to fix whatever was wrong with a person. Research has no life without people and stories. I wanted that story in my dissertation.

How could I tell about the tears that came as one woman told of her monthly pilgrimage to see her son who had been jailed for throwing rocks at soldiers? She would leave before dawn in the morning to board a bus that would make the trip to the jail. There were checkpoints along the way where the passengers in the bus were counted, made to disembark, searched, had their packages searched and the bus searched, counted again as they reboarded and continued to the next checkpoint. On the best days, the passengers would be allowed off the bus in groups of ten or so to go in and spend twenty or thirty minutes with their relatives before returning to the bus and waiting for each small batch to have their short visit. It would be night before they arrived back home. On other days they would be met by the announcement that some prisoner had misbehaved and there would be no visits that day. The relatives were sometimes allowed to look through a pile of letters that had been written by their sons/brothers/husbands.

"You cannot imagine how I feel," she had said, "having to ask someone else if there is a letter for me. The worst part is not knowing if that person really knows how to read well enough to find my name or is just saying there is no letter." I wanted that story in my dissertation.

My solution was to take portions of various interviews that touched on particular issues that crossed through multiple stories and weave them into short vignettes. The vignettes are not truly fiction since every event or circumstance described really happened. On the other hand, no vignette describes any single woman in the study. The word "fictionalized" seemed appropriate. Each vignette took aspects of different women and joined them into a whole piece through the embroidery of my words. After each vignette I discussed how it illustrated the issue and connected it with the literature in the field as well as actual quotes from the interviews. Thus the literature became an integral part of the results chapters. Yes, I had more than one results chapter.

The women I interviewed ranged in age from twenty to forty-five and I realized quite early that there were clear differences in their stories based on age. I also realized that, since I had asked about their parents and their children, I also had data that stretched for several generations—and that generational differences were accompanied by differences not only in educational level, but also in their beliefs and attitudes. My decades of familiarity with the culture and the politics of the region helped me make connections between the background events and the attitudinal changes, but I realized that most readers would not make the same connections. I considered that connection to be a vital part of the whole picture—so I added a chapter that gave a chronology of important events and changes within the political situation and tied it to the attitudes of the population toward literacy and education. Again, I made extensive use within the chapter of existing literature to reinforce my own findings.

This chapter, originally meant to be the final Big Picture chapter, left me feeling that it was still unfinished. I went back to my chairman and told him that the only thing that I felt would be a suitable ending would be to tie the results to my ultimate goal of literacy centers within the camps. I needed to show how the results of my study indicated the need for such centers, the desire of the women for the centers, and the direction the centers should go to best serve the population. I felt (and I hesitate to voice this heresy) that my research was not significant in and of itself. The *women* were the significant element and the research would gain significance only if it could lead to an improvement in some aspect of the lives of the women and their children. I was prepared to argue my point but my chairman smiled and told me that was exactly the right ending for my dissertation. That developed into two more chapters. One told what the women wanted and why, and the other outlined the plan for the center and tied it to my research results.

I have heard many people talking about the dissertation process as a lonely and solitary process. They advise students to form support groups so they can talk over their work and share their frustrations. I felt no need for such a group. Not only was my husband a wonderful supportive companion who supplied me with countless gallons of tea as I wrote, but the women seemed to be a constant presence in my mind. They had opened windows into their lives and I owed it to them to portray what I had learned as faithfully and effectively as I possibly could. That was the motivation behind my choices of how I would present my dissertation.

شكراً جزيلاً يا أخواتي .

Thank you, my sisters and brothers.

"In my own backyard"

Denise Purnell's story

with Rodney Beaulieu, Bob Dick, Kath Fisher, and Renata Phelps

---

- Participatory action research
- Researcher activism
- Participant voice
- Explicit use of story
- Working in one's own community
- Poetry
- Critical race theory

Dr. Samson: Now it is my pleasure to introduce our second to last dissertation story presenter of the conference, Dr. Denise Purnell. In 2006, Denise received her EdD from Fielding Graduate University in Educational Leadership and Change. The title of her dissertation is "A Critical Race Theory Analysis of Parents' Rights in the Aftermath of the Pennsylvania State Takeover of Chester Upland School District."

Denise: Thank you Dr. Samson, Runner and all who have come to this conference to help pave the way for future ways to "research" and create dissertation projects that can help meet the many challenges that we face in the world today. Dr. Samson has asked me to be brief and I'll try my best, but I would like to start my story with a poem I call "Whose Dissertation is it Anyway?"

Do I forfeit my nagging desires?
Or conspire
to act on my intuition
and bring to fruition
what I think the dissertation should be?

I'll take a stand and do the dissertation I want to do
Not for me or for you,
But for them!
It may not be immediately understood
This dissertation is for the greater good!

During my educational journey I had contemplated numerous dissertation topics. I relentlessly reverted back to wanting to study the condition in Chester Upland School District (CUSD). The district had been plagued with a multitude of social problems, which include but are not limited to poverty, violence, teen pregnancy, low parental involvement, and two state takeovers. Parents had typically taken the brunt of the blame for these problems. My perception was that parents were being used as scapegoats while structural inequities were being ignored as contributing factors. More specifically, I believed that the state takeover affected parents' involvement, as well as their voting and civil rights. The takeover of CUSD took power away from the school board, which is made up of elected officials. This act basically erased voters' votes and limited parent involvement. I felt an insatiable desire to commit myself, as a scholar practitioner and as advocate for social justice, to this community.

Chester Upland School District, in the state of Pennsylvania, educates approximately 6,000 mostly poor, minority students from single-parent households. Grandparents manage many of these single parent households. CUSD is notorious for fiscal mismanagement, providing inadequate education to impoverished minority students prone to violence, and long referred to as the worst district out of 501 in the state of Pennsylvania. In 1994, the Pennsylvania State Legislators enforced Act 46 allowing the state of Pennsylvania to manage CUSD due to fiscal mismanagement. In the year 2000, six years after the initial state takeover, the state of Pennsylvania declared Chester Upland an empowerment district and then took over academic responsibility by reporting that half its students scored in the lowest range on the Pennsylvania Systems of School Assessment (PSSA) evaluation. At that time, a three-panel board was appointed to oversee the school district, financially and academically. In addition, Edison Schools Inc., the nation's largest private for-profit manager of public schools was hired.

Although there is so much more to reveal, suffice it to say that Edison made matters even worse on all counts. Then Edison pulled out of their contract early making the 2004–2005 school year their last with CUSD. During Edison's last year their stock prices plunged. Their shares slid from $21 to less than 50 cents on the Nasdaq. Edison was threatened with removal from Nasdaq if the price didn't rise above $1. Subsequently, Edison auctioned off textbooks, office furniture, lab supplies, and musical instruments, leaving students with decade-old books and little to no equipment. Edison's premature exodus left the two party control board to manage the district after the third control board member resigned.

I found the aforementioned deeds insultingly in need of being addressed, and was interested in what parents thought, how they felt, and if they desired to do anything about the conditions their children were being subjected to. I wanted to investigate how their parental rights were being protected and how meaningful parental participation was encouraged in the policy environment created by the Pennsylvania state takeover of the Chester Upland School District.

I did not really have the confidence at the beginning to know the power that would emerge from allowing people to tell their stories, and was not sufficiently knowledgeable about alternative formats that might help me capture that power. In fact, I went through the difficult task of changing respected committee members midstream because together we had not been able to find the vision that lurked in my soul. With the help of this first committee, I put together a new "team" and with its guidance began to formulate a plan. Although I am a poet and had thought much about how to use poetry in my dissertation, I did not know about arts-based research at the time and the work all of you have been doing. I did use some poetry, though not enough, but it was part of the traditional dissertation format, you know, with the lit review, five chapters and all. My participatory action research approach did seem appropriate to my goals, however.

My study addressed two questions: Are parental rights protected, and meaningful parental participation encouraged in the policy environment created by the Pennsylvania state takeover of the Chester Upland School District? And, what actions might parents wish to take regarding the conditions in their school district? As a result of the study and the parents' responses to these questions, they are now a strident force in the decision-making processes for school reform and for holding CUSD and federal administrators accountable.

I should also mention that after the first cycle of participant narrative, I came to realize that the conditions in Chester Upland School District existed largely because of racism. This led me to Critical Race Theory, which acknowledges that racism is imbedded, and permanent in American life. CRT also asserts that American society values property rights rather than human rights. CRT employs story telling to expose how policies and institutions promote inequality. The way in which a disenfranchised people tell a story can have significant impact. This is what I wanted to capture. I wanted to give them an opportunity to tell their story.

The way in which the parents told their stories of mistreatment and the inadequate provision of education their children are subjected to in CUSD were powerful. They eloquently protested their objections of overcrowding, lack of text books, insufficient amount of teachers, fiscal mismanagement, two unsuccessful takeovers, and no mechanisms set in place by CUSD officials to protect parental rights. It was as if they had waited a lifetime for someone to simply ask: What do you think? They argued their case as a lawyer would before a judge and a jury. They offered me testimony after testimony. One person's story would generate and inspire another person's story. I'm telling you, these parents were a wealth of information. Their information was rich in data, and their words were genuine. I believe their statements were unaffected and unrestricted because they were fearless of retribution or consequence. And they were correct. There was no one in the room who could punish them or their children for their feelings and opinions. I could not have gotten this information in any other setting. This is what I consider rigor. The oratory data spoke volumes. It was the passion in their intonation, the disgust in the pronunciation, and their spirits in their proclamations of mistreatment that is irreversible. Had they written the words down on a survey their written experiences would have been absent of truth.

The ultimate benefit to the participants was in going from feeling powerless to powerful. Participants were able to express themselves, acknowledge problems in a flawed system, and create a list of solutions to combat and resolve the problems. Participants were empowered as they implemented some of the tasks, maintaining ongoing dialogue with the American Civil Liberties Union (ACLU), National Association for the Advancement of Colored People (NAACP), and the National Education Association (NEA) to keep them abreast of the situation and to obtain support and direction on how to proceed. The parents decided to mobilize to change the conditions in which their children are educated. Participants reported they felt more prepared to take on the issues and hold others accountable for providing their children with an inadequate education. Some of the parents who participated in this study joined with a moderate parents group and are now in the process of suing to have to control board removed.

I also believe my project offers a blueprint for other superintendents and school officials in urban school districts that are being threatened with or involved in takeovers to follow for prediction, avoidance, and solutions. I had to learn how to keep my own emotions and ideas at bay, and to effectively organize and facilitate the PAR process was significant. I also learned how to facilitate and be responsive to dialogue within a dramatic and chaotic environment. Academic shadows that caused me to worry about whether this work would be concrete enough, or valid enough, were burned away by the hot light of the participants' stories. The power of oral communication, such as story telling and a person's lived experience was underestimated. The parents substantiated and validated one another. They did not need percents and ratios to authenticate how they felt.

Runner: Thank you Denise for sharing your story and the stories of those empowered by your work.

Dr. Samson: I wonder, everyone, if this example can really be considered "alternative." I mean, action research is not new. Kurt Lewin recommended this approach for solving social problems in the 1940s. In the 1970s, Paulo Freire brought forth the idea of participatory action research that Denise used as a way to empower the poorest members of community. I think that its use has more often related to organizational change, but the kind of emancipation orientation so obvious in Denise's work has been there from the beginning. Lewin's work, if I recall, was even about minority problems. Anyway, what's new or "alternative" here?

Runner: I think the problems that Denise had, even at a very progressive university, reveal that it may still be a bit of a challenge to orthodoxy when used for a doctoral dissertation. Basing a dissertation so much on the voice of the participants' stories is an alternative to most academic research. There are many things in education that were introduced long ago that remain ignored, like most of John Dewey's ideas about teaching. Also, I think you are correct about action research applications being more related organizational improvements. In any case, I think what Denise did is more than participatory action research because of the strong activism component. I would rename her "methodology" a "collaborative anti-racist activism research" or something.

Unnamed person in audience: Actually, I think that particular phrase exists already. There is a journal entitled, *Turning The Tide: Journal of Anti-Racist Activism Research and Education*.

Dr. Samson: I think this is a good time for others to join in the conversation, and I would like to introduce Dr. Rodney Beaulieu. Rodney is a co-founder of the School of Educational Leadership and Change at Fielding Graduate University, where he serves as a Professor. He is also a co-founder of the Human Development Program at California State University, San Marcos, where he served as an adjunct professor. He consults for several organizations, evaluating educational programs throughout California, has several publications, and is now writing a textbook that is aimed to help graduate students write an action research dissertation.

So you are also from FGU. You weren't on either of Denise's committees were you Rodney?

Rodney: No, but I know Denise and certainly commend her on the work she has done, and I understand the difficulties she faced in moving forward on her path. Interestingly, Fielding was established in an action-oriented tradition. Its founders challenged traditional education models, traditional views of clinical psychology, and traditional perspectives on organizations. In ELC, we assume that dissertations will be action-oriented. At the same time, faculty members are very conscientious about rigor and, frankly, most of us were trained as doctoral students in traditional methodologies, so we don't always have a large repertoire of alternative approaches to draw from, such as, for example, story telling. As dissertation chairs, we may sometimes limit our students from achieving great things because we, ourselves, are limited in our training and in our view of what's possible.

There is also the matter of dissertation formats. I admit that I have been a bit uncomfortable with a number of the formats that have been presented at this conference. I just would need to know more about them and why a student would use one to answer the dissertation question. I am willing to consider them if a candidate gives me sufficient reason. I am now working on a book that shows why the traditional five-chapter format works for action research and I was happy to see that Denise used the traditional five-chapter model for hers.

Denise: Yes, but I have to admit, it was because I did not know I had an option until I came here. Just last night, sitting with a number of my colleagues from Canada, I realized I could have incorporated poetry, which I find useful for conveying feelings and ideas in ways that I lose with academic writing. Or I perhaps could have used video documentary to better capture the work. Even just using journaling would have made the process serve my goals for learning better. And for sure the final product would have been more meaningful for future audiences. Instead of waiting until the end of my work in the field to write the dissertation, I could have written as I went. I could have found resources in the literature based on my experiences instead of doing them as a precursor to my work in the field.

Rodney: Well, that is why we are here, to talk about these things. But I want to argue for using the five-chapter form for action research. In most social/behavioral graduate programs, the dissertation is typically structured along the five-chapter, traditional format: introduction, literature review, methodology, findings, and discussion. There are many positive aspects to this dissertation structure. For example, readers can easily find specific sections of the dissertation; the format is standardized. Accordingly, if we wanted to know about the participants in a particular dissertation, we could find them introduced somewhere in the middle of Chapter 1, and again toward the beginning of Chapter 3. It's a predictable structure.

Runner: Are you saying that nontraditional formats such as those Denise learned about last night aren't as effective as traditional approaches because they are not predictable?

Rodney: Bob Kaplan addressed this several days ago when he said that readers or faculty who are not used to other formats might turn away. If most readers are expecting a five-chapter format, then anything else would potentially be disorienting. I want naïve readers to find information in a convenient way, and the five-chapter format is the most widely known approach.

Runner: For sure, but I think the whole idea of this conference is to show that this expectation, or maybe we should call it a habit, is preventing candidates from putting forth work that can get us out of many of the ruts our world is in perhaps because of such "conveniences" or expectations?

Rodney: If a student were to approach me with a dissertation proposal that is unconventional, I would encourage that student to develop the ideas further, assuming that s/he had a solid rationale for taking this approach. I appreciate creative and novel ways of representing knowledge, and don't want to discourage anyone who has clear ideas and is educated about research methods.

Denise: But Rodney, this isn't just about representing the knowledge, at least as I am beginning to understand it. I think if I had been able to write my dissertation with the narrative and poems and random ideas and even with literature sources that emerged way after I did my lit review chapter, this work might have been more meaningful both to me and to people who would have maybe been more likely to read it!

Rodney: This gets us back to the ideas about rigor that you shared as being an issue with the committee. I am not receptive to an alternative dissertation format if it does not reflect rigorous scholarship. By rigorous, I mean the dissertation proposal must include at least several important features. First, I would want a comprehensive review of published literature, including theories about the particular topic(s), and research that has already been done. This does not prevent someone from referring to new sources later. I would also want details about how the data will be collected and analyzed. Are they reliable and valid methods? I would also want to know how the student plans to structure the entire dissertation. If the five-chapter format is being rejected, what will be the alternative approach, and will this approach ensure that the findings are presented in a logical, meaningful way? The idea of your approach emerging, if you presented that to me, would have made me very nervous!

I remember that as a graduate student, I was curious to learn more about autoethnography after overhearing two professors praise a particular student's autoethnographic dissertation and discuss its controversial position in the academic world. Scanning this autoethnographic dissertation myself, I became very surprised to see it only had two chapters. The first chapter included theories about health care, followed by a lengthy philosophical discussion about research methods and a rationale for using autoethnography for dissertation research. The second chapter was a detailed narrative of the author's personal experiences in overcoming breast cancer, chronicled like journal entries. This format was disorienting, stirring lots of emotional reactions in me. I wondered why the author chose this particular approach, rather than the traditional five-chapter format that the academic world recognizes and reproduces. Was she self absorbed, focusing too openly on herself as the object of study? Was she unfamiliar with traditional dissertation approaches and didn't know how to apply "scientific" methods for research? Did she naïvely choose autoethnography by default? She reduced the dissertation process to personal "navel gazing," exploring her own experiences, rather than drawing from other knowledgeable informants on the topic. How could she possibly assume that her own voice was appropriate for data collection? I was trained to assume that empirical data should be drawn from a larger sample of participants, and the researcher should never place her/himself in the text. "Avoid the personal pronoun," I was told.

I tried to imagine this student in my head. Did she choose "soft" research methods because she flunked research methods? Why did her dissertation committee approve this work? Why did they allow her to "talk her way out" of writing a real dissertation? Why wasn't she coached to transfer to journalism or the English department instead, where she could apply her writing skills in a more appropriate academic arena? Why were they praising her work?

These questions inspired me to learn more about alternative forms of research methods, methods that are not traditionally applied in graduate programs. I shared my distaste for autoethnography with colleagues who directed me to a few convincing articles. Now, years later, I have a broader perspective of research methods and encourage my own graduate students to be familiar with many research approaches. I know there is a lot of research in support of first-person writing. But, in any case, if a student isn't able to write a fine dissertation, then it will reflect poorly on the entire dissertation committee and on the university. I know this from my own snobby biases. Like most scholars, my assumptions about "good" research methods come from my own training. I believe that the traditional five-chapter dissertation format is useful, so I recommend it to my graduate students who struggle with conceptualizing a format. I don't think I could effectively advise any other dissertation format since I have so little experience with alternative formats. This is perhaps an unfortunate but important-to-note fact. As a graduate student myself I wanted to do action research, but did not know how. I was expected to merely report my research findings. Applying the findings to improve professional practice, for example, was not something that was encouraged. My mentors didn't know how to guide me in structuring such a dissertation. There were no printed manuals about action research or many examples of action research dissertations to consider during this time.

Because action research itself is not formulaic, my thinking is that a solid, proven structure for presenting is needed. It can help the candidate organize their questions, such as: "What is the scope of the problem that I want to address?"; "What resources are available to me, both material and human? How can the planning process proceed?"; "What is the desired outcome? What are the short- and long-term implications?"

It's an exciting time in social/behavioral research. In the past, we struggled to apply research methods that originated in physical science to our field. These were the best tools of the time—we thought. We're now critically questioning the value of those traditional approaches because they haven't always led to "truth" or helped us improve the quality of life. For the most part, the dissertations of the past continue to sit on university library shelves, collecting dust, and most have made few practical contributions. To see so many scholars now considering alternative approaches that might offer unique insight about our complex world is good, and we can use the knowledge that is generated to improve the quality of life for everyone. We should welcome this.

Dr. Samson: Thanks Rodney. I would now like to introduce Bob Dick, who came all the way from Australia to be with us, and who may have a somewhat different view than Rodney's. Bob divides his time between independent scholarship, an adjunct appointment at Southern Cross University, and work as a facilitator and consultant in the field of change. His interests include action research and the use of story. He is also the author of *Rigour Without Numbers* and *Values in Action*.

Bob: I'll offer a few comments on Denise's approach, and then respond to Rodney's advocacy of the five-chapter thesis structure.

A growing number of thesis candidates, like Denise, use research as a vehicle for giving a voice to those who often lack it. They help participants bring about desired changes. I'm encouraged by the growth of such research. It can make an immediate difference in the world. It contributes to bringing the academy and the community together. It integrates research and practice. These are some of the reasons for my own interest in action research.

I'm also pleased to hear about the explicit use of story in Denise's research. In my experience it allows multiple levels of meaning to be expressed. Story and action research go well together, in my view.

Rodney argues that there is some risk in departing from accepted practice in structuring a thesis. I agree with this, as I agree with his identification of the advantages of a conventional structure. There are also advantages in adopting an alternative approach. I'll come to them in a moment.

If you look at the action research web site at Southern Cross University you'll find two papers on thesis structure. One, by my friend and former colleague Chad Perry, recommends a conventional five-chapter structure. You'll find it at www.scu.edu.au/schools/gcm/ar/art/cperry.html. Another, which I wrote, suggests that for action research a less conventional structure may be justified. It further suggests that such a thesis can be organized around the contribution to knowledge that the thesis makes. The paper is at www.scu.edu.au/schools/gcm/ar/art/arthesis.html. These papers are intended to offer candidates a choice; I don't wish to be an evangelist for either approach. I do wish to see both traditional and non-traditional approaches chosen on their merits.

In probably a large majority of research studies, existing theory and the literature guide the choice of topic and methodology. This is true of some action research too. A conventional five-chapter thesis structure then works well. Because of the advantages that Rodney identifies, it may be safer to be traditional.

Other action research studies are shaped more by the situation and the participants. This seems to be true, for instance, of Denise's thesis. A pressing concern motivated the study. I suggest, first, that action research is a particularly apt choice of methodology for such a study. Action research offers researcher and participants high flexibility and responsiveness to the situation. Second, I don't believe a five-chapter structure does justice to such an action research study.

I have two main reasons for this belief. At the beginning of such a study it's unlikely that a candidate understands the research situation well. The participants may not yet be well known either. It's hard to design in detail a methodology to fit well to a poorly known situation. It's often better to fine-tune the methodology as you proceed—as you learn more about the situation. The second reason is similar. Without a good understanding of the situation you are unlikely to know which literature is going to be most relevant to your action outcomes and your research findings.

To my mind, a conventional structure implies that literature and methodology together decide much of what happens. If they do, then like Rodney I'd encourage candidates to consider using a conventional structure unless they have a good reason to depart from it.

Many candidates choose action research because it allows them to engage more flexibly with the situation and the participants. It then makes more sense to adopt an approach, and a structure, that capitalizes on that flexibility. I don't believe a conventional thesis structure does so.

As Rodney says, departing from convention carries risks and other disadvantages. Fortunately, there are ways of reducing these. Candidates can explain why they have departed from convention. They can cite methodological literature that supports less traditional approaches. They can provide informative previews—signposts—that let readers know where they will find the information. They can take care that they situate their findings in the relevant literature. They can relate their theory to other relevant theories.

Runner: Thanks Bob. Also here from Southern Cross University in Australia are Dr. Kath Fisher and Dr. Renata Phelps. Kath is the Associate Dean of Graduate Studies at Southern Cross University and works in a support capacity with postgraduate students from across the university and is currently supervising students doing action research. Renata is Senior Lecturer in Educational Information Technology and her action research focuses on supporting teachers' professional development in IT. In 2007, together with a third colleague, they published a book for postgraduate research students on organizing and managing research. In 2006 they wrote a three-act play that was published in *Action Research*, which I personally found very enlightening. You can tell by the title alone how well it fits this conversation, "Recipe or Performing Art: Challenging Conventions for Writing Action Research Theses." Thanks so much for joining us Kath and Renata!

Renata: Thanks for the invitation. We are excited about this conference and appreciate the dialogue we have heard about what constitutes quality research. There is a growing paradigmatic debate across the humanities and social science disciplines that questions the nature of "knowledge" and the need for a uniform criteria of validity. I've brought a list of references that I'll post later, but I'm now thinking of Bradbury and Reason, as well as Winters. I think one of the problems with all qualitative research is the constant need to seek its justification within someone else's framework.

Kath: I agree, of course. The play form with our imaginary characters that we used for the article we wrote for *Action Research* itself proved to us the efficacy of alternative ways of writing. I don't think we could have explored the tensions and incongruities between conventional thesis presentation and the principles of action research as well in a strictly academic format. Our approach in the article is an example of "presentational knowing," which although rarely seen in an academic journal, allows the text to "speak out" and challenge convention. Action research is not just cathartic, it is political. Our "play" challenges orthodoxy because it is possible that a formulaic approach to academic writing, as required by both journal and dissertation conventions, can restrict the authenticity and integrity of research that is dynamic and emergent.

Renata: Yes, although Rodney is right about it being safer to follow established convention, I challenge the capacity of traditional research to adequately address the many social problems facing our world today. I think that engaging the spirit of action research requires letting go of having things go in a particular way. Conventional research tends to leave mistakes and "dead ends" out of the final presentation. But such dead ends can be a critical part of the learning, change, and theory development process!

Runner: So you agree with Bob about the potential problems with, say, a standard five-chapter literature review?

Renata: Yes. Literature references should reflect the emergent process and the thesis that comes from conducting action research. Literature should be woven through the developing arguments and interpretations. Reading can inform different stages of the research process and the reflection, insight, application process then provides the framework for structuring the thesis in the same way that this cycle informed participants to solve problems.

Dr. Samson: Rodney referred to the problem of "navel gazing" that can possibly detract from the rigor of the kind of dissertation you seem to be describing.

Kath: If I may, I understand Rodney's point and it is indeed important for us to help doctoral candidates distinguish authentic inquiry and understanding from indulgent navel gazing. We need to know how to assist them in identifying key turning points in the narrative, rather than just allowing them to give blow-by-blow descriptions. But this is a better option than just giving in to the standard orthodoxy surrounding academic research and writing.

Dr. Samson: This has been a great dialogue, and a good introduction really for our next and final dissertation story about a representative format presented long ago that is still not, even in my conservative perspective, where it should be! But before we move on, let's give Denise, Rodney, Bob, Renata, and Kath a big hand.

(Applause)

"Flight of ducks"
Electronic dissertations
Simon Pockley's story

with Glen Gatin

- Web-based dissertation
- UNESCO
- Streams of conversation
- Institutional tension

Students who remain persistent in their efforts to provide broader access to their research and/or to challenge what counts as knowledge in the academy by experimenting with non-linear structure and visual or auditory forms of information in publishing their work defy assimilation to the cultural model of the research professor.

(Jude Edminster. See 'Resistance to ETDs in Academe' at www.bgsu.edu/cconline/edminster/resetds.htm)

Dr. Samson: Our last dissertation presentation before our closing speakers is also a biographical "participant story" of sorts, though it is a story about the author's father and his expedition across the plains of Australia. It is also our only electronic dissertation representative. In fact, it was the world's *first* electronic, web-based dissertation as far as we know. Yes, Dr. Simon Pockley was responsible for the world's first online doctoral thesis, "The Flight of Ducks," which you can access on the World Wide Web. I'll write it down for you now: www.duckdigital.net/FOD/. Simon receives invitations to speak at National and International forums where he speaks, and also writes about, values in the ecology of information management. He was a contributor to UNESCO's Guide to Preservation and Digital Heritage as well as the UNESCO Guide to Electronic Theses and Dissertations. He lives in Australia and is in demand as a PhD supervisor, examiner, and student mentor. He works from time to time as a consultant.

Dr. Samson: I must admit I'm nervous about this movement to electronic and other non-print dissertations. Our academy is founded on publication of the written word in English and with a certain prescribed and accepted format. I for one am worried that the Internet will cause us to forget this basic tool of scholarship!

Runner: The benefits of non-print dissertations allow for greater expression and creativity, for keeping research alive and open-ended, for a universal reach that is accessible for many to learn from and build upon. I think we had better let Simon tell his own story. Simon, welcome to the United States.

Simon: Thanks Runner and Dr. Samson. I'm grateful to be invited. As to your concerns, Dr. Samson, I think they are misplaced. The written word is alive and kicking. When it comes to publication, the written word has never been more widely accessible. I think what you mean is that your academy was founded on maintaining restricted access to the printed page. I suspect that this was more to do with control than scholarship. Although many of the conventions of paper text have been carried into the electronic domain, when it comes to form, a properly conceived electronic thesis or dissertation is actually an intelligent organism capable of adapting to the needs of its readers. Scholarship is necessarily attended by discipline, rigor, fearlessness, and the ability to build bridges between disciplines. Scholarly texts are really mutable streams of thought, open to annotation, revision, re-presentation and part of the very fabric of their community of interest.

To the best of my knowledge, the *Flight of Ducks* was the first fully online doctorate in that it was publicly conceived, researched, developed, submitted, examined—and since 1995 has been stored—online. For the last ten years it has attracted an annual audience of over two million individuals. This is a brief description of how it came about. There's more, but you'll have to go to the Web for that.

The research began in 1990 when my father died. I extracted from his belongings a collection of artifacts, a pile of photographs, and journals relating to a camel expedition into Central Australia in 1933. I'd grown up with stories from this trip and I felt a duty to protect the integrity of this collection.

In 1933 my father was only twenty years old when he wrote his field journal. He never sought to have it published. Indeed, he insisted that it was not of sufficient interest (or quality) to warrant publication. At first glance, he was right. The original is, by itself, little more than a few sparse jottings.

Nevertheless, as part of the journey of the son around the father, I spent many nights over the next three years typing up an annotated version of the journal that combined the original with subsequent versions. To my surprise, I found that many of the stories I had grown up with were (through the process of elaboration) imaginary. When I started looking at other people's accounts of central Australian journeys, I discovered that his journal was typical, that most of the desert journeys were actually spiritual journeys assembled from the imagination, field notes, and previous accounts.

Herein lies the significance of the title, the *Flight of Ducks*. It refers to a song at the heart of the expedition journal, to imaginative flight, and to the shape and form that the project began to assume after I found that I had lost all my typing to a corrupted hard drive and began to use the World Wide Web as a space to hold the story.

I chose the Web as a repository as a pragmatic way of ensuring that my digital files would be there when I wanted them. It enabled me to build a deeply layered work where the files were laid out in a series of parallel lines to reflect the topography of the landscape through which the expedition travelled. As the site evolved, I began to traverse a datascape and to write about my own journey of discovery. These reports took on some of the characteristics of the explorer's journal. They were like streams of conversation and they had a poetic that lay somewhere between a postcard and a phone tap. I hadn't anticipated that other people would find the material and talk back to it. My research into how the central story could be best accessed and preserved rapidly became encrusted with other people's stories and observations. I guess this inclusive aspect also make it the first blog. It is easy to forget that in late 1994, any understanding of a Web-enabled poetic was drawn more from the vision of such prescient thinkers as Vannevar Bush and Ted Nelson than from actual experience. Back then, the Web was a novelty: there were very few personal digital repositories, neither semantic nor syntactic consensus for metadata, and most "interactive" writing took little account of the implications of having two-way communications—particularly over scholarly material.

In 1995 I became a "mature-age" PhD student with a vaguely defined archival project based on preserving my father's material in a digital domain. But it was enough to give me access to a server. As I recall, each student was entitled to an email account with a megabyte of storage space. Through luck rather than skill, I found my way into a newly established research lab with access not only to a server but also to a $100k Silicon Graphics workstation. It was computing heaven if you wanted to work on high-end 3D graphics, but I didn't and I never took this Maserati out of first gear. I just used the text editor (Notepad equivalent) and taught myself HTML the hard way. At that time there weren't any books or tutorials on Markup. The way to learn was through a process of reverse engineering where you would copy someone's source code and modify it to suit.

The values underlying this form of shared collaborative learning, involving unbridled appropriation, proliferation, re-use and re-presentation have become the values of the Electronic Thesis and Dissertation (ETD) movement. But at the time, I was barely aware that for information to be knowledge it required a social and cultural dimension. The hands-on work of writing and learning Markup languages meant that when I scanned the images and fragmented the texts I was necessarily engaged in an iterative methodology akin to sculpting. I'd once worked as a puppeteer and I could not help but see the screen as a small theater. The challenges of working with these constraints led to my involvement in the development of the shadow language of descriptive containment known as the Dublin Core Metadata Standard.

The application of metadata was one of several interrelated areas of research that constituted the focus of my doctoral research. The others were: long-term access strategies, networked narrative structures, and the complex arena of Aboriginal representation online. There was an obvious tension between the institutional requirement for fixing an exegesis in time and the evolving nature of the research. The paper entitled *Killing the Duck to Keep the Quack* describes some of these challenges.

The University not only lacked the infrastructure to accommodate an online thesis but also lacked any insight in to how it might be examined. Eventually, I had to write my own protocols. I think that Virginia Tech, in the U.S.A., adopted them. The Higher Degrees Committee insisted that I also submit a bound paper thesis and a CD-ROM of the site. On the eve of submission, a politicized University Ethics Committee deleted the entire site from the University server. Such was the level of controversy that my Australian examiners withdrew and I became an academic untouchable.

My research into long-term access had encouraged me to engage in proliferation as a preservation strategy. This meant that the site could be accessed through several servers in Australia and the U.S.A. In addition, the National Library of Australia had chosen the *Flight of Ducks* as a pilot for their archive of sites of national significance. After nine months the Ethics Committee conceded their mistake and in 1998 the doctorate was examined in the U.S.A. at MIT and UCLA. This was the first of a series of politically motivated assaults on the site. It is now hosted in Hong Kong.

Regardless of the institutional dysfunction, or good fortune, that has kept the *Flight of Ducks* "in the wild," it remains outside the custodial influence of the university that approved my research and awarded my doctorate. As a consequence, the rationale behind *proliferation*, as a demonstrably successful digital preservation strategy, has extended to values that can be characterised as open, transparent, unprotected, and responsive.

That the *Flight of Ducks* is still "live" and still growing is not necessarily at odds with existing academic and administrative requirements. The imperative to freeze the doctoral thesis in time, for the purpose of examination, is easily accommodated. But why should it end there? The more time passes, the more likely it is that there will be more to say and more to understand about any chosen area of research.

That an electronic thesis should be open to annotation and responsive to change is not only dependent on its architecture, but on its genuine connections to human activity and thought. If we acknowledge the passion and endurance that is required to complete a higher degree of substance, then there is a discontinuity in the expectation that the momentum of scholarly discourse should stop at the point of submission for examination.

Doctoral research inevitably leads to professional and academic practice. The *Flight of Ducks* demonstrates that the electronic thesis can also serve as a personal repository for containing the revisions, expansions, and contractions of post-doctoral thought—as well as locating articles and conference papers within a contextual framework.

For me, the thoughtful human interaction that occurs almost every day as a result of having an openly accessible dissertation on the Web is not only a source of delight but inevitably leads to what one contributor described as, "the flesh meeting." This is a tendency towards physical meeting as a consequence of networked communication. It is a phenomenon at odds with the notion of disconnection invariably associated with an intellectual life.

Runner: What a fascinating history. Thanks so much Simon. Are there any doctoral candidates here who are planning on an electronic dissertation? Glen, would you introduce yourself and tell us a little about what you are doing?

Glen Gatin: I am an educator from Canada who uses web-based technologies for teaching and learning. I have long been interested in the potential of the Internet to extend human consciousness. Teihard de Chardin, in The Future of Man, proposed the concept of the noosphere or the sphere of collective consciousness. Others have suggested that the Internet may be a manifestation of an evolving sphere of collective consciousness mediated by electronic networks. My participation in various online, collaborative communities has deepened my conviction that this is the case and I believe that our understanding of human knowledge and its expression will need to incorporate this alternative perspective. I'm currently working on my doctorate at Fielding Graduate University in Educational Leadership and Change, with a concentration on Media Studies and I hope to use a wiki to compose my doctoral dissertation.

Dr. Samson: Can you explain to everyone what a "wiki" is Glen?

Glen: A wiki is a Web-based collection of electronic documents that is set up in an application that allows easy access, editing, and sharing. It is ideal for collaborative work between people at a distance. You set up an account with a wiki host and begin writing pages with a text editor. You can easily create hot links between other pages that you create or links to documents and resources stored elsewhere.

With a wiki format for my dissertation, rather than referencing the living authors who are practicing in my field of interest, I can record interviews and embed video or audio clips. In my mind this would be much more authentic and verifiable than footnotes and bibliography entries that reference past publications. I am very pleased that my dissertation committee at Fielding Graduate University has agreed to consider this alternate dissertation, which essentially represents an evolutionary step in the discovery of and contribution to human knowledge.

A wiki can be set up to have multiple contributors. As Simon said, this allows a dissertation to be a "living" work, so to speak. The best thing about a wiki is the idea that it represents a living document and embodies the spirit of scholarship and the collaborative development of ideas. The scholar–practitioner values of the doctoral program are complemented by the democratic nature of the wiki tool. The wiki makes co-production of knowledge a real possibility. In an open wiki there is a sense of trust and regard for the ideas and values of other participants.

Usually the originator of the wiki has the administrative rights to the overall wiki and has the ability to determine the number of contributors and the privileges that each enjoys. Some can be invited to read only, others can be given the right to contribute material and edit their own contributions, still others can be given the right to edit all content. If the wiki is open to the general public, the administrator often reserves the right to vet each contribution, which means that a new addition to the page notifies the administrator who has the ability to accept or refuse the new content.

Some institutions of higher learning have been piloting a variety of projects investigating the possibilities of electronic formats for academic purposes. An increasing number of institutions are insisting that any thesis or dissertation be published and presented in an electronic format. Proquest is a major publisher of academic works and has an extensive electronic database including electronic dissertations from 2005-2006.

I think for a doctoral student there are many advantages to an ETD format and many universities now have guidelines in place for doing so. For example, you can go to the University of Vermont's ETD Web site and actually go through a tutorial.

Runner: Would you get that Web site address for me, Glen?

Glen: Actually, I have it here in my notebook. It is http://etd.vt.edu/etd tutorials/.

Anyway, the advantages are many. An ETD facilitates the dissemination of ideas worldwide. More people have access to the ideas and information expressed in such a dissertation. This practice would enhance a more equitable access to academic resources, as many of the publication formats for academic publications are difficult to navigate and expensive to access. It also allows for more creativity and artfulness. It allows, as I've said, for an interactive process that keeps the research alive and growing. From an environmental perspective, ETDs have a much lower impact given that there is no need to transport and store reams of costly high quality, acid-free paper in a comparatively large and expensive temperature-controlled environments. Digital storage servers and the energy costs to maintain them represent a fraction of the environmental cost. In terms of the economics of higher education the monetary savings realized in this way could be reinvested in many of the priority areas that are emerging.

Anyway, I didn't mean to give a sales pitch for ETDs, but I'm sure after hearing Simon's remarkable story, many of us here are going to want to look more carefully at this alternative!

Closing remarks

with Rita L. Irwin, Stephanie Springgay, Alex de Cosson, and Tony van Renterghem

We must reconstrue our curriculum to focus on knowledge-in-action rather than knowledge-out-of-context. . . . As we move through life, we learn to draw upon many different traditions that provide alternative, often complementary, ways of knowing and doing—of defining the world and of existing within it.

(Arthur N. Applebee, from *Curriculum as Conversation: Transforming Traditions of Teaching and Learning*, 1996, p. 3)

Dr. Samson: We have arrived at the close of our remarkable week together. I must say that in spite of my skepticism about "arts-based" and other forms of research and representation, I now understand the potential of this movement. Perhaps we lost something along our higher educational path in spite of the fact that this path has nonetheless led us to some amazing places. Yet, perhaps it is past time to consider other ways of knowing for this highest level of education.

We have had the great opportunity to listen to a remarkable group of scholars, scholars whose courageous passion for their subject expanded boundaries in higher education. In addition to the personal stories that informed these dissertations, from the first fictional work to the first web-based project, we have also listened to the comments of many distinguished scholars about ways of knowing, research, and representation that stand outside the status quo boundaries of the academy. Now we close with some words of wisdom from four others whose authentic lives and leadership have, in one way or the other, helped pave the way for all of us to challenge the status quo when the status quo is no longer working in the positive.

Our first three speakers include Rita L. Irwin, Stephanie Springgay, and Alex de Cosson. They will talk briefly about their long-time experiences with arts-based research and with what they call "a/r/tography." Then, our final invited guest, Mr. Tony van Renterghem, will share some final thoughts for us to ponder.

Introducing the three distinguished scholars from left to right we have Dr Rita L. Irwin. Rita is a Professor and Associate Dean of Teacher Education, Faculty of Education at the University of British Columbia. She is an artist, researcher, and teacher who is committed to the arts as living inquiry. As such, she continues to create art, conduct research, and practice her pedagogy in ways that are integrative, reflective, and full of living awareness.

Stephanie Springgay is an Assistant Professor of Art Education and Women's Studies at Penn State University. Her research and artistic interests include the body, phenomenology of touch and desire, aesthetics, visual culture, feminist epistemologies, social justice in the arts, and a/r/tographical research. Her artistic installations incorporate human hair and felt. Stephanie was awarded the 2005 AERA Arts and Learning SIG Dissertation Award and the 2004 UBC, Ted T. Aoki Outstanding Dissertation Prize.

Alex F. de Cosson is a sculptor with a PhD from the University of British Columbia; he has been on the faculty of the Ontario College of Art and Design since 1989 and is concurrently a Sessional Instructor at UBC in Art Education, Department of Curriculum Studies. His research interests include arts-based and autobiographical arenas. Alex was awarded the Gordon and Marion Smith Award in Art Education, from UBC in 2003.

(*Speaking to the panel*) It's all yours!

Rita: Inspired by the many conference presentations I listened to during the week, I am honored to sit briefly with my colleagues here to reflect on our own journeys as they relate to mentoring doctoral students. Our collective conversation with(in) a (s)p(l)ace of un/knowing seeks questions not answers, finds comfort in discomfort and imagines the possibilities of what I call, "a/r/tographical research." A/r/tography, in brief, is a process of unfolding image and text together (image in this sense could mean poetry, music or other forms of artistic inquiry). It is a research methodology that intentionally unsettles perception and complicates understandings. It is really a living practice, a life-creating experience examining our personal, political, and/or professional lives. Many, if not all of the presentations we listened to this week are examples I think.

It doesn't seem that long ago when I completed my doctorate. I wanted to use action research as my methodology but was unable to do so given there wasn't a critical mass of professors at my university to support me. Four years later, after completing my degree and working at another university, I returned to my alma mater as an assistant professor. During my first semester on campus I stepped out of the mold and integrated action research into one of my courses. The students became so involved with their projects they wanted to continue after the course was finished. This group became my first group of arts-based researchers. During those years, we began to conceptualize what research would look like if it began from art and action research. We wrote articles, read theory, and practiced our teaching and art making. Our monthly dinner meetings at my home became a very special time for all of us.

Alex: As I struggled to write my dissertation I was buoyed by a lifeline to similar-minded people. I remember well, my committee member Carl Leggo telling me that I must cultivate a pool of support and allow time to take its course. "You most probably will not find it all in one place. (I didn't realize, at the time, how he was referring to both time and people.) You have to put it together as you attend conferences and meet others interested in similar issues." It was this liminal "(s)p(l)ace" of connection that slowly materialized and became a driving force in my dissertation writing.

Stephanie: This reminds me of a student who arrived in my office to speak with me about the possibilities of "performing" an arts-based dissertation. To prepare for this journey she had undertaken the task of working on an independent study, the outcome of which will be an artful comprehensive exam. She is excited by the prospects of thinking with(in) this "(s)p(l)ace," but also heavy with hesitation as she will be among the first to do so at her institution. I'm conscious of the fact that while my arts-based dissertation was encouraged and respected, she and others like her will face challenges as they work their way through the tenure process, colleague's words of rigor and standards brushing against their ears. This is why conferences like this one are important.

Alex: In fact, it was at my very first conference when I met Gary Knowles, another one of the pioneers in this movement that recognizes the many forms of art in the research process. He stood in the lobby area animating a kinetic sculpture with controls held behind his back. There were two other sculptures on view in the same area. The intrigue struck me immediately. I stopped to observe as he called out to conference goers, "Does this resemble your experience of teaching?" Some passed with a, *don't bug me, I'm on a mission that doesn't include some harebrained piece of whatever that is*, expression. They hurried to their sessions; the idea that art could have a place in these research corridors seemed foreign to some. However, there were many who were interested; who stopped or came back after their sessions and engaged with these wonderfully playful and insightful works. They talked with Gary and others who gathered, conversations were traded; the art was working as it should—creating places and spaces for new understandings to be co-created. Meanings unfolded for those present as they engaged with the sculptures and each other. Dialogues of real-life teaching were heard echoing from the ceilings.

As this was my first conference, little did I know the significance of what I was experiencing. I have been to many conferences since and I have yet to see something so immediate; as sessions are presented behind closed doors, tiptoed into after the assigned start time. I now realize that the use of the lobby, the medium of expression, the delivery method, were all innovative and challenging to the accepted norms of conference gatherings. That I was engaged in *living* research has grown with me as an example of the powerful effect arts-based research can have.

Rita: In a time span of twenty years since completing my doctorate, I have witnessed an epistemological shift and a methodological transformation at the University of British Columbia. Whereas I used qualitative ethnographic techniques in my doctoral research, students are now participating in the creation of a methodology called a/r/tography as a precursor to their doctoral research work. The conditions for this fundamental shift can be attributed to several important points. First of all, as a faculty member I was in a good position to experiment with new research methods and to support students. Second, while I tested the waters among my colleagues, I pursued my interests with like-minded graduate students. This supported our mutual desire to grow while giving all of us the courage to transform our research traditions. With that courage I was able to learn how to debate with those who were unaware of our innovations. Third, and perhaps more importantly, our work was beginning to have an impact on others. Starting out in a small community of graduate students committed to change, we collaboratively gathered strength, ideas, and creativity from one another. We were stronger together than we were apart. As a result of the incremental development of the research methods within the faculty as a whole, students were able to identify committees that supported arts-based educational research.

Stephanie: During my graduate program I met regularly with colleagues at UBC in a research group, one that was dedicated to understanding our own connections to the world of the arts-based dissertations. We met weekly for a number of terms, presented at conferences together, and debated the many issues that arose from what we were seeing and reading. As we were all visual artists it meant that our understandings were coming from a similar framework. This tightness of focus allowed us to conceptualize and formulate a/r/tography as a research methodology from which dissertations could be (art)iculated and defended.

At the time of writing my dissertation I remember how frustrating it was to be in a place of not only thinking through research questions, but one where simultaneously I/we were creating a new methodology. I recall the anxiety I felt trying to explain to faculty and students that my methodology was not "complete," that it was not this package that I could apply to my research site and text. While struggling to analyze and grasp the effects of my research project in a local secondary school, I was also trying to articulate the intricacies of doing a/r/tographical research with others. There were so many moments of hesitation, of uncertainty, and fear. I know that I often retreated to my studio where the texture of hair and red pigments that stained by fingers blood red, allowed me new points of departure, and helped me wade through the thickness of un/knowing my research. This leads me to think about the conceptual narrative I describe in my dissertation. At one point in my committee meetings someone mentioned that my writing read like too many "dropped threads." It was a wonderful metaphor that interconnected with numerous conversations I had had with the classroom teacher.

In pondering this notion of "dropped threads" I discovered an image of Bronwyn, the art teacher, sitting in the class un/knitting. I also remember my grandmother having to unknit something because she had "dropped" a stitch, which meant that there was a mistake in her pattern, a place that she needed to return to so that she could re-knit her project. This form of unknitting is linear, traveling a path backwards to a place of origin, to a dropped, missed stitch, in order to repair and correct the knitting. Bronwyn's un/knitting was altogether different. These were not dropped threads that she was trying to mend, but rather she was involved in an active process of "dropping threads"— intentional acts of disruption. Using previously knitted objects, Bronwyn un/knits, and I use the slash in this instance to "image" the idea of unknitting and knitting simultaneously, in order to create something new. Her knitted art pieces are interwoven combinations of "dropped threads," entangled wools of different colours and textures.

Bronwyn's un/knitting is aesthetic inquiry, it is a process of interrogation, and because she intentionally questions, examines, and reflects on its meaning in relation to her art practices and pedagogy, it also becomes an a/r/tographical gesture. Jean Luc Nancy articulates this concept of un/knitting when he argues that meaning is created when it "comes apart." This philosophical shift is important because common sense posits meaning as a linear assemblage, as something that is added to and built upon. Instead, un/knitting insists that meaning is an exposure, a rupture that emphasizes an opening up.

Rita: With my graduate students and supportive colleagues we have managed to stretch our ideas collectively while maintaining our independent research, teaching, and art-making activities. What has been incredibly exciting for me has been witnessing the development of these ideas over time and with different groups of people, while cherishing the commitment by everyone to ensure the conceptual and philosophical premises of our epistemological change.

We began to understand that a/r/tography is committed to emphasizing the process of inquiry in addition to the representational form; to the evolution of ongoing research questions; and to collaborative yet critical engagement as a research collective. As students embrace these and other ideas, I feel compelled to participate to the same degree. Imagining an a/r/tographical (s)p(l)ace I create and write alongside others.

Alex: Witnessing the evocative presentations at this conference, I know the three of us are mindful of the paths taken and the new directions to come through a/r/tographical research. Although each of us has a different story to tell about navigating, writing, and mentoring arts-based dissertations, it is through collaboration and the collective nature of living inquiry that a/r/tography is materialized, embodied, and given form.

Runner: Let's give a round of applause to our panel.

(*Applause*)

It is now my great privilege to introduce you to Tony van Renterghem. Tony, now at age 88, was a young officer in the Dutch Cavalry and he fought the Nazi invaders of his Netherlands home. He spent five years in the Dutch Resistance and ran the Dutch Resistance's Underground Camera photo unit. He received many honors, including being awarded Israel's Yad Vashem medal for saving Jewish lives from the Holocaust. He is the author of the acclaimed book, *When Santa Was a Shaman*, and was the research advisor for both the Pulitzer Prize-winning play and the Hollywood motion-picture, *The Diary of Anne Frank*, and was director of research, working with Carl Sandburg, for the movie *The Greatest Story Ever Told*, although he tells me that the producer/ director, George Stevens Sr., was pressured by religious groups not to use much of their painstaking research about the "man" Jesus. Tony is also the only surviving participant and chairman of the 1949 World Federation of Liberal and Radical Youth founding conference at Cambridge University, and was recently honored by them. There is so much more I could say about his life experiences, but Tony just whispered to me that if I talk much longer he will be too tired to talk himself. So without further ado . . . (*Applause*)

Tony: It has been good to see the courage behind many of the dissertation projects here. Courage to do relevant work to make the world healthier. Courage to challenge the status quo and risk repercussions. I have said that, nowadays, the ivory towers of the academy, with their cautious kittens, hardly qualify as lion's dens, but you may be proving me wrong. Still, you all seem to be the exception and the resistance to what you are doing seems significant. What concerns me is the kind of one-dimensional spin our academic system seems to have been forced into.

The original meaning of the word academe/academic as referring to a place of learning is no longer its key meaning. Where, at one time, students gathered around some wise, experienced person, to listen and walk with him, and *to exchange* ideas under a star-lit sky, while watching far-borne waves crashing on a rocky shore . . . that is a dream of the past; nowadays, academic learning, too often, has become synonymous with stuffy, pedantic, dull, linear, one-way communication achieved through take-it-or-leave-it hand-outs or on-line learning.

How did this change take place and what caused it to change? Knowledge is a gift, to be shared and passed on. The first shaman who discovered how to keep and make fire, shared his/her knowledge with the young tribal members, together with the tricks of hunting, and the facts of puberty and pro-creation. But soon some less-principled shaman came to realize that his knowledge could be used for personal power, privilege, and wealth. Thus, a priesthood came into power and together with their partner—the warrior chief/king/dictator—gained control over their clan, tribe, or nation! And now we have, "The Academy."

Too much linear thinking and "thinking inside the box" create an academic coffin of lethal security, respectability, and tenure. Yet trying to think outside the box also means having to disassociate oneself from the comforting approval of the foundations of one's theories by respected predecessors and colleagues; maybe even having to disprove some of them. It may also require disassociating oneself from the even more comforting possibility of recognition and acclaim by those who had hoped to see you as an ally for their own causes.

I have been so disheartened by what I am seeing happening in our world today. But hearing the stories that I have heard this week has given me hope for the future if more like you will climb out of the safe playpen of academic security, and if more scholars begin to teach on the cutting edge of reality and conventional sanity, venturing beyond, as did Galileo, Columbus, and Einstein; probing and proving the existence of other dimensions and realities in the same manner that brain synapses reach out non-linearly to probe for other, different, and perhaps better, paths of achievement.

When I was in high school I saw how academic conservatism at first violently opposed such thinking and teaching, as when Alfred Wegner saw Earth as a red-hot, center-gravitated ball of glowing molten stone, with, on its surface, tectonic, continental plate crusts floating around and bumping into each other. It was hardly academic research per se when he noticed on a map how the world's continents seemed to fit into each other like pieces of a puzzle. I remember one bold teacher who tried to present his theory at my high school, but was prohibited from doing so as "not being based on proper academic thinking." It took fifty years for his idea to be finally accepted.

Painting God into man's image (rather than the other way around) creates a false foundation and in many ways this is what conventional academics try to do. The worst teaching and the worst research stems from this kind of fundamentalist approach whereby researchers build on ideas they consider absolute. The true charm of academic knowledge should be that it remains flexible and open to change by new and, yes, even radical thinking, pro-vided it can then be verified by present knowledge of reality and is situated contextually in present reality. If it cannot, it is either false or present know-ledge is insufficient and needs to be re-examined and re-adjusted; but never just on the basis of academic orthodoxy. American education is fragmented, too irrelevant to what is going on in our world. Students emerge from schools able to do well on multiple-choice questions but poorly in critical thinking about what matters. Academic teaching is also too often controlled, or browbeaten, by irresponsible governments with imperial ambitions. Institutes of higher learning and their teachers have become guilty accomplices, by practicing omission and invoking mindless requirements to memorize hegemonic mandates.

When during WW-II in 1941 the Nazi occupiers of the Netherlands required that all academic teachers sign, under oath, that they would never teach anything opposed to the Führer and the Nazi Occupation Forces or else would lose their jobs and their tenure, they almost unanimously refused and walked out rather than becoming Nazi accomplices. Most of them privately continued teaching out of their homes. The prime task for a teacher *is* to bear witness to the truth, not to ignore it or look the other way when, for instance, one's fellow teachers are fired and sent to death camps with their families. Yes, teaching is a vocation that not only requires knowledge, but courage and solidarity as well. And if applying the arts to research, or if, for instance, allowing for Indigenous ways of knowing, or presenting data in alternative ways will do something to help clean our air, stop wars and global warming, reduce prejudice and greed, then the courage and solidarity I have seen at this conference must spread like a wildfire before it is too late.

(*Applause*)

Runner and Dr. Samson: Everyone please rise as our invited Indigenous drummers and singers offer our closing song. We wish all of you safe journeys and express our deepest appreciation for your participation in this event.

End of recorded transcript.

Bibliography

People who try to please or otherwise gain acceptance seldom make important discoveries, for they limit their endeavors to contexts and channels that have been established by others. For this reason any academic fields in the humanities and social sciences, whose arguments are not scientifically demonstrable and whose denizens, therefore, are rewarded only when they have gained acceptance by respectable elders and specialized scholarly journals, are currently all but barren of real discovery . . .

   This state of affairs discourages bold advances and disciplinary self-questioning (especially in younger scholars), instead encouraging conservative projects, patriarchism, faddism, and groupiness. It paves the way for a politicization of scholarship, a damper on free inquiry. Instead of developing an open forum, these factors have nurtured a bureaucracy of letters, a vast system of categories, departments, and subspecialties devoted to narrow and formalized discourse, inimical to questions of wholeness, and resistant to any evolution except the incremental proliferation of its own complexity.

   (Robert Grudin, *The Grace of Great Things*, pp. 31 and 169)

In his book, *The Courage to Create*, Rollo May says that whereas moral courage is about righting wrongs, creative courage is about discovering new forms, new symbols, and new patterns on which a new society can be built. With this in mind, the contributors to this book might be considered as courageous as any discoverer. In addition to these individuals, there are also many other courageous scholars who have written books or articles specifically attempting to challenge the barriers to more creative research in the Academy that Grudin describes above. The following list of readings are from such individuals and may help further pave the way for future students so as to minimize these barriers for them to create or discover vital knowledge for bringing health and harmony back to our world.

Barman, N. and Piantanida, M. (2007) *The Authority to Imagine: The Struggle Toward Presentation in Dissertation Writing*. New York: Peter Lang.

Barone, T. (2000) *Aesthetics, Politics, Educational Inquiries: Essays and Examples*. New York: Peter Lang.

Bentz, V.M. and Shapiro, J. (1998) *Mindful Inquiry in Social Research*. Thousand Oaks, CA: Sage Publications.

Blumenfeld Jones, D.S. (1995) "Dance as a mode of research representation," *Qualitative Inquiry*, 1(4): 391–401.

Brown, L. and Strega, S. (eds) (2005) *Research as Resistance: Critical, Indigenous and Anti-oppressive Approaches*. Toronto: Canadian Scholars Press.

Cajete, G. (1994) *Look to the Mountain*. Durango, CO: Kivaki Press.

Cajete, G. (1999) *Native Science: Natural Laws of Interdependence*. Santa Fe, NM: Clear Light Publishers.

Center for Arts-informed Research Newsletter. Available online at http://home.oise. utoronto.ca/aresearch.

Christians, C.G., Ferre, J.P., and Fackler, P.M. (1993) *Good News: Social Ethics and the Press*. New York: Oxford University Press.

Cole, A.L., Neilsen, L., Knowles, J.G., and Luciani, T. (eds) (2003) *Provoked by Art: Theorizing Arts-informed Research*. Halifax, NS: Backalong Books.

Collins, Patricia Hill (2000) *Black Feminist Thought: Knowledge, Consciousness, and the Politics of Empowerment*. London: Routledge.

Cosson, Alex (ed.) (2005) *A/r/tography: Rendering Self Through Arts-based Living Inquiry*. Vancouver, BC: Pacific Educational Press.

Daignault, J. (2005) "Mixed autobiography or the acousmatic modality," *Educational Insights*, 9(2). Available online at www.ccfi.educ.ubc.ca/publication/insights/v09n02/intro/daignaultautoeng.html.

Deck, A.A. (1990) "Autoethnography: Zora Neale Hurston, Noni Jabavu, and cross-disciplinary discourse," *Black American Literature Forum*, 24(2): 237–256.

Dei, G.J.S., Hall, B.L., and Rosenberg, D.G. (eds) (2000) *Indigenous Knowledges in Global Contexts: Multiple Readings of our World*. Toronto: University of Toronto Press.

Deloria, V. (1973) *God is Red*. Golden, CO: Fulcrum Publishing.

Denzin, N.K. (1989) *Interpretive Biography*. Newbury Park: Sage Publications.

Denzin, N.K. (1999) "Interpretive ethnography for the next century," *Journal of Contemporary Ethnography*, 28(5): 510–519.

Denzin, N.K., Lincoln, Y.S., and Smith, L.T. (eds) (2008) *Handbook of Critical and Indigenous Methodologies*. Thousand Oaks, CA: Sage Publications.

Dissanayake, Ellen (1990) *What Is Art For?* Seattle, WA: University of Washington Press.

Duke, N.K. and Beck, S.W. (1999) "Education should consider alternative formats for the dissertation," *Educational Researcher*, 28(3): 31–36.

Eisner, E.W. (1991) *The Enlightened Eye: Qualitative Inquiry and the Enhancement of Educational Practice*. New York: Macmillan Publishing Company.

Eisner, E.W. (1997) "The promise and perils of alternative forms of data representation," *Educational Researcher*, 26(6): 4–10.

Eisner, E.W. and Barone, T. (1997) "Art-based educational research," in R.M. Jaeger (ed.), *Complementary Methods for Research in Education* (pp. 73–79). Washington, DC: AERA.

Ellis, C. and Botchner, A. (eds) (2002) *Ethnographically Speaking: Autoethnography, Literature, and Aesthetics*. Walnut Creek, NY: AltaMira Press.

Ellis, C. and Bochner, A.P. (2000) "Autoethnography, personal narrative, reflexivity: researcher as subject." In N.K. Denzin and Y.S. Lincoln (eds), *Handbook of Qualitative Research* (pp. 733–768). Thousand Oaks, CA: Sage.

Emmison, M. and Smith, P. (2000) *Researching the Visual: Images, Objects, Contexts and Interactions in Social and Cultural Inquiry.* Thousand Oaks, CA: Sage.

Ermine, W. (1995) "Aboriginal epistemology." In M. Battiste and J. Barman (eds), *First Nations Education in Canada: The Circle Unfolds.* Vancouver, BC: University of British Columbia Press.

Ettling, D. (2000) "Reclaiming the feminine principle in research." Paper presented at the University of Texas Arlington Conference, "The female principle: eclipses and re-emergences," March 30–April 1.

Finley, S. and Knowles, G.J. (1995) "Researcher as artist/artist as researcher," *Qualitative Inquiry*, 1(1): 110–142.

Four Arrows, aka Jacobs, D.T. (2006) *Unlearning the Language of Conquest: Scholars Expose Anti-Indianism in America.* Austin, TX: University of Texas Press.

Four Arrows, aka Jacobs, D.T. (in press) *The Neuropsychology of Indigenous Wisdom.* Netherlands: Sense Publishing.

Gabbard, D. (ed.) (2007) *Knowledge and Power in the Global Economy: The Effects of School Reform in a Neoliberal/Neoconservative Age.* Mahwah, NJ: Lawrence Erlbaum.

Garmen, N.B. and Piantanida, M. (eds) (2006) *The Authority to Imagine: The Struggle Toward Representation in Dissertation Writing.* New York: Peter Lang.

Gerber, B. "Consideration of an alternative dissertation format." Available online at www.ed.psu.edu/ci/journals/2000aets/00file1.asp. (*Author's note*: this article describes what is referred to as a "journal ready" dissertation in which a collection of published journal articles or potential journal articles ready for publication, written by the dissertation author, are presented and defended. Arguments for this type of alternative dissertation are that it better prepares doctoral program graduates to write for peer reviewed journals and more realistically prepares them for post-doctoral work.)

Goldman, R., Pea, R., Barron, B., and Derry, S. (eds) (2007) *Video Research in the Learning Sciences.* Mahwah, NJ: Lawrence Erlbaum Associates.

Graveline, F.J. (1998) *Circle Works: Transforming Eurocentric Consciousness.* Halifax, NS: Fernwood.

Greene, M. (1995) *Releasing the Imagination: Essays on Education, the Arts, and Social Change.* San Francisco, CA: Jossey-Bass Publishers.

Grudin, Robert (1990) *The Grace of Great Things: Creativity and Innovation.* New York: Houghton-Mifflin.

Hampton, E. (1995) "Towards a redefinition of Indian education." In M. Battiste and J. Barman (eds), *First Nations Education in Canada: The Circle Unfolds* (pp. 5–46). Vancouver, BC: University of British Columbia Press.

Harding, S. (1998) *Is Science Multi-cultural? Postcolonialisms, Feminisms, and Epistemologies.* Bloomington, IN: Indiana University Press.

Hawisher, G. and Selfe, C. (1999) "English at the crossroads: rethinking curricula of communication in the context of the turn to the visual." In G. Hawisher and C. Selfe (eds), *Passions, Pedagogies and 21st Century Technologies.* Logan, UT: Utah State University Press.

Hesse-Biber, S.H. and Leavy, P.L. (2006) *Emergent Methods in Social Research.* Thousand Oaks, CA: Sage.

Hirsh, Marianne (1997) *Family Frames: Photography, Narrative, and Postmemory.* Cambridge, MA: Harvard University Press.

hooks, b. (1989) *Talking Back: Thinking Feminist, Thinking Black*. Boston, MA: South End Press.

hooks, b. (1994) *Teaching to Transgress: Education as the Practice of Freedom*. New York: Routledge.

Husserl, E. (1970) *The Crisis of European Sciences and Transcendental Pheomenology: An Introduction to Phenomenological Philosophy*. Evanston, IL: Northwestern University Press.

Irwin, R.L. and de Cosson, A. (eds) (2004) *A/r/tography: Rendering Self Through Arts-based Living Inquiry*. Vancouver, BC: Pacific Educational Press.

Jacobs, D.T. (1998) *Primal Awareness: A True Story of Survival, Awakening and Transformation with the Raraumuri Shamans of Mexico*. Rochester, VT: Inner Traditions International.

Jipson, J. and Paley, N. (eds) (2006) *Daredevil Research: Re-creating Analytic Practice*. New York: Peter Lang.

Johnson, B.D., Parker, D.O., Lunsford, M., and Henderson, L.J. (2008) *Dimensions of Learning: Education for Life*. Reno, NV: Bent Tree Press.

King, T. (2003) *The Truth About Stories: A Native Narrative*. Toronto: Dead Dog Café Productions, Inc.

Kirby, S. and McKenna, K. (1989) *Experience Research Social Change: Methods From the Margins*. Toronto: Garamond Press.

Knowles, J.G. and Cole, A.L. (2002) "Transforming research: possibilities for arts informed scholarship?" In E. O'Sullivan, M. O'Conner, and A. Morrell (eds), *Expanding the Boundaries of Transformative Learning* (pp. 199–214). New York: Palgrave.

Knowles, J. and Cole, A. (eds) (2008) *Creating Scholartistry: Imagining the Arts-informed Thesis or Dissertation*. Halifax, NS: Backalong Books.

Leggo, Carl (2001) "Research as poetic rumination: twenty-six ways of listening to light." In Lorri Neilsen, Ardra L. Cole and J. Gary Knowles (eds), *The Art of Writing Inquiry* (pp. 173–195). Halifax, NS: Backalong Books.

Linds, W., Hocking, B. and Haskell, J. (2001) *Unfolding Bodymind: Exploring Possibility Through Education*. Burlington, VT: Foundation for Educational Renewal.

Louv, R. (2006) *Last Child in the Woods: Saving Our Children From Nature-deficit Disorder*. Chapel Hill, NC: Algonquin Books.

Lovitts, B.E. (2005) "How to grade a dissertation," *Academe Online*. Available online at www.aaup.org/AAUP/pubsres/academe/2005/ND/Feat/lovi.htm?PF=1.

MacDougall, D. (2006) *The Corporeal Image: Film, Ethnography, and the Senses*. Princeton, NJ: Princeton University Press.

McKibben, B. (1993) *The Age of Missing Information*. New York: Penguin.

MacMillan, Gail. (2002) "The digital library." Available online at www.vala.org.au/vala 2000/2000pdf/McMillan.PDF.

McNiff, Shaun (1998) *Art-based Research*. London and Philadelphia: Jessica Kingsley Publishers.

May, Rollo (1975) *The Courage to Create*. New York: Norton.

Mayo, P. (2003) "A rationale for a transformative approach to education," *Journal of Transformative Education*, 1(1): 38–57.

Merleau-Ponty, Maurice (1968) *The Visible and the Invisible*. Translated by Alphonso Lingis. Evanston, IL: Northwestern University Press.

Mezirow, J. (2003) "Transformative learning as discourse," *Journal of Transformative Education*, 1(1): 58–63.

Mihesuah, D.A. and Wilson, A.C. (eds) (2004) *Indigenizing the Academy: Transforming Scholarship and Empowering Communities*. Lincoln, NB: University of Nebraska Press.

Miller, J.P. (2007) *The Holistic Curriculum*, 2nd edn. Toronto: University of Toronto Press.

Mohanty, C. (1991) *Under Western Eyes: Feminist Scholarship and Colonial Discourse*. Bloomington, IN: Indiana University Press.

Monaghan, P. (1989) "Some fields are reassessing the value of the traditional doctoral dissertation," *Chronicle of Higher Education*, 35, March 29: A1, A16.

Murray, L.J. and Rice, K. (eds) (1999) *Talking on the Page: Editing Aboriginal Oral Texts*. Toronto, Buffalo, London: University of Toronto Press.

Myers, N. and Kent, J. (2005) *The New Gaia Atlas of Planet Management*. London: Gaia Books.

Nash, R.J. (2004) *Liberating Scholarly Writing: The Power of Personal Narrative*. New York: Teachers College Press.

Nicholsen, S. (1997) *Exact Imagination: Late Work: On Adorno's Aesthetics*. Cambridge, MA: MIT Press.

Palmer, P. (1998) *The Courage to Teach*. San Francisco, CA: Jossey-Bass.

Park, Peter (ed.) (1993) *Voices of Change: Participatory Research in the United States and Canada*. Westport, CT: Bergin and Garvey.

Richardson, L. (1990) *Writing Strategies: Reaching Diverse Audiences*. Newbury Park, CA: Sage.

Richardson, L. (1997) *Fields of Play: Constructing an Academic Life*. New Brunswick, NJ: Rutgers University Press.

Rogers, Everett M. (1995) *Diffusion of Innovations*, 4th edn. New York: The Free Press.

Schratz, M. and Walker, R. (1995) *Research as Social Change: New Opportunities for Qualitative Research*. London and New York: Routledge.

Slattery, P. (2006) *Curriculum Development in the Postmodern Era*. New York: Routledge.

Smith, L.T. (1999) *Decolonizing Methodologies: Research and Indigenous Peoples*. London: Zed Books.

Springgay, S., Irwin, R.L., Leggo, C. and Gouzouasis, P. (eds) (2008) *Being with A/r/tography*. Rotterdam: Sense Publishers.

Starhawk (1997) *Dreaming the Dark*. Boston, MA: Beacon Press.

Truman, C., Mertens, D., and Humphries, B. (eds) (2000) *Research and Inequality*. London: UCL Press.

Walker, R. (1993) "Finding a silent voice for the researcher: using photographs in evaluation and research." In M. Schratz (ed.), *Qualitative Voices in Educational Research*. Washington: The Falmer Press.

Weis, L. and Fine, M. (2000) *Speed Bumps: A Student Friendly Guide to Qualitative Dissertations*. New York: Teachers College Press.

Wilhelm, J.D. and Edmiston, B. (1998) *Imagining to Learn: Inquiry, Ethics, and Integration Through Drama*. Portsmouth, NH: Heinemann Educational Books.

Winston, Morton (1995) "Prospects for a revaluation of academic values." In Joseph M. Moxley and Lagretta T. Lenker (eds), *The Politics and Processes of Scholarship*. Westport, CT: Greenwood Press.

Author index

Subject index

aboriginal youth 123–5; *see also* children
academic gatekeepers 3, 95, 188, 213, 214, 215
academy, critique of the 105, 246–7, 249
accessibility 163, 175, 176, 177; of Web-based dissertation 234, 235, 236, 237, 238, 239
accountability, ethics of 199
accoustmatic text 156, 159
action 93
action research 4, 222, 224–7, 229, 230, 231, 232, 242
activism 66, 196, 217, 222, 226
Adodaroh 43
aesthetic play 111, 113–14, 115–16
aesthetics 53, 107, 108, 109, 112, 119, 245
Africa *see* South Africa
Africanization 86
alternative dissertation movement 3
alternative forms of data representation 56, 151
alternative ways of knowing and doing 241
American Educational Research Association (AERA): awards 51, 66, 76, 84, 98, 117–18; conferences 55, 62, 68; task force 71
anthropocentrism 2, 5
anti-oppressive pedagogy 162, 163, 164, 165
anti-oppressive research 4, 217, 226
appreciative inquiry 201, 202, 203, 204, 206
Arabana people 21–7
Arabic 219

art, moral function of 121
art as autobiography 185
artistic knowledge 129, 130
a/r/tography 54, 241, 242, 244, 245
arts 2, 4, 6, 57–60; *see also* collage; drama; film; music; novels; photography; poetry; story telling; theater
arts-based research 4, 54, 61, 63–4, 66, 68–75, 243–4; action research and 242; "art informs the research and research informs the art" 155; choosing 157; defending 160; description of 57; distinction between arts-informed research and 69–70; ethical guidelines for 159; lack of attention to aesthetics in 107, 109; in mathematics education 83, 84, 87; in mixed methods research 139; storied dissertation 150
art theory 117, 118, 130
"assimilative intent" 21, 24, 25, 26
assumptions 3, 5, 11, 74, 87, 168, 229
attunement 111, 112, 116, 206, 208
audience participation 158–9, 160, 170, 171
Australia, Arabana people of 21–7
Australia, expedition across central 234–6
authentic biographies 213, 215–16
authorized knowing, folly of 99, 100
autobiography 4, 6, 149, 211; all art as 185; epistolary novel as 52, 53; defined 11; Four Arrows 14; Karen Lee 150, 152; Adair Linn Nagata 206, 207
autoethnography 4, 6; Jeanie Cockell 201, 202; critical 187, 189–90; criticism of 228–9; defined 11; ethics and 163, 164;